The Second Practice of Nineteenth-Century Tonality

The Second Practice of Nineteenth-Century Tonality

Edited by William Kinderman and Harald Krebs

University of Nebraska Press, Lincoln and London

Acknowledgments for the
use of previously published
material appear on page ix.
© 1996 by the University
of Nebraska Press
Library of Congress
Cataloging-in-Publication Data
The second practice of
nineteenth-century tonality /
edited by William Kinderman
and Harald Krebs.   p.   cm.
Includes bibliographical
references and index.
ISBN 0-8032-2724-8 (alk. paper)
1. Tonality.   2. Music—19th
century—History and criticism.
I. Kinderman, William.
II. Krebs, Harald, 1955–
ML3811.S43   1995
781.2′6′09034—dc20
95-16160   CIP   MN

to Professor Christopher Lewis *in memoriam*

Contents

Acknowledgments

This book would not have come into existence without the support of many individuals and several institutions. Most of the essays began as papers read at the international symposium "Alternatives to Monotonality" held at the University of Victoria, British Columbia, in February 1989. Several excellent papers presented at the conference could not be included in the book, since they concerned tonal practice after the end of the nineteenth century or other topics too distant from the main focus of the volume. The conference participants not represented here include Joan Backus, Robert Bailey, Elmar Budde, Reinhard Gerlach, John Glofcheskie, and Deborah Stein. Coordinated with the symposium were performances by Eva Solar-Kinderman, pianist, and by Susan Young, soprano, with Harald Krebs, pianist. Financial support for the conference was supplied by the Social Sciences and Humanities Research Council of Canada, the Deutsche Forschungsgemeinschaft, and the University of Victoria. During the years following the symposium, this book took shape through an extended process of revision; the editors are grateful to the several anonymous readers who offered helpful suggestions. Special thanks go to Sharon Krebs for her invaluable assistance in helping to prepare the final typescript, and to Brenda Dalen for her careful editing of the chapter by Christopher Lewis.

The Second Practice of Nineteenth-Century Tonality

Introduction

WILLIAM KINDERMAN

1

The evolution of tonal practice between the music of Beethoven and Schubert in the 1820s and the post-tonal works of Schoenberg and Berg written a century later poses challenges that traditional analytical methodologies and theoretical systems have not fully met. One such challenge is the phenomenon of musical works beginning in one key and ending in another or otherwise embodying the practice of directional tonality, tonal pairing, or the double-tonic complex. Such works depart from the principle of a unified tonal framework organized around a single tonic key, which informs nearly all earlier tonal compositions in the various basic genres. Even though Haydn may begin in the "wrong" key, or Beethoven may preface a piece with a harmonic curtain initially obscuring the main key (as in the First Symphony), the first section of a classical work is almost invariably in the tonic. The improvisatory genre of the fantasy may violate this principle in favor of an additive sequence of keys (as in Beethoven's Fantasie op. 77), but this is exceptional. In all other genres the tonic key normally provides both the initial and final points of orientation.

The monotonal orientation around a single governing tonic is weakened by the middle of the nineteenth century and sometimes replaced in the succeeding decades by a controlled tonal ambiguity, whereby extended passages are based on the tension between two key centers, most often a third apart. This expanded tonal practice, with its alternatives to monotonality, is the focus of the present volume. Many of the chapters are derived from papers read at the symposium "Alternatives to Monotonality" held at the University of Victoria, British Columbia, in February 1989. The symposium brought together theorists and historians to assess new approaches to the understanding of nineteenth- and early-twentieth-century tonal practice. These approaches derive above all from

Professor Robert Bailey of New York University, whose influence as a teacher has equaled or surpassed the influence of his published writings. Several of the authors, in their explications of directional tonality, tonal pairing, and the double-tonic complex, are deeply indebted to Bailey's ideas, although they apply these concepts in ways by no means identical to his own.

In his essay on Chopin in this volume, Jim Samson argues that the problem of alternatives to monotonality appears in a different light when regarded from a historical rather than an analytical perspective. William Benjamin makes a related point in his essay on Bruckner by stressing the impact that the complex aesthetic context of much late-nineteenth-century music has on our perception of its large-scale tonal relations. Some of the issues involved are subtle and even elusive, and they have always remained controversial. For that reason, it may be helpful to review the critical reaction that these matters have received from the middle of the nineteenth century up to recent times. (Readers who wish to skip the following detailed introductory discussion can turn to section 3 for a brief overview of this volume's chapters.)

A revealing perspective comes from a composer and critic who was closely associated with Liszt and Wagner, Felix Draeseke. On 8 August 1861 Draeseke delivered a lecture at Weimar entitled "Die sogenannte Zukunftsmusik und ihre Gegner" (The so-called music of the future and its opponents), which was published later that year in the *Neue Zeitschrift für Musik*.[1] In this essay Draeseke identifies harmonic and tonal practice as the "showplace of the liveliest recent controversies" and characterizes the crux of the matter as bound up with the "suspension of the main tonality [*Aufhebung der Haupttonart*]."[2] Hostility to the so-called music of the future, he argues, arose out of a misguided fear that a triumph of the newer music would bring about a destruction of the tradition. Draeseke criticizes this opposing view on historical grounds as overlooking the dynamic, evolving nature of "the modern tonal system . . . the study of whose distinctive features had still occupied the Vienna School." Draeseke continues with a political, revolutionary metaphor: "and so it was not surprising that Beethoven's third period seemed destined to shake the absolutist regime of the main tonality for the first time, and that thirty years had to pass before that system was actually put aside."[3]

"Undoubtedly the alert observer of the recent history of harmony notices a consistent striving to fuse the separate tonalities [and] to further expand the tonal relations, gradually sweeping away the notion of foreign opposition [to the tonic]. [This] striving, which inevitably leads to the suspension of diatonic writing, had to bring with it the freest treatment of harmony."[4] Here Draeseke describes the central concern of the present book, namely, the fusion of keys as a manifestation of the expanded tonal system. As Draeseke points out, Beethoven not infrequently replaced the tonic-dominant polarity of Mozart and Haydn's age with tonal relations a major third above or below the tonic. The use of key relations at the minor third, he adds, opened up even more distant tonal paths, such as the connection of C with the diminished fifth above, G♭, through E♭. Keys formerly regarded as remote and harshly contrasting were thereby brought into juxtaposition.

"Could then the system of the main tonality, without inner deception, be preserved?" asks Draeseke.[5] His provocative image for the singular tonality in this expanded web of relations is that of the lines of latitude and longitude on a geographical map, which lack power over the actual musical landscape. It is in this sense that the main tonality has been suspended, canceled, or annulled; Draeseke uses the term *aufgehoben,* a term that Hegel favored and that Schoenberg employed a half-century later to describe his voyage into the sea of pantonality.[6] The gravitational pull of the main tonality ceases to exercise control at that historical moment when music has become "dialectical."

2

Some of the same controversies that dogged Draeseke still persist, as is readily illustrated through a brief review of analytical scholarship on Richard Wagner, probably the most influential figure in the evolution of nineteenth-century tonality. The issues at stake are by no means confined to harmony and tonality but touch on matters of formal integration and dramatic symbolism. The key to a fresh reappraisal of these perennial questions lies in what Draeseke described as a fusion of tonalities and what some recent analysts, following Bailey, have termed tonal pairing or the double-tonic complex. Rarely discussed in the older theoretical literature, these matters find perhaps their most significant mention in the brief section entitled "Fluctuating and Suspended Tonality" in Schoenberg's *Theory of Harmony,* first published in 1911. Schoenberg describes suspended tonality [*schwebende* or *aufgehobene Tonalität*]" as "not readily illustrated by little phrases because it involves the articulation of distinct parts of a composition"; in citing examples, he refers the reader to works by Beethoven, Schumann, and Mahler, among other composers.[7] In the same context Schoenberg cites Wagner's *Tristan* and pieces of his own in which the implied tonic key is scarcely, if ever, confirmed through the appearance of its triad. A subsequent study touching on some of these issues is Edwin von der Nüll's *Moderne Harmonik* (1932), with its description of successive and simultaneous bitonality in Schoenberg's music.[8]

The reluctance of more recent commentators to probe these concepts in any detail may be linked to problems of methodology and particularly to the failure of established analytical systems to address adequately the musical practice of the later nineteenth century. Carl Dahlhaus has drawn attention to one aspect of this problem through his critique of Ernst Kurth's influential concept of chromatic alteration in *Tristan*. As Dahlhaus rightly asks, if "the essential element in the association of chords is semitonal connection and not root progression (and it can hardly be disputed that it is the function within the association that determines the harmonic significance of a phenomenon), then 'alteration' is strictly an inadequate term, as it seems to imply that chromaticism is secondary and derivative. Rather, chromaticism has achieved a degree of independence from its origins in alteration."[9] Similarly, it will not do to regard the expanded tonal structures of many nineteenth- and twentieth-century works merely as deviations from earlier practice. Before I explore these issues in more detail, however, it is appropriate to consider some of the underlying assumptions of analysis along these lines, which easily comes into conflict with the deconstructionist tendencies fashionable in some recent scholarship.

The editors of a recent collection of essays on Wagner and Verdi, Carolyn Abbate and Roger Parker, have attacked analytical studies that emphasize "autonomous structure, or coherence, or organic unity in a work," claiming that "many critics assume a priori that the musical object, to be of value, *must* be unified in certain conventional ways. This assumption is, of course, related to a naive insistence that interpretation can and ought to be wholly detached from its context."[10] Their polemics are directed particularly at the analyses of Alfred Lorenz, who attempted in his monumental four-volume work *Das Geheimnis der Form bei Richard Wagner* to reveal the "secret" of later Wagnerian form as a succession of tonally closed, symmetrical units.[11] The shortcomings of Lorenz's work are serious, as is widely recognized, but the flaws in no way establish that large-scale formal and tonal relations are absent in Wagner's works from *Tristan* to *Parsifal*. One of the most artificial features of Lorenz's approach stems from his habit of fixing the ends of his "periods" at a passing recurrence of the original key, with this alleged "tonic" of a section often having relatively little sway over the intervening music.[12] The shortcomings of his methodology compelled Lorenz to propose formal divisions on the basis of a limited and essentially outmoded concept of tonality, sometimes yielding not much more control over the music than the lattice lines of Draeseke's landscape map. Of tonality understood as a process involving a fusion of keys, with passages based on the tension between key centers, Lorenz had little or no conception.

An approach sensitive to the structural aspects of modulation and tonal polarity is indispensable here because it can reveal correspondences between harmonic detail and the larger tonal architecture, on the one hand, while also illuminating expressive and dramatic features, on the other. One of Wagner's favorite devices, for instance, is to foreshadow the large-scale tonal progression of an entire act at the outset of an orchestral prelude.[13] Hence, in the *Tristan* prelude the rising minor third relation of the two opening phrases, which pause on the dominant-seventh sonorities of A and C, corresponds to the overall tonal progression from A to C in the first act as a whole. In the more diatonic world of *Die Meistersinger* the two opening thirteen-measure phrases beginning on C and F at the head of the overture similarly parallel the overall tonal framework of the first act, which ends in F major. In *Götterdämmerung* the first two chords of the prelude, E♭ minor and C♭ major, anticipate the tonal polarity between the tonalities of E♭ and B—the enharmonic equivalent of C♭—with the first act closing in B minor. In *Parsifal* the opening harmonic progression from A♭ to C is composed out not only in the tonal shift from A♭ major to C minor in the ensuing statements of the Communion theme in the prelude but also in the overall move to C major as the central tonality of the first Grail scene at the end of the act. Each of Wagner's major works beginning with *Tristan* employs this procedure, which represents but one aspect of a complex network of musical relations.

There can be no intrinsic danger of slighting "context" through such an approach, which belongs to the mainstream of analytical criticism. Adequate analysis needs to avoid excessive abstraction, lest it come to resemble "a railway schedule whose trains never run," in Pierre Boulez's apt formulation.[14] Nonetheless, it would be a mistake to dismiss analysis as such as inevitably reductionist. The scheduled trains often do depart on their journeys; analytical reflection may help to illuminate aspects of these artistic processes that would otherwise remain obscure. Properly conceived and practiced, analysis leads not to a preoccupation with abstractions but to an enhanced engagement with contextual features.

Consider, for instance, the dramatic and symbolic meaning assumed by Wagner's paired tonalities. At the end of the first act of *Tristan,* the alternation of the keys of A and C is coordinated with the duality between the inner world of the lovers and the outer, social world centered on King Marke. The contrast of thematic material and orchestration is reinforced here through the duality in sound created by the paired keys. In the first act of *Götterdämmerung,* Wagner creates a subtle dramatic effect through the abrupt modulation from B to E♭ at Brünnhilde's shocked response to Siegfried when he appears in the likeness of Gunther, after having been transformed by the magic of the Tarnhelm, whose associated tonality is B minor. The use of such tonal polarity to underline psychological conflict between characters occurs elsewhere in Wagner; another example is found in the Wotan-Erda dialogue in act 3, scene 1, of *Siegfried,* where the central tonality of Erda's last three passages is E♭ and the main key for Wotan throughout is G. In *Parsifal,* on the other hand, the C-minor inflection within the opening Communion theme at the outset of the work proves to have far-reaching dramatic consequences connected to the threat to the Grail.

Thus, although analysis posited along these lines gives attention to the integration of musical relations and gestures and their large-scale connections or correspondences, it is hardly "trapped in a tautological cage of value judgements predicated on musical unity."[15] The most valuable results of analytical criticism are context dependent; clearly, readers need to test claims about musical and dramatic relations against their own aesthetic experiences. Analysis needs to be flexible enough to be applied convincingly, and even transparently, to its aesthetic objects. One is compelled here to question the previously cited claim that "many critics assume a priori that the musical object, to be of value, *must* be unified in certain conventional ways." The precise means of musical integration in Wagner's later works, for example, are hardly conventional in the sense of following a priori rules. Procedures such as his signaling at the outset of a work the tonal polarity to follow permit very different realizations in differing musical contexts. Nevertheless, the critique offered by Abbate and Parker should be welcomed inasmuch as it exposes the "tunnel vision" of analysts whose overreliance on systematic method can obscure the rich complexity of works of art.

The critical approach sketched here and exemplified in some chapters of this collection requires neither that the artwork be divorced from its context nor that conventional strictures be imposed on it. Instead, what is sought is a more flexible approach to the essentially new system of harmonic and tonal relations embodied in many nineteenth-century works, an approach whereby these pieces may be analyzed on their own terms. The evolution in tonal practice may be seen as involving the virtual replacement of the twenty-four major and minor keys by twelve chromatic modes, whereby the "diatonic musical space" of much earlier music tends to be supplanted by "chromatic musical space," to state matters in the formulation of Patrick McCreless. Harmonic sonorities marginalized in earlier music, such as the augmented triad, assumed enhanced importance, as R. Larry Todd shows in his chapter on Liszt. A familiar strategy in surveys of music history is to trace the role played by increasing harmonic dissonance in musical expression: the evolutionary sequence from Schumann's *Kreisleriana* to Liszt's *Faust* Symphony and Wagner's *Tristan,* leading on to Richard Strauss and Schoenberg, is irresistible. Nevertheless, such evolutionary descriptions risk oversimplifying the actual sequence of events. The older diatonic practice remained in use beside the newer practice, with both often coexisting in a given work, and to a notable extent artistic products of earlier generations served as important models for the newer style. For Wagner, Mozart was "the great *Chromatiker,*" and Beethoven's later works provided an inspiration for Wagner's own innovations.

A work such as Beethoven's C♯-Minor Quartet, op. 131 (1826), is a case in point, for it already raises some of the same issues of tonality and large-scale form as does *Tristan.* Beethoven sustains a large-scale tension over the seven interconnected movements of the quartet by delaying the first strong cadential downbeat in the tonic until the outset of the last movement and recalling thematic, textural, and tonal features of the opening fugue in the finale. Vital to the aesthetic idiom of this work is the tonal ambiguity of the slow fugue, whose initial subject entries are heavily weighted toward the subdominant and Neapolitan and whose powerful harmonic drift to the Neapolitan D major prepares the shift to that key in the second movement. Beethoven thus sets into motion a complex narrative sequence whereby powerful contrasts are held in delicate structural balance, with each of the movements before the finale yielding up part of its formal autonomy in support of the unity of the work as a whole.

What bears comparison to *Tristan* here is Beethoven's initial treatment of the principal key of C♯ minor, which is somewhat obscured through the emphasis on pitches belonging to D major; this is surely one of the moments in Beethoven's later music that already "shake[s] the absolutist regime of the main tonality," as Draeseke puts it. Beethoven's op. 131 illustrates the broader historical tendency for musical works to lead from an initial ambiguity to a final clarification, summation, or apotheosis. Many pieces—from the "Depiction of Chaos" in Haydn's *Creation* to Beethoven's Ninth Symphony and from Schumann's D-minor Symphony to Bruckner's Eighth—reflect this tendency, which is often associated with programmatic or symbolic designates and large-scale narrative patterns suggesting the presence of archetypal meanings.

Directional artistic patterns whereby the beginning of a work is shad-
owed in obscurity, characterized by a sense of struggle or agitation, or
given a dreamlike, tentative, or preparatory quality can lend themselves
to a tonal practice challenging an overall unity of key. Not surprisingly,
texts harboring these implications are often a prime motivating factor,
whether in the music dramas of Wagner or the directionally tonal songs
of Schubert. In addition, however, there is a considerable number of instrumental works that employ analogous devices, and these by no means
stem only from the most famous and successful masters. For a characteristic example we may turn once more to Felix Draeseke, namely, to his
Sonata quasi Fantasia for piano, op. 6, which was begun the year after his
lecture, in 1862, and finished and published in 1869.[16]

In his sonata Draeseke combines a motto technique somewhat remi-
niscent of Schumann with a type of directional tonality, with the main
tonal polarity—between E major and C♯ minor—exposed immediately
in the initial four-measure motto (see ex. 1a). The "heroic" chords of the

Example 1a. Felix Draeseke, Sonata quasi Fantasia, op. 6, beginning.

first half of the motto imply a cadence in E without supplying the chord
of resolution; the continuation reinterprets the last melodic pitches of
this opening fanfare—G♯ and F♯—as the springboard for a rising chromatic progression to C♯, which is realized only within a striking overall
drop in register, in a virtuosic, Lisztian pianistic texture. The bare, un-
harmonized C♯ octaves concluding this bipartite motto anticipate or are
expanded into the funeral march in C♯ minor forming most of the first
movement. The E-major fanfare, on the other hand, recurs many times
in the massive finale, with the triumphant close in that key reserved for
the last moments (ex. 1b).[17]

Draeseke originally supplied a poetic motto for the work, which he
later suppressed, but the expressive connotations of his tonal duality
are perfectly clear—perhaps too much so, for his sonata may overuse
the dualistic opening motto and rely too heavily on loose, mosaic-like
construction. Extended passages such as the fantasy-like continuation

Example 1b. Felix Draeseke, Sonata quasi Fantasia, op. 6, end of finale.

following the opening motto are based on the principle of semitonal connection noted by Dahlhaus, although without much connection to the duality of keys exposed at the outset. Apart from the motto itself and the association of its two halves with the first and last movements, there is a much less thorough treatment of tonal pairing here than in the previously cited Wagnerian examples. This reminds us of the need to avoid premature generalization in the application of analytical concepts. As Schoenberg once wrote, referring to examples of suspended tonality, "if one takes a look at them, one will know what I mean [by the term *schwebende Tonalität*] and what rich resources must be on hand to bring it about."[18]

Draeseke's sonata is but one instance in a whole category of pieces that begin in one key and end in another, a practice illustrated in several of Gustav Mahler's symphonies, such as the Fourth, Fifth, Seventh, and Ninth. Dika Newlin described the procedure as "progressive tonality" in her book *Bruckner, Mahler, Schoenberg* (1947).[19] Another term apart from directional or progressive tonality that has been applied to this phenomenon is "interlocking tonality," a formulation used by Graham George in his 1970 study *Tonality and Musical Structure*.[20] Unfortunately, the value of George's work is often diminished by his tendency to regard tonalities as abstract entities apart from concrete musical contexts. The risk of an overly abstract treatment of tonal relations can be avoided only through careful attention to the context of the music and the manner in which keys are connected to one another. This brings us back to the issues raised by Samson and Benjamin, namely, the extent to which

an assessment of directional tonality or tonal pairing as a progressive development needs to be balanced by careful consideration of the historical
and aesthetic context. The mere fact that a work begins and ends in different keys is in itself no proof of a progressive orientation.[21] Conversely,
a bold treatment of tonal relations can occur in works that begin and
end in the same key.

The directional tonality in Mahler's symphonies is bound up with
what Theodor W. Adorno describes as their affinity to narrative genres
like the novel or ballade.[22] Just as the two-key scheme of Chopin's Ballade op. 38 is a function of its narrative unfolding, the tonal designs in
some of Mahler's balladelike symphonies demonstrate a similar correspondence. In the Fourth Symphony Mahler does not place his concluding setting of the *Wunderhorn* song "Das himmlische Leben" in G major,
the initial tonality of the work; he casts it instead in E major, a key with
celestial associations in earlier music.[23] In the Fifth Symphony the key
of the initial funereal trumpet call, C♯ minor, acts as point of departure
but not as tonal destination of the overall narrative design: the central
key, D major, is unveiled in the climactic brass chorale heard near the
close of the second movement, a passage that is reaffirmed in the finale.
As Adorno points out, the placement of the finale of Mahler's Seventh
Symphony in C major is conditioned by the "harmonic macrocosm" of
the entire composition, and particularly by the tonal balance between
its opening movement in E minor and the weighty inner movements.
Consequently, the key of the finale corresponds not to the first movement but to the following "Nachtmusik."[24] The ultimate tonality of the
symphony is C major, which is also the key of an earlier work whose influence is felt in Mahler's finale: Wagner's *Meistersinger*.

3

The organization of this book is broadly chronological, and the term
"nineteenth-century tonality" is taken to refer to origins rather than historical limits: indeed, some of the principles explored here could be applied to music of the recent past and will continue to apply to music that
has not yet been written. The major emphasis falls on the period between
the suspension of the main tonality that Draeseke described in 1861 and
the more sweeping suspension of tonality inaugurated by Schoenberg
nearly fifty years later. Important directionally tonal works also date from
earlier in the nineteenth century, however, and the first chapters address
several such pieces from contrasting critical perspectives. Harald Krebs's
analysis of the two versions of Schubert's "Meeres Stille" and of "Der

Wanderer" explores structural and expressive features of tonal pairing, as well as the poetic motivation for this tensional ambiguity in the texts. In a succinct essay Jim Samson attempts to place Chopin's tonal practice in its historical context by suggesting how the *stile brillant* and improvisatory practice weakened an overall tonal regulation of events. For Samson, even the two-key scheme of the Second Ballade may be regarded as "an extension of, rather than a major departure from, the dynamics of [Chopin's] normative practice" and is "as much a residue of the past as a premonition of the future." The longer study by Kevin Korsyn compares examples of directional tonality by Chopin and Brahms, from before and after the midpoint of the nineteenth century, and analyzes the nature of their kinship using criteria for intertextuality drawn from Harold Bloom's literary theory. Korsyn also examines Chopin's Second Ballade, but unlike Samson, he merges historical and analytical categories into a dynamic critical stance wherein directional tonality is regarded as "a reinterpretation of prior tonal language" not untouched by that quintessentially modern condition, "the anxiety of influence."

The chapter by Patrick McCreless confronts the issue of a second practice of nineteenth-century tonality by probing the emergence of chromatic space distinct from the diatonic space of earlier music. The comprehensive arguments he presents call for reevaluation of the often too monolithic view of later-nineteenth-century tonal practice that is enshrined in many theoretical studies and some histories of music. In later chapters certain issues McCreless raises are explored in analyses of specific works. Christopher Lewis examines the impact of harmonic progressions rooted in more than one tonic on our temporal perception of music and discusses the apparent interruption or dislocation of this temporal unfolding in a number of pieces by Bruckner, Schoenberg, Pfitzner, and others. Like Korsyn, Lewis deepens the critical context of his analyses by venturing a provocative analogy to another art form, namely, to Maurizio Nichetti's film *The Icicle Thief* [*Ladri di saponette*], a work whose engagement with Vittorio de Sica's 1949 film *The Bicycle Thief* [*Ladri di biciclette*] helps to create a narrative structure of temporally independent cinematic levels that gradually interact or fuse with one another. When analogous dualistic or multilevel structures occur in musical works, these can be manifested at least partly through alternatives to monotonality.

The following chapters concern the two major proponents of the so-called music of the future: Liszt and Wagner. R. Larry Todd explores Liszt's growing preoccupation with the augmented triad, an interest that generated the celebrated opening of the "Faust" Symphony and brought Liszt in later works to the brink of atonality. Todd also considers the changing perception of the augmented triad in nineteenth-century theoretical writings, especially those by Carl Friedrich Weitzmann. My own study examines the manner in which Wagner uses tonal pairing in connection with large-scale recapitulation to articulate central dramatic concerns in *Tristan* and *Parsifal*.

The final chapters focus on some of the boldest works by Hugo Wolf and Anton Bruckner. John Williamson examines tonal ambiguity and harmonic structure in a series of songs by Wolf, seeing in them "the most convincing synthesis after Wagner of chromaticism, enharmony, and where it suited [Wolf], monotonality." William Benjamin analyzes harmonic, rhythmic, and tonal relations in Bruckner's Eighth Symphony, exploring their expressive significance in a stimulating reassessment of Bruckner's style. In his conclusion Benjamin argues that, by the 1890s, such music had "worked its way into the very center of European intellectual life" by "symbolically countering alienation," by making whole again the "fractured existence of persons in an increasingly urbanized, industrialized, and bureaucratized society." The integrating power of Bruckner's tonal dualism is thus seen as binding divergent, even contradictory forces in a "sonic order" whose potential symbolic meaning has assumed an increasing relevance in our own time.

The emphasis in the present volume has fallen on Austro-German music. Because of the broad scope of the topic, some key figures associated with that tradition, such as Mahler and Richard Strauss, could be given little or no detailed attention here. It is hoped that future studies may find the analytical approaches developed here to be of value for French, Russian, and other musical repertories of the nineteenth and twentieth centuries.[25] To guide further study, Harald Krebs has compiled a selected bibliography of publications related to tonal practice. All translations are the author's unless otherwise specified.

NOTES

1. Felix Draeseke, *Neue Zeitschrift für Musik* 55 (1861), hefte 9 and 10. The full text has been reprinted in *Felix Draeseke, Schriften 1855–1861*, ed. Martella Gutiérrez-Denhoff and Helmut Loos, 315–36 (Bad Honnef: Gudrun Schröder Verlag, 1987). This volume is the first of an ongoing monograph series issued by the International Draeseke Society (Internationale Draeseke Gesellschaft), of which five volumes have so far appeared.

2. Ibid., 324–27.

3. "Lange genug hatte es freilich gedauert, das moderne Tonarten-System abzuschließen, das Studium seiner Eigenthümlichkeiten hatte ja sogar noch die Wiener Schule beschäftigt; und so war es denn nicht zu verwundern, daß Beethoven's dritte Periode erst berufen schien, an dem absolutistischen Regime der Haupttonart zu rütteln, und

daß dann noch weitere dreißig Jahre vergehen mußten, ehe dasselbe wirklich beseitigt ward" (ibid., 327).

4. "Unzweifelhaft tritt dem aufmarksamen Beobachter das in der neueren Geschichte der Harmonik andauernde Streben entgegen, die einzelnen Tonarten zusammenzuschmelzen, die Verwandtschaftsverhältnisse weiter auszudehnen, den Begriff des fremd Gegenüberstehenden allmählig hinwegzuräumen: ein Streben, welches nothwendiger Weise zur Aufhebung der diatonischer Schreibart führen, die freieste Bewegung auf harmonischem Gebiete nach sich ziehen mußte" (ibid., 326).

5. "Könnte da noch, ohne innerliche Lüge, das System der Haupttonart aufrecht erhalten werden?" (ibid., 326).

6. Draeseke's *aufgehobene Haupttonart* [suspended main tonality] corresponds almost too neatly to Schoenberg's *aufgehobene Tonalität* [suspended tonality]; in both cases the German term retains some connotations of preservation together with the basic meaning of abolishment or cancellation, and for that reason, "suspension" is probably the best rendering in English of *aufgehoben*.

7. Arnold Schoenberg, *Theory of Harmony,* trans. Roy E. Carter (Berkeley: University of California Press, 1978), 383–84.

8. Edwin von der Nüll, *Moderne Harmonik* (Leipzig: Fr. Kistner and C.F.W. Siegel, 1932), 102–9.

9. Carl Dahlhaus and John Deathridge, *The New Grove Wagner* (London: Macmillan, 1984), 119. Dahlhaus's essay was previously published in *The New Grove Dictionary of Music,* ed. Stanley Sadie (London: Macmillan, 1980).

10. Carolyn Abbate and Roger Parker, "Introduction: On Analyzing Opera," in *Analyzing Opera: Wagner and Verdi,* ed. Abbate and Parker (Berkeley: University of California Press, 1989), 3.

11. The four volumes of Lorenz's *Das Geheimnis der Form bei Richard Wagner* were published at Berlin by M. Hesse between 1924 and 1933; they were reprinted at Tutzing by Hans Scheider in 1966.

12. For a specific example of this problem in Lorenz's analysis of *Götterdämmerung,* see my article "Dramatic Recapitulation in Wagner's *Götterdämmerung,*" *19th-Century Music* 4, no. 2 (fall 1980): 112.

13. Robert Bailey has drawn attention to this practice in Wagner in his article "The Structure of the *Ring* and Its Evolution," *19th-Century Music* 1, no. 1 (July 1977): 59.

14. Pierre Boulez, "Musikdenken heute," 1, in *Darmstädter Beiträge zur Neuen Musik* (Mainz, 1963), 5:14. Cited in the excellent survey of music analysis by Elmar Budde, "Funktionen und Methoden der musikalischen Analyse" and "Analyse und Interpretation," chapters 3 and 4 of *Funk-Kolleg Musik,* ed. Carl Dahlhaus and others (Frankfurt: Fischer, 1981), 1:57–129; quotation on 58.

15. Abbate and Parker, "Introduction," 3.

16. The 1869 edition of the sonata has been reprinted recently by the International Draeseke Society as *Felix Draeseke, Sonate für Klavier zu zwei Handen op. 6,* ed. and with a foreword by Udo Follert (Munich-Gräfelfing: Verlag Walter Wollenweber, 1988).

17. A detailed discussion of the sonata is provided in my article "Draesekes Klaviersonate op. 6" in *Zum Schaffen von Felix Draeseke: Instrumentalwerke und geistliche Musik. Tagungen 1990 in Coburg und 1991 in Dresden,* ed. Helmut Loos, 3–17, vol. 5 of Veröffentlichungen der Internationalen Draeseke-Gesellschaft (Bonn: Gudrun Schröder Verlag, 1994); an English version of this article appears in the booklet accompanying the recent recording of the sonata by Claudius Tanski (Altarus AIR-CD-9030).

18. Schoenberg, *Theory of Harmony,* 383–84.

19. Dika Newlin, *Bruckner, Mahler, Schoenberg* (New York: Kings' Crown, 1947).

20. Graham George, *Tonality and Musical Structure* (London: Faber & Faber, 1970).

21. This point needs to be stressed in the light of some influential recent studies. For

example, Susan McClary's argument in *Feminine Endings: Music, Gender, and Sexuality* (Minneapolis: University of Minnesota Press, 1991), 158–61, that Madonna subverts narrative and tonal closure is both too rigid in characterizing traditional procedures and uncritical in assessing the extent to which such constraints apply to popular music.

22. Theodor Adorno, *Mahler: Eine musikalische Physiognomik,* in Adorno's *Gesammelten Schriften,* ed. Gretel Adorno and Rolf Tiedemann (Frankfurt: Suhrkamp, 1986 [1961]), 13. Adorno's discussion of narrative design in Mahler's symphonies is found in his chapter entitled "Roman," 209–29.

23. An example of the celestial connotations of E major is Beethoven's "Abendlied unterm gestirnten Himmel" (Evening song under the starry heavens), WoO 150, from 1820. Analogous associations invest the slow movement of his String Quartet op. 59, no. 2, in E major, which Beethoven reportedly composed while "contemplating the starry heavens and thinking of the music of the spheres" (see Alexander W. Thayer, *Life of Beethoven* [Princeton: Princeton University Press, 1964], 408–9).

24. See Adorno, *Mahler,* 176.

25. A number of authors have employed a dualistic approach to twentieth-century analysis. See, for instance, Joseph Straus's discussion of Stravinsky's Serenade in A as a response to Chopin's Ballade no. 2 in *Remaking the Past: Musical Modernism and the Influence of the Tonal Tradition* (Cambridge: Harvard University Press, 1990), 149–55.

Part 1: The Origins and General Principles of Tonal Pairing and Directional Tonality

Some Early Examples of Tonal Pairing: Schubert's "Meeres Stille" and "Der Wanderer"

HARALD KREBS

S chubert's exploration of alternatives to monotonality, particularly in the lieder of 1815–17, has been the focus of a number of recent studies.[1] All these investigations have dealt with Schubert's use of directional tonality, which is a significant component of his tonal practice in the lieder of those years. It is not as well known, however, that another nonmonotonal practice—tonal pairing—is also found in Schubert's early songs.

The term "tonal pairing," along with the synonymous term "double-tonic complex," originates with Robert Bailey, who applies these terms to situations where two keys simultaneously occupy the highest position in a tonal hierarchy. In an analysis of the first act of *Tristan und Isolde,* for example, Bailey refers to the double-tonic complex A/C as "the controlling tonic." In a brief discussion of the operation of tonal pairing on the surface level of a work, he remarks: "Either triad [of the pair] can serve as the local representative of the tonic complex. Within that complex itself, however, one of the two elements is at any moment in the primary position while the other remains subordinate to it."[2] This statement clarifies the distinction between tonal pairing and what is commonly known as bitonality: a work involving tonal pairing does not generally sound bitonal, since one of the keys predominates at any given point on the surface. Tonal pairing is rather an association of two tonics at the highest level, the level of controlling tonic.

Other writers have elaborated on Bailey's concept of tonal pairing and have demonstrated its importance in late-nineteenth-century works. In his studies of Wagner's music dramas William Kinderman defines tonal pairing, in a manner quite similar to Bailey's, as "the juxtaposition of two key areas which together comprise the tonal center for an extensive musical unit" and as "the basing of large sections . . . not on one stable sonority but on the tension between two tonal centers."[3] The reference to tension hints at the dramatic potential of tonal pairing, a topic to which I return later.

In his monograph on Mahler's Ninth Symphony Christopher Lewis provides a lucid discussion of tonal pairing, including a list of the ways in which tonal pairing is commonly manifested on musical surfaces: (1) juxtaposition of musical fragments implying the two tonics in succession or alternation; (2) mixture of the two tonalities, exploiting ambiguous and common harmonic functions; (3) use of a tonic sonority created by conflation of the two tonic triads; and (4) superposition of lines or textures in one key on those in another.[4]

This chapter draws attention to procedures similar to those outlined by Bailey, Kinderman, and Lewis in two works from the early nineteenth century, namely Schubert's songs "Der Wanderer" (1816, D.489) and "Meeres Stille [Calm at sea]" (1815, D.216). Lewis's list and the remarks of Bailey and Kinderman provide a framework for my analyses.

An examination of the foreground level of "Der Wanderer" reveals a persistent alternation between prolongations of the C♯-minor and E-major harmonies. Although the functions of the harmonies are somewhat ambiguous, the first fourteen measures can be heard as prolonging the C♯ harmony via the progression I (mm.1–7)–IV (mm.8–12)–V (m.13)–I (m.14). The authentic cadence to C♯ in mm.13–14 is immediately followed by another cadence, this one leading to E major (mm.15–16), and the latter harmony is prolonged on the surface until m.19. From this point onward fluctuation between expanded E and C♯ harmonies is continuous. Measures 20–22 restore the C♯ harmony; the sustained dominant of C♯ in m.22 resolves as expected, and C♯ continues to govern the first seven measures of the following section (mm.23–29). At m.30, however, the cadence to C♯ that concluded the first phrase of the section (see m.26) is replaced by a cadence to E, and the latter harmony is prolonged in mm.30–61. Measure 62 brings another shift to C♯ harmony, which can be heard as being expanded until m.66. (I discuss a different hearing of mm.65–66 later.) The final phrase of the song returns to E-major harmony and closes therewith.[5]

The alternation of prolonged E-major and C♯-minor harmonies (which are heard as surface key areas) throughout "Der Wanderer" is the most obvious indication that a pairing of these keys underlies the work. The pairing is also manifested by Schubert's use of sonorities that are composed of the union of the tonic triads of the two keys (see Lewis's third point). Measure 16 provides a simple example; in the vocal line the E-major triad is embellished by the upper neighbor C♯, resulting in a blending of the E-major and C♯-minor triads, both within the melody and in the total texture. The same melodic idea is immediately repeated in the bass in m. 18 and also in mm. 58 and 60 (which correspond musically and textually to mm. 16 and 18), resulting in further conflation of the tonics. In m. 49 a conglomerate of the two triads arises from the superposition of C♯ on vertical statements of the E-major triad.

In each of the conglomerates mentioned thus far, E major is clearly the predominant triad, C♯ being a neighboring tone. A more striking conflation of the two triads, within which they have equal significance, occurs in mm. 65–66. Here Schubert abruptly shifts from a chordal texture to *all'unisono,* partly, no doubt, in response to the word *Geisterhauch* [ghostly exhalation]. The scale segment thus highlighted by a change in texture (in fact, by a shift to a texture that occurs nowhere else in the work) can be heard as arpeggiating either the C♯-minor or the E-major triad. Both interpretations make perfect sense in context. If the scale segment is heard as an arpeggiation of the C♯-minor triad, it provides the expected resolution of the preceding dominant harmony. If it is heard as an E-major arpeggiation, it provides a good continuation for the G♯-major harmony in terms of voice leading and also connects logically with the following cadence in E major. The passage, strategically placed near the end of the song, beautifully encapsulates the double-tonic complex E/C♯.

One more manifestation of the surface-level pairing of C♯ and E must be mentioned, namely the frequent use of ambiguous and common harmonic functions (see Lewis's second point). Two harmonies that are prominent throughout the song, namely, F♯ minor and A major, have potential functions within the keys of C♯ minor and E major: F♯ minor can act as IV of C♯ and as II of E, whereas A major can act as VI of C♯ and as IV of E. Thus, each use of the F♯ and A harmonies creates a tonal crossroads; after each statement of these harmonies, the progression could turn toward the keys of either E or C♯. The prolonged F♯-minor triad at mm. 8–12, for example, could be followed by an authentic cadence to E or to C♯. Schubert actually explores both options here; he initially opts for a C♯-minor cadence, which he states emphatically in mm. 13–14, but immediately undercuts this cadence by a second one to E (mm. 14–16). The passage in mm. 23–30 (famous because of its incorporation into the *Wanderer Fantasy*) further illustrates the double function of the F♯-minor triad. In the first phrase of the passage, the F♯-minor triad leads to an authentic cadence to C♯ (mm. 25–26). Schubert follows this phrase by a parallel one in which the F♯-minor triad prepares an authentic cadence to E major (mm. 29–30).

Another example of the exploitation of harmonic ambiguity as a mani-

Example 1. Schubert's
"Der Wanderer" (D.489),
analyzed in terms of
(a) C♯ minor and
(b) E major.

festation of the C♯–E pairing is found at m.66. Not only the aforementioned *all'unisono* scale segment (mm.65–66) but also the chord to which it leads—an F♯-minor seventh chord   could belong either to the keys of C♯ minor or E major; the chord could function either as II$^6_5$ in E or as IV$^6_5$ in C♯. Schubert chooses to employ the chord in its E-major sense, leading it to V$^4_2$ of E. He could just as easily have led the chord to the dominant of C♯ and ended the song in that key; this alternative resolution of the F♯-minor seventh chord and a hypothetical C♯-minor ending are shown at the end of ex.1a.

Schubert employs not only the ambiguity of the secondary triads of F♯ minor and A major in forging a C♯–E pairing but also the ambiguity of the C♯-minor and E-major triads themselves. The significance of the C♯/E ambiguity becomes evident when one investigates subforeground tonal structure, that is, when one attempts to discover the matrix (to use Carl Schachter's term) around which the prolongations investigated thus far are organized.[6] The surface prolongations can be gathered about two different matrices, namely, those of C♯ and E. The basis for this large-scale dualism is the capacity of each of the two tonics to function as a subordinate harmony within the other; the E-major triad can be the mediant of the key of C♯ minor as well as the tonic of E major, and C♯ minor can be the submediant of E major as well as the tonic of C♯ minor. Schubert keeps both functions of both triads, and hence an E and a C♯ matrix, active in virtually all portions of the song. Schenkerian voice-leading sketches demonstrating the two interpretations of the functions of the C♯ and E triads and the two matrices are shown in exs.1a and 1b.[7] Although it is most convenient to discuss the two interpretations separately, it must be stressed that they are simultaneously active and that they intertwine as one experiences the song.

In mm.1–22 the succession of large-scale harmonies, C♯–E–G♯ major, appears to establish a C♯ matrix, within which E is the mediant (see ex.1a). The emphasis on C♯ minor at the outset, both by extensive foreground prolongation and by the high dynamic level of the cadence at mm.13–14, renders this C♯ matrix readily perceptible.

The passage in mm.23–31 is, because of the preceding music, easily heard as another incipient arpeggiation of the C♯-minor triad; the C♯ harmony of mm.23–29 sounds like the tonic, and the E major of mm.30–31 sounds like the mediant of C♯ minor. The mediant, prolonged for some time, eventually leads to the dominant of C♯ at m.63.[8] The possibility of interpreting mm.65–66 as a foreground arpeggiation of the C♯-minor triad was mentioned earlier (see the slurring of this passage in ex.1a); this C♯-minor triad is the final tonic of the large arpeggiation of mm.23–64.

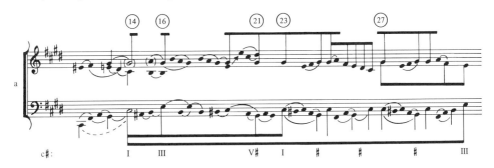

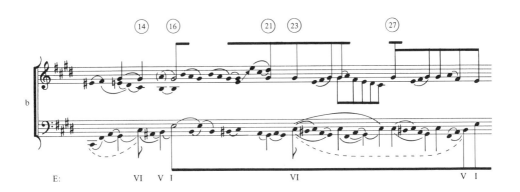

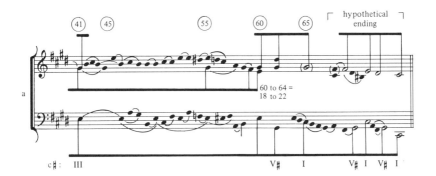

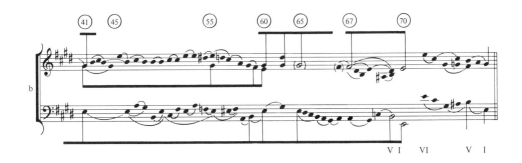

Theoretically, the E-major harmony of the final measures could be understood as mediant harmony in C♯ minor. This interpretation, however, would imply that the song sounds incomplete, which in my opinion it does not. Schubert has in the course of the song imbued the E-major harmony with sufficient "tonic power" that one is prepared by the end to hear it as a tonic rather than as a mediant. Let me verify this point by reexamining the song's harmonies from the standpoint of an E-major rather than a C♯-minor matrix (see ex. 1b).

The initial prolongation of C♯ is shown as a submediant in ex. 1b, and the first E-major harmony in mm. 16–19 is shown as the large-scale tonic. Several factors permit hearing the opening of "Der Wanderer" in this way. As was mentioned, the harmonies of mm. 1–14 function somewhat ambiguously; it is unclear whether the C♯-major harmony of mm. 1–7 is a tonic or a dominant and hence whether C♯ or F♯ is the governing foreground harmony. When E major arrives in mm. 15–19, on the other hand, it is presented in an entirely unclouded fashion. Moreover, Schubert highlights the arrival of E major by placing it within a piano interlude and suddenly dropping the dynamic level. It is therefore quite possible to hear the opening as an introduction of a typically ambiguous nature and mm. 15–19 as the point of establishment of a controlling E-major tonic. It must also be remembered that many early-nineteenth-century works begin with submediant pseudo-tonics, so that a prolongation of C♯-minor harmony at the opening of a work in E major is not at all unusual.

The prolongation of C♯ minor in mm. 20–29 can be interpreted as submediant harmony within E major; it moves in mm. 29–30 to the dominant of E, thus acting, as submediant harmonies often do, as an upper neighbor to the dominant. The following prolongation of E (mm. 32–61) is easily heard as tonic of E major. The G♯-major harmony at m. 64 can be interpreted as III♯ or V/VI in E, and the final measures of the song lie comfortably within that key as well. Note the use of C♯ minor as VI of E in the piano postlude; the first notes of the piano after the end of the vocal line arpeggiate the C♯-minor triad, which leads through vii^7/V to V in E. The final harmonic event in the song, then, is a firm attachment of the C♯-minor triad to the matrix of E.

I have shown that it is possible to hear "Der Wanderer" as being controlled by a C♯-minor as well as an E-major matrix; both keys are active on the highest level of the song. A case could certainly be made for the lesser significance of C♯ minor and for E major as sole tonic; the fact that E major concludes the work is the most important point in favor of that argument. The impression of a C♯-minor matrix created by the frequent enclosing of E major within C♯-minor arpeggiations, however, seems to me to be a vitally important aspect of the song's tonal structure. An analysis that fails to take that aspect into account misses much of the song's subtlety and expressiveness.

Investigation of the text supports a dualistic tonal analysis. The prominent themes of Schmidt's poem—incessant searching, restlessness, and the inability to be content in a given location—are beautifully reinforced by the tonal structure: the tonality is, until the very end, not permitted to settle in any one place but remains torn between two poles.[9] The keys of the double-tonic complex, in fact, seem to act as symbols of the two worlds with which the poem deals; C♯ minor suggests the cold and bleak world of the wanderer, and E major, the world of hope, friendship, and life for which he searches. The association between E and the goal of the wanderer's quest becomes especially clear in the long E-major passage of mm. 32–58, during which the text describes his dream world in detail.

I turn now to Schubert's "Meeres Stille." Schubert wrote two settings of Goethe's famous poem of that name in 1815, one on 20 June and the other on 21 June.[10] The settings are deceptively simple; both melody and accompaniment are unusually static for Schubert, and the tonal structures of both versions seem, at first glance, quite straightforward. Both begin and end with C-major triads and thus appear superficially to be in that key. Recent studies of the song, while unveiling many of its subtleties, have accepted the C-major tonality at face value. Peter Gülke suggests that there is something mysterious or puzzling ("rätselhaft") about the harmonic progression but refers to the song as a "C-Dur-Lied."[11] Although Timothy Jackson's discussion of "Meeres Stille" focuses not on tonal structure but on differences between the two versions in terms of motivic development, the accompanying voice-leading sketches indicate that he regards both versions as being ultimately in C major.[12] Lawrence Kramer believes that the song "is based on a recursive principle of enclosure: C major surrounds E major, which in turn surrounds A minor." C major, then, has primary status in Kramer's tonal analysis as well. From his perspective, E major is presented in a "surprisingly feeble" manner, "start[ing] off strongly and then disintegrat[ing]."[13]

An approach based on the search for matrices around which the various key areas are organized leads to an entirely different assessment of the roles of C major and E major: E major emerges as a tonal center equivalent in importance to C, with the result that the song is governed by the complex C/E rather than just by its initial and final tonic of C major.

A brief look at the tonal structure of the first version provides an instructive starting point for my discussion of "Meeres Stille." I agree with

Jackson's assessment of the first version: it does seem to be controlled by the single tonic C (although, as will be shown, there are forces working to weaken that tonic). As shown by the voice-leading sketch in ex. 2a, there are no obstacles to interpreting all the work's harmonies in terms of a C matrix. The C-major to E-major progression of the first phrase (mm. 1–4) is followed by the prolongation in the second phrase (mm. 5–8) of the F-major harmony. The following phrase (mm. 9–16) consists almost entirely of a rising chromatic sequence; since this sequence leads to another F triad (now F minor) in m. 15, it continues the prolongation of F harmony initiated in m. 6. In m. 16 the phrase comes to rest on a C-major triad. In retrospect, mm. 1–16 can be regarded as having prolonged the opening triad of C major (see the large slur in the bass of ex. 2a); the large-scale harmonic progression C–E–F–C, or I–III♯–IV–I in C, can be further reduced to I–IV–I in C and ultimately to the framing triad of C.

In m. 21 Schubert destabilizes the C-major harmony by adding a seventh, and the resulting seventh chord is employed in m. 22 as a German sixth chord leading to the dominant of E. That dominant resolves to an E-minor triad in m. 25, which drops abruptly to the C-major harmony in m. 27 as the opening music returns (with slight modifications). Since the E-minor key area of mm. 21–26 is enclosed by the significant cadential and recapitulatory C-major harmonies of mm. 16 and 27, one can interpret the E-minor harmony as being subordinate to C major; such oscillation between a given harmony and one of its third relations is a common prolongational technique in nineteenth-century music.[14]

The final section of the song (mm. 27–35) prolongs C major in an even more obvious manner. The I–III♯ progression of mm. 27–30, almost identical to the opening phrase of the song, is followed once again by IV (m. 31). The subdominant harmony this time moves through a French sixth chord to the dominant of C, which in turn resolves to the tonic. The underlying progression of the final section, then, is I–III♯–IV–V–I in C, a traditional arpeggiation expanding the C-major harmony. The first version of "Meeres Stille," in short, contains three substantial prolongations of the C-major harmony. These prolongations, along with the use of C major as initial and final triad, lend a high profile to the C harmony and establish over the course of the song a clearly perceptible C-major matrix to which all harmonies in the song are subordinate.[15]

Although it can be regarded as monotonal, the first version indicates that Schubert was beginning to toy with tonal dualism. At the beginning of the song, for example, Schubert sets up an ambiguity between the keys of C and F; that is, it is not immediately clear whether the harmonies are to be regarded as forming a C-major or an F-major matrix.

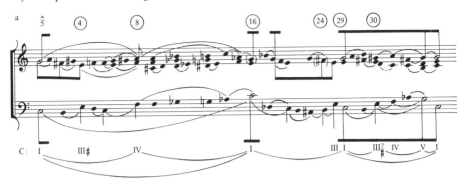

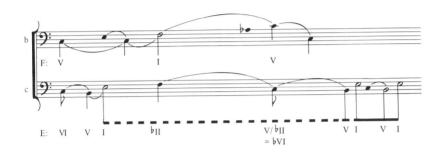

Example 2. Schubert's "Meeres Stille," first version (D.215a), analyzed in terms of (a) C major, (b) F major, and (c) E major.

The C-major and the F-major and -minor harmonies in mm.1–21 can be interpreted not only as I and IV in C, respectively (as in ex.2a), but also as V and I in F (see ex.2b). Schubert fuels this ambiguity by avoiding the G-major harmony in these opening measures. One strong presentation of that harmony could have swung the tonal pendulum away from the key of F and toward that of C, but although he comes within touching distance of the dominant of C in mm.13–14, Schubert does not actually state it during the opening section. Only at the very end of the song, within the aforementioned arpeggiation of the C-major triad (mm.27–35), does Schubert lead the F-major harmony to that of G major, thereby placing F major, now definitely heard as a subdominant, within the C-major matrix.

The E harmony is an even more significant rival to the tonic of C than F is. The strong cadence to E in the first phrase, for instance, could certainly suggest that E, rather than the weakly presented initial C harmony, is the song's tonic; that is, the progression of the initial phrase can be heard not only as I–V/III♯–III♯ in C but also as VI–V–I in E. The sustained dominant of E in m.24, by far the most conspicuous dominant in the song, and its subsequent resolution are further ripples in the E-major undercurrent. Finally, the progression resulting from the connection of the E-minor triad in m. 25 with the returning opening music of mm. 27–30 (E–C–B–C) can be heard not only as III–I–V/III–III in C but also as I–VI–V–I in E. *preferably*

Example 2c shows an interpretation of mm. 1–30 in terms of a controlling tonic of E. There are some difficulties with this hearing, however; the prominent F-major harmony, in particular, subverts it. Without that harmony the large-scale progression of mm. 4–24 (E–C–B) could easily be heard as I–VI–V in E. The presence of the F harmony between E and C renders the progression somewhat illogical in terms of an E matrix (whereas it can be accommodated within a C matrix). *but it is there*

At the end of the first version, the vaguely suggested matrix of E is firmly counteracted. The nature of the chord in m. 30—a seventh chord rather than a stable triad—weakens the impression that E is the controlling key. The destabilization of the E harmony, along with the aforementioned absorption of the E harmony into the final arpeggiation of C, grants C major a definite supremacy over E and permits it to function as a satisfying final tonic and as the sole controlling tonic of the song. It is primarily because the rival tonics of F and E are ultimately engulfed by the tonic of C that the first version is a piece in C major rather than a piece based on a pairing of keys.

When Schubert set "Meeres Stille" a second time, he preserved many aspects of his setting of 20 June. The harped chord accompaniment is common to both versions, although it is more consistently employed in the second. Both versions begin and end with C-major triads. Both have a cadence to E major near the opening (although it occurs four bars earlier in the first version) and a cadence to the dominant of E near the end (mm. 23–24 in both versions, with identical melodies and chords). The melody at "ungeheuren Weite" and both piano and voice parts at the final cadence are virtually the same in the two versions as well. In terms of tonal structure, however, Schubert radically transformed the song when he returned to it on 21 June: by making a number of telling changes, he established E as a second large-scale tonic, paired with C.

The revised opening already hints at the pairing; whereas in the first version he skims through the C and E harmonies quite rapidly within the first phrase (mm. 1–4), Schubert begins the second version with a juxtaposition of prolongations of the C and E triads, allotting a four-measure phrase to each (mm. 1–4 and 5–8, respectively). The broadened presentation of juxtaposed C and E harmonies in the second version suggests their increased importance not only as individual entities but as a pair.

Additional changes in the second version undermine the key of C and allow the key of E to become equally significant. In the first version the initial cadence to E is followed by prolongation of F harmony in mm. 5–15 and a cadence to C in m. 16. This series of events reinforces the overall key of C and subverts E in two ways. First, it permits the interpretation of C as tonic and of E as a subordinate harmony (a mediant within a large plagal prolongation of C). Second, the prolonged F harmony in itself, more easily heard in terms of a C than of an E matrix, encourages the perception of C, not E, as overall tonic. In the second version, however, the progression from E to F to C is eliminated; the initial cadence to E is followed not by F and C harmonies but by prolongations of A minor (mm. 9–12) and F major (mm. 13–16), whereupon a stepwise succession of passing chords draws a direct line from the F triad to the B-major harmony at m. 24.[16] This revised progression entirely alters the tonal situation. Since there is no cadence to C comparable to that of the first version's m. 16, the initial harmonies do not form a progression prolonging C major, and the E triad is not, as at the beginning of the first version, subordinated to C. Furthermore, the new prolongation of A minor, unlike the prolongation of F major that appears at the corresponding point of the first version, is equally readily heard in terms of a matrix of C or E; A minor is VI of C and IV of E.

In the first version the B-major to E-minor motion of mm. 24–26 is followed by a significant assertion of C-major harmony in the form of a return of the opening material. That recapitulatory C-major harmony connects with the C-major triad of m. 16 to create a large prolongation of C. The C-major harmony at m. 27, furthermore, initiates an arpeggiation of the C-major triad within which the E-major harmony functions as a mediant. In the second version Schubert excises the return of the opening, thereby altering not only the form of the song but also its tonal structure; the elimination of the recapitulatory C-major harmony does away both with the oscillatory prolongation C–E–C and the arpeggiation C–E–G–C that occurs in the first version. The removal of the first version's large prolongations of C major, within which E is subordinate to C, drastically affects the roles of the C and E harmonies; since the E harmony is never subordinated to C, it gains the capacity to assert itself as a tonic equally as significant as C.

An additional small change in the second version also bolsters the key of E. Whereas the E harmony is destabilized near the end of the first version by the addition of dissonance (m. 30), that harmony remains a stable triad and thus a potential tonic even within the final measures of the second version (see mm. 25, 28–29).

The preceding discussion has drawn attention to the changes in the second version that enable E to assume the role of a controlling tonic alongside C. The following remarks clarify how the pairing of C and E operates in the second version and how this pairing relates to the text of the song. The reader can see in ex. 3a that the matrix of C, although it is much less clearly perceptible than in the first version, does not completely fade out of the picture in the second version. The fact that C major retains the role of initial and final triad certainly suggests that this harmony still plays a significant role. Furthermore, the increased emphasis on the C-major harmony in the initial measures of the second version encourages a C-oriented interpretation of the succeeding harmonies: the prolongations of C major, E major, A minor, and F major (mm. 1–16) could be interpreted as I–III♯ (= V/VI)–VI–IV in C. On the other hand, C receives no obvious corroboration as overall tonic between m. 16 and the end. Schubert could easily have supplied such corroboration; for example, had he stated the dominant and tonic of C after the initial harmonies of C, E, A, and F, a clear C-major matrix would have emerged. He refrains, however, from using the dominant at this point. In fact, he avoids the dominant of C entirely, except within the cadences in mm. 3 and 31.

Instead of linking the A and F harmonies of mm. 9–16 to the dominant of C to establish an obvious matrix of C, Schubert connects them to the dominant of E and then resolves that dominant to E major (subsequently converted to E minor). The harmonies of mm. 8–29 (E, A, F, B, and E), then, unlike the internal harmonies of the first version, are not directly involved in prolonging C major, and a matrix of C is therefore much less clearly perceptible.

Although the harmonies of mm. 8–29 cannot be heard as directly prolonging C, they do form a logical prolongation of E major (see the bass slurs in ex. 3a). It could be argued that the initial C-major prolongation, the large internal E-major prolongation, and the cadential dominant and tonic of mm. 31–32 form an all-encompassing C-major matrix; the dotted bass beam and the lower roman numerals in ex. 3a show this interpretation.[17] As the use of a dotted beam suggests, I am uneasy with this neat and tidy Schenkerian interpretation. It is "correct" in the abstract, but it does not accurately reflect my experience of the song, particularly of its conclusion. In most tonal works a dominant-to-tonic motion near the end has great structural significance; this motion, leading the music to its expected and longed-for point of conclusion, resolves all tensions generated within the work and thus deserves to be highlighted by stems and beams within a voice-leading sketch. The G-to-C progression at the end of the second version of "Meeres Stille," however, does not sound like a

Example 3. Schubert's "Meeres Stille," second version (D.216), analyzed in terms of (a) C major and (b) E major.

long-awaited, expected resolution. It lacks conviction as a final cadence; it is somewhat unstable and unsatisfying, quite unlike the final cadence of the first version. (I am not, of course, suggesting that Schubert's ending is a mistake; I discuss the reasons for this vaguely troubling conclusion in due course.) Since I hear the C-major ending as unstable, I am reluctant to treat it as an event of structural primacy and to portray the song as being based on an overarching C-major matrix. The interpretation in terms of a C-major matrix is, in my opinion, at most a half-truth.

Example 3b shows the other half of what I perceive to be the tonal structure: all the harmonies of the song, not only those of mm. 8–29, can easily be gathered around an E matrix. As I mentioned earlier, the harmonies of mm. 8–29 can be heard as prolonging E major; the progression E–A–F–B–E is I–IV–♭II–V–I within E. This large prolongation of E is shown here not as an expanded mediant of C, as in ex. 3a, but as the core of an E matrix. The I–V–I framework of this matrix is clearly articulated in the music; the initial tonic is the goal of the first strong cadence in the song (m. 8), the dominant is the only internal harmony that is sustained by a fermata (m. 24), and the final tonic is a substantial prolongation (mm. 25–29).

The beginning and ending of the song, although not literally enclosed within the E matrix, are easily drawn into it. As was already shown in connection with the first version, the initial C–B–E progression can be regarded as VI–V–I of E. What of the final three measures of the song? Because the E matrix is so clearly presented in the song's first twenty-nine measures, that matrix is able to absorb even the C-major harmony of the final measures; that is, the final C-major harmony sounds like the submediant of E rather than a tonic.[18] The end of ex. 3b shows a hypo-thetical E-major ending for the song within which Schubert's unstable C-major harmony is actually treated as a submediant; it is led, as at the beginning of the song, to the dominant of E, which resolves to the tonic. This ending sounds, to my ears, more satisfying than Schubert's C-major conclusion; this is the resolution toward which the music seems to strive but that Schubert deliberately avoids.

With the establishment of a true tonal pairing in the second version of "Meeres Stille" (achieved by the significant weakening of the origi-nal tonic of C major and concomitant strengthening of E major), and with the unstable conclusion made possible by that pairing, Schubert more powerfully addresses certain ingredients of Goethe's text than in the monotonal first version: conflict, helpless paralysis, and anxiety. Like "Der Wanderer" (and like many of the poems that Schubert chose to set to music), the poem deals with a protagonist in conflict with his envi-ronment; hostile natural forces have placed him in a position of utter helplessness and have prevented him from reaching the goal for which he set sail. The tonal conflict between E and C is an appropriate musical symbol for the collision between man and nature. The final cadence to C major in a context that gravitates toward E, furthermore, not only par-allels the sailor's inability to attain his goal[19] but also evokes an intense sense of disquiet. As his directions to the performer in both versions in-dicate ("*ängstlich* [anxiously]"), Schubert viewed anxiety and apprehen-siveness as the primary mood of the text; in his second setting he was much more successful in conveying it. It is a remarkable aspect of the second version of "Meeres Stille" that the conclusion on the opening harmony does not result in a sense of resolution and long-awaited ar-rival but rather functions as a musical representation of tension and the inability to reach a desired goal.[20]

I have studied two examples of Schubert's employment of tonal pair-ing, a technique that was to become a cornerstone of late-nineteenth-century tonal practice. I have shown that his manner of establishing tonal pairings is in some respects similar to that of later composers: the first three points on Lewis's list of common manifestations of tonal pairing, a list based on late-nineteenth-century practice, can to some extent be applied to Schubert's songs. To be sure, there are some important differences between Schubert's pairings and those of later composers. Whereas Schubert's juxtapositions of the two tonics, as illustrated particularly by "Der Wanderer," do not differ from those found in late-nineteenth-century works, his way of mixing the two keys by exploiting ambiguous functions (Lewis's second point) is not necessarily identical to that of later composers. I have shown that in "Der Wanderer" and "Meeres Stille," Schubert employs harmonies that function within two tonics to create progressions that simultaneously prolong both. Although such dualistic prolongations can be found in some late-nineteenth-century works,[21] much late-nineteenth-century harmony is not clearly prolongational in nature; ambiguous harmonic functions may thus operate differently in late-nineteenth-century tonal pairings. (Much more research of tonal pairing in late-nineteenth-century music will be required before the precise nature of the differences can be determined.) Conflation of two tonics, the third technique on Lewis's list, is much less significant for Schubert than for later composers; such conflation occurs only in "Der Wanderer," and even there, with one exception (the passage at mm. 65–66), in an incidental manner. The fourth technique mentioned by Lewis, "superposition of lines or textures in one key on those in another," is not represented in the songs studied here (nor, to my knowledge, in any of Schubert's songs). The techniques of superposition, and of the conflation of two tonics, were not able to flower until a more liberal approach toward dissonance evolved in the later nineteenth century.

Although Schubert uses tonal pairing somewhat differently than later composers do, his reasons for employing the practice seem to be identical to theirs. William Kinderman points out that Wagner uses tonal pairings to "reflect the underlying tensions of the drama" and to "underline psychological conflicts between characters."[22] In "Der Wanderer" and "Meeres Stille" the young Schubert similarly utilizes tonal pairing to represent tensions and conflicts inherent in his texts. He does so on a much smaller scale, but certainly no less skillfully and no less effectively than Wagner and other later composers.

NOTES

1. See, for example, Thomas Denny's article "Directional Tonality in Schubert's Lieder," in *Franz Schubert—Der Fortschrittliche? Analysen-Perspectiven-Fakten,* ed. Erich W. Partsch, 37–53 (Tutzing: Hans Schneider, 1989), and my article "Alterna-

tives to Monotonality in Early Nineteenth-Century Music," *Journal of Music Theory* 25, no.1 (spring 1981): 1–16.

2. Robert Bailey, "An Analytical Study of the Sketches and Drafts," in *Prelude and Transfiguration from "Tristan and Isolde,"* ed. Bailey, 113–46 (New York: Norton, 1985), 121–22.

3. William Kinderman, "Dramatic Recapitulation in Wagner's *Götterdämmerung,*" *19th-Century Music* 4, no.2 (fall 1980): 102n and 106.

4. Christopher Lewis, *Tonal Coherence in Mahler's Ninth Symphony,* Studies in Musicology no.79 (Ann Arbor: UMI Research Press, 1984), 6.

5. Since the song begins with a substantial prolongation of C♯ and ends by prolonging E, a case could be made for referring to it as directionally tonal. The techniques of directional tonality and tonal pairing are not, of course, mutually exclusive.

6. See Carl Schachter, "Analysis by Key: Another Look at Modulation," *Music Analysis* 6, no.3 (Oct. 1987): 291.

7. The use of Schenkerian analysis, an approach firmly rooted in monotonal practice, in connection with nonmonotonal works may strike some readers as methodologically problematical. The application of the approach to nonmonotonal early-nineteenth-century works is, I believe, justified by the adherence of these works to many aspects of the prevailing monotonal practice (e.g., to the use of linear progressions or tonic-dominant axes). That is, these works display so many similarities to the contemporary works to which Schenkerian analysis is routinely applied that the approach remains applicable to them as well. The tonal dualisms of the works discussed here cannot be captured in detail in a single sketch; I have therefore employed pairs of sketches that are vertically aligned.

8. The fact that the music toward the end of the arpeggiation in mm. 58–64 is identical to that at the end of the first C♯-minor arpeggiation (mm.16–22) might make one hear the second, much larger arpeggiation as an expansion of the first.

9. Schubert does bow to the musical conventions of his time, providing an unambiguous ending in spite of the unresolved textual conflict. At the end of the second version of "Meeres Stille," however, Schubert responds to a similarly unresolved textual conflict in quite a different manner, as will be shown.

10. The earlier setting of "Meeres Stille" was first reproduced by O. E. Deutsch in "Ein unbekanntes Goethe-Lied von Schubert" (An unfamiliar Goethe-song by Schubert), *Schweizerische Musikzeitung* 92, no.11 (1 Nov. 1952): 446–48. It can now also be found in the *Neue Schubert-Ausgabe* 4, *Lieder* (Basel: Bärenreiter-Verlag Kassel, 1970), 1b:197.

11. Peter Gülke, *Franz Schubert und seine Zeit* (Regensburg: Laaber-Verlag, 1991), 118.

12. Timothy Jackson, "Schubert's Revisions of *Der Jüngling und der Tod,* D.545a–b, and *Meeresstille,* D. 216a–b," *Musical Quarterly* 75, no.3 (fall 1991): 336–61. Although Jackson's voice-leading sketches on p.354 are similar to my C-major interpretations (exs.2a and 3a), some important differences exist. In his sketch of the first setting, for example, Jackson does not allot structural significance to the C-major harmony of m.27, treating the bass note at that point (which he erroneously shows as an A) as a mere neighbor note to B. I feel that because the C-major harmony of m.27 introduces a return of the opening, it is comparable in significance to the initial C-major harmony; I therefore connect it to the bass beam in ex.2a rather than treat it as a neighbor note. I discuss other differences between Jackson's and my interpretations later.

13. Lawrence Kramer, "The Schubert Lied: Romantic Form and Romantic Consciousness," in *Schubert: Critical and Analytical Studies,* ed. Walter Frisch, 200–236 (Lincoln: University of Nebraska Press, 1986), 211.

14. I have listed many examples of such oscillatory third progressions in chapter 2

of my Ph.D. dissertation, "Third Relation and Dominant in Late Eighteenth- and Early Nineteenth-Century Music" (Yale University, 1980). My final example in that chapter is the second version of "Meeres Stille"; I there interpreted the song quite differently than I do here, namely, as reducing to the large-scale oscillatory third progression C–E–C (and ultimately to C itself).

15. Note the absence of a final descent in exs. 2 and 3. I have not been able to arrive at a convincing fundamental line for either version of the song. Jackson's sketches similarly lack a descent from the primary tone G. The open-ended effect resulting from the nonconnection of scale degree 5 to scale degree 1 is likely intended to contribute to a sense of unresolved tension at the end of the song.

16. By referring to this progression as having an embellishing function, I do not mean to contradict Kramer's various comments on the significance of individual chords within the progression ("Schubert Lied," 212–13), nor do I wish to deny that this progression, with its associations of sinking into the abyss of death, exerts a strong emotional impact.

17. Timothy Jackson, in "Schubert's Revisions," interprets the second version in this manner, as does Oswald Jonas in the appendix to Elisabeth Mann Borgese's translation of Schenker's *Harmonielehre* [Harmony] (Cambridge: MIT Press, 1973), 374.

18. I disagree with Kramer's statement that the E triad is "demoted to a diatonic step within C major" at the end of the song ("Schubert Lied," 211). It is precisely because no clear demotion of E from tonic to mediant takes place that C major is unable to function as a strong tonic at the end of the second version.

19. The latter idea was suggested to me in 1980 by Jeffrey Stirling, then an undergraduate music student at Yale University.

20. Other authors have interpreted the relation between music and text in "Meeres Stille" quite differently. Kramer makes many convincing observations about the manner in which the harmonies of the song reflect the poem's anxiety and its terror. His suggestion, however, that the surrounding of A minor by E major, and the surrounding of E major by C major, creates a "schematic portrait of the ship that the poem [*sic*] imagines enveloped by the 'monstrous breadth' of the ocean" ("Schubert Lied," 210) conflicts with my perception that C major does not surround E but is, on the contrary, subsumed by it. Jackson's motivic analysis ("Schubert's Revisions," 350–55) leads him to conclude that the second version, unlike the first, ends with a suggestion of hope and thus takes Goethe's optimistic poetic sequel, "Glückliche Fahrt [Prosperous voyage]," into account. I cannot hear the ending of the second version in the positive sense that Jackson proposes but agree with Gülke's observation (*Franz Schubert,* 118) that the song's abrupt withdrawal into silence renders it incompatible with a succeeding "prosperous voyage."

21. See, for example, Lewis, *Tonal Coherence,* 69.

22. Kinderman, "Dramatic Recapitulation," 106.

Chopin's Alternatives to Monotonality: A Historical Perspective

JIM SAMSON

This chapter is based on a study written for a symposium entitled "Alternatives to Monotonality," and Chopin is an appropriate and even obvious choice of composer to illustrate such a theme. There are already several published articles on Chopin's alternatives to monotonality, including the one from which the conference took its name.[1] In this chapter I seek a different methodological orientation in approaching the subject. Almost all the existing literature has been analytical or theoretical in thrust, asking how the alternative tonal structures function. I ask instead where they came from and what made them possible, questions that require an investigation of context.

It is worth expanding on this distinction in aims and methods. History and structure offer complementary modes of understanding that may be mutually enriching, provided we remain clear about their separate areas of competence. There are, of course, meeting points between them at a very basic level of inquiry. Analytical tools depend on normative categories that emerge from history, just as historical subject matter properly includes musical structures. Ideally we might seek other meeting points in a calculated enterprise of mediation between history and structure. This is currently a major project in cultural theory,[2] and it is all the more interesting and challenging in that the mediation may penetrate even the underlying premises. There are also meeting points of a less happy kind, however, resulting from a lack of clarity about the scope and limits of the two modes of inquiry, such that research of the one is allowed to generate conclusions about the other. Such conclusions will almost certainly lack refinement.

Consider the competence of analytical inquiry. That competence is first and foremost to reveal elements of structure in the terms of an underlying theory. This latter point is important. Virtually all worthwhile analysis proceeds from an underlying theory, even when the analyst does not recognize that theory. Although analysis also has a bearing on other fields of study, notably stylistic history and music perception, its explanatory power is limited in these fields. I think that it is worth stressing this limitation, since some analysts still contend that their results should be validated by perception or that they may usefully inform music history.

From an analytical perspective alternatives to monotonality may well represent a major departure from norms of structure. It does not follow that they represent an equally major departure from norms of perception, however, or indeed from norms of style. This chapter does not address matters of perception, which belong within the cognitive psychology of music, but concentrates on the issue of style, which is properly a subject of historical investigation. Rather than examine the relevant works of Chopin through detailed analysis, I address their stylistic context, hoping to identify some of the factors that enabled his alternatives to monotonality. This investigation, in turn, may suggest a need to qualify any notions of a generalized early-nineteenth-century ancestry of progressive or directional tonality.

Chopin's musical style was grounded in a postclassical concert repertory that emerged in the early nineteenth century in response to rapid changes in the socioeconomics of musical life. This repertory was addressed to a specific taste-public, located in the benefit concert and the middle-class salon; it was designed to be popular and ephemeral; its producers willingly accepted its commodity status. Favored genres were independent rondos, ornamental variation sets, fantasies, potpourris, and concertos, and favored style sources were contemporary French and Italian opera, folk song, and folk dance.

Two aspects of the repertory served to weaken an overall monotonal regulation of events. The first is the influence of improvisation on composition. Within the world of "pianist's music," which Fétis, in his review of Chopin's first concert in Paris, was careful to distinguish from "pianoforte music,"[3] improvisation was of central importance, playing a role in the decoration of cantilene, in the practice of "preludizing," and in extempore performances on a given theme. There are many accounts of improvisation in method books and contemporary criticism[4] that offer a fairly clear picture of its typical practices and of the ways in which it influenced composition. To avoid belaboring points that have been well made elsewhere,[5] I refer here only briefly to some areas of influence. There is the influence on composed-out ornamental melody; on the extended, deliberately teasing introductions to variation sets and rondos; and on the frequent changes of mood, tempo, and tonal region that characterize pieces in "free" style (caprices and above all fantasies). In all these areas the practice of improvisation, by stretching the conventions, was a determinant of style.

Chopin's mature music both transcended and remembered such associations. The transcendence is obvious enough. To appreciate it we need only consider his approach to three genres that obviously connote improvisation, the prelude, impromptu, and fantasy. In this context not only did he engage in projects of generic renovation, giving substance and weight to genres whose conventions were weakly defined; he also employed cyclic techniques in these genres (and only in these genres), most notably in the impromptus.[6] In all three cases his concern for integration within the work and within the cycle spelled out his rejection of the genre titles' obvious connotations. The mature Chopin was defiantly a composer, not a pianist-composer.

For all that, however, improvisation remained a primary style-historical source for Chopin's music, a fact that would have been obvious enough to his contemporaries (although it scarcely registers today). It can be illuminating to examine even the major late works within this context, mapping their characteristic procedures against the documented archetypes of improvisation. There is the succession of type-conscious thematic treatments in the Fourth Ballade, op. 52, juxtaposing plain, canonic, and cantabile-decorative presentations. There is the calculated formal discontinuity of the Polonaise-Fantasy. There is the play on styles and genres at the opening of the Fantasy op. 49, reinforced by explicit intertextual connections with the Impromptu in F♯ Major, op. 36, and the Prelude in G Major, op. 28, no. 3. In different ways all evoke the typical practices of contemporary improvisation.

The harmonic freedom encouraged by improvisation is particularly relevant to the theme of this volume. I confine my observations in this chapter to a single issue: the common practice of extempore preludizing as applied both to extended improvisations and to composed works. Czerny identified several types of improvised prelude and remarked of the longer ones: "It is not necessary to begin in the same key in which one must conclude. . . . Daring, remote modulations are appropriate in these preludes, and whoever possesses a thorough knowledge of harmony can easily indulge in the most interesting ventures in this respect."[7] He offers several examples, including some that define the home key only at the end. Chopin's Prelude in A Minor, op. 28, no. 2, really takes its origins in this characteristic keyboard expression of a conventional recitative principle: the novelty here lies only in the transformed generic context.

The improvised prelude informs as well many of the composed introductions to variation-sets, fantasies, rondos, and even sonatas produced by pianist-composers in the early nineteenth century, the young Chopin among them. It was far from uncommon for such introductions, as in many a recitative, to begin outside the tonic key either in a tonally ambiguous area or in an alternative key. Examples could be multiplied: Czerny himself in his Brilliant Fantasy on English National Airs, op. 545, and his Brilliant Potpourri on Themes from Spohr's "Faust"; Kalkbrenner in his Brilliant Rondo, op. 61; Herz in his Swedish Air with Brilliant Variations, op. 23; Moscheles in his Fantasy, Variations and Finale, op. 46; and many others.

Several stages in Chopin's absorption of this conventional practice into his composed music can be identified. In early works, such as the Rondo in E♭ Major, op. 16, or the Bolero op. 19, the tonally inductive prelude is cleanly separated from the rest of the work, as in the pieces by the previously cited composers. It is in the spirit of such pieces that Chopin was able later to place the Andante Spianato before the Grande Polonaise. The next stage includes works like the Scherzo in C♯ Minor, op. 39, which preserves a thematically discrete prelude that functions as a tonal anacrusis but is inseparably linked to the substance of the piece, and the Second Scherzo, op. 31, whose opening paragraph retains the tonal function of an inductive prelude while utterly transforming its formal function. Finally, in the Fantasy op. 49 the formal function of a prelude is maintained, but it is no longer congruent with an ambitious tonal anacrusis that extends well beyond the prelude to the later stages of the work.[8] In all these pieces, even in the Fantasy, the tonal practice takes its origins in, and retains some memory of, the inductive prelude.

Not so in the Second Ballade, op. 38, Chopin's only work, I submit, to employ a two-key scheme—one in which the key actually shifts—and therefore quite different in organization from the other works mentioned. The enabling factors here lie not in extempore preludizing but in a second aspect of the repertory: the formal methods characteristic of extended works of the so-called brilliant style—concertos, rondos, fantasies, and so forth.

The term *brilliant style* was used initially by late-eighteenth-century theorists to identify one of the several components of contemporary compositional practice.[9] As the century turned the term was applied to a manner of playing associated particularly with the qualities of the Viennese piano[10] and then more widely to identify the music of the pianist-composers who came into prominence in the 1820s. This repertory had a sharply defined and widely recognized individual profile in contemporary perceptions. It was described as a "modern school" whose sole object seemed to be "to play the greatest possible number of notes in a given time," in contrast to the "grave and well considered works of Dussek and Clementi and the more thoughtful and less mechanical creations of Beethoven and Weber."[11]

The brilliant style encompassed a dual impulse of display and sentiment; in technical terms that meant bravura figuration and popular melody, respectively. Often the melodic basis of these pieces was a familiar operatic aria or folk song (as in the many fantasies, variations, and potpourris on well-known themes) or an independent tune grounded in a popular genre—a dance type, barcarolle, march, berceuse, or siciliano. Formally, melodies tended to be squared off against passagework, with a good deal of internal repetition and sharply defined sectional divisions, the whole at times amounting to little more than a linked chain of relatively self-contained melodic or figurative paragraphs. Ornamentation was an essential ingredient of this music, and characteristically there was a marked disjunction between structure and ornament. Among the many exponents of the brilliant style were Kalkbrenner, Herz, Pixis, Moscheles, and Klengel. It was given its finest expression in certain "public" works by Hummel, Weber, and the young Chopin.

Although these pieces are usually monotonal, the stylistic features I have outlined work decisively against the kind of long-range tonal control that we associate with Viennese classical composers and their successors in Austro-Germany. This circumstance is well demonstrated by the repertory's resistance to voice-leading analysis. In the first place the severely sectional construction, together with the high level of literal repetition, often results in a juxtaposition of discrete structures, and even of discrete *Ursatz* forms, with no obvious way of assigning priority. In the second place the lack of integration between an underlying harmonic framework and the ornamental detail it supports makes it difficult to establish any genuine prolongational relationship of middleground to background. As a result, the final tonic, whatever its referential value, is seldom a completion of extended tonal spans. Thus, the formal methods of the brilliant style were singularly well placed to promote alternatives to monotonality.

Such alternatives are easily found in this repertory. Predictably, they are most common in potpourris and fantasies based on operatic themes or folk songs. I will confine myself to a few examples: Czerny's Fantasy on "La Muette di Portici" and his Caprice and Brilliant Variations on "Torquato Tasso"; Blahetka's Fantasy and Variations on a Dutch Folk Song, op. 33; and Moscheles's Second Fantasy on "The Siege of Rochelle." Of more significance, however, are the directional schemes found in independent single-movement pieces, for example by Clementi, Hummel, and Kalkbrenner. Here we have a pertinent context for the Second Ballade; I return to it later.

It must be emphasized that the early works of Chopin, in particular his rondos, ornamental variations, and polonaises, belong to the brilliant style. Like other pieces from the same world, they are composed formally, that is, in relatively discrete, tonally closed components linked together with little attempt to assimilate detail to whole. Monotonal regulation of the structure is accordingly weak. The same is true throughout the Polish period, even toward its end, when Chopin was beginning to achieve real compositional mastery (as the eccentric tonal organization of the Piano Trio and the Concerto in E Minor suggests).

As was the case with improvisation, the formal methods of the brilliant style were both transcended and remembered by Chopin. He transcended them by shifting priority from formal design to tonal structure, a process that has been traced with exemplary clarity in John Rink's dissertation, the most comprehensive and detailed analysis of Chopin's early music that has been undertaken.[12] Chopin remembered the formal methods of the brilliant style in that the starting point for his mature structures often remains an alternation of lyrical and figurative paragraphs that optimize tonal closure. This point may be demonstrated both by style-critical analysis, as in Józef Chominski's study of the Sonata in B♭ Minor,[13] and by genetic analysis, as in studies of the Polonaise-Fantasy by Wojciech Nowik, Jeffrey Kallberg, and myself.[14]

Such analysis suggests not only that emaciated traces of the brilliant style's formal methods underlie the structural wholes of Chopin's mature music but also that these formal methods were often the initiating and enabling impulse of a work. Chopin's willingness to adjust the tonal settings of extended paragraphs at a very late stage of the creative process (as in the Polonaise-Fantasy) is strong evidence that his arrival at an organic whole was at least partly a matter of the arrangement and adjustment of already composed formal components.

If we view the Second Ballade against this background of alternating, tonally enclosed lyrical and figurative paragraphs, its two-key scheme may be viewed as an extension of, rather than a major departure from, the dynamics of his normative practice, a practice that derived ultimately from the brilliant style. Whatever its structural implications, the two-key scheme was not an enormous step in style for Chopin. Indeed, as intimated earlier, such schemes were not at all uncommon in the repertory of the brilliant style.[15] It is illuminating, for instance, to compare the Ballade's use of interlocking third-related regions (F major and A minor in double sequence) with the directional schemes of Kalkbrenner's Grand Fantasy, op. 68, or Hummel's Fantasy op. 18. In these works there is a similar double sequence of interlocking thirds, D_{minor}^{major} and F major in the Kalkbrenner and Eb major and G minor in the Hummel. The Hummel work, composed in 1805, in fact, offers the same tonal sequence as the Chopin Ballade, although a tone lower. In addition, it seems to foreshadow several other aspects of the mature Chopin. Whereas its two-key scheme looks to the Second Ballade, its formal design anticipates the Polonaise-Fantasy; it similarly comprises a slow introduction, an interrupted first theme, a slow movement, and an unexpected return of the introduction. There are also several gestural details that foreshadow Chopin's works, notably the sequence of chromatic chords followed by a pregnant pause preceding the bravura coda, a moment that is uncannily close to the Fourth Ballade.

This complex of connections with the Hummel Fantasy offers a rather specific instance of Chopin's general stylistic indebtedness to the postclassical concert music of the early nineteenth century. Chopin transformed but never entirely renounced this musical world. This perception is essential to an understanding of his wider significance. Unlike Hummel, Chopin did not seek his project of greatness in other musical worlds. Instead, he transformed the elements of popular concert music until they could themselves contribute to a project of greatness, taking their place alongside more prestigious private or epic musics. Rather than reject the popular in favor of the significant, he transformed the popular into the significant. It is necessary to stress this point because the brilliant style is often represented as merely a passing phase in Chopin's evolution, a phase that left few significant traces. On the contrary, it was the foundation on which he built his mature musical language. The two-key scheme may be understood at least partly in relation to it; it is as much a residue of the past as a premonition of the future.

There is another aspect to the historical perspective on the Second Ballade: a second context. Although his musical style was grounded in postclassical concert music, Chopin simultaneously responded in his own way to aesthetic dimensions of the newly emergent world of early romanticism. These dimensions, too, had a bearing on his tonal practice. I examine two issues related to this point in this chapter. The first concerns the relationship between popular genres and high art music. It has become a commonplace of criticism that "popular" and "significant" musics became increasingly incompatible in nineteenth-century bourgeois society, establishing an opposition between conventional language and an incipient avant-garde. It is less often remarked that in some nineteenth-century music this opposition was actually embodied within the individual work, as popular genres increasingly took on a parenthetical role in art music, rather than a supportive or an enabling one.

Chopin played a major part in this development, extending the play of "topics" (to use Leonard Ratner's term) [16] within classical and post-classical music until it became a counterpoint of generic referents, most commonly based on popular genres—march, funeral march, waltz, mazurka, barcarolle, chorale. Moreover, the genre markers of such referents are counterpointed not only against one another but also against those of the controlling or host genre of a work. The effect of this counterpoint was to isolate the popular genre, to give it boundaries and to place it in a dialogue with the norms of art music. This counterpoint of genres was to be taken much farther at the end of the century; in the music of Mahler and later composers the tension between a controlling genre and the popular genres that invade it often results in a kind of displacement and fragmentation of traditional generic content.

Chopin's counterpoint of genres contributed to a more deeply rooted dialectic within his music, a dialectic between factors that encourage continuity and factors that stabilize and therefore distinguish the individual formal segments of a work. His persistent allusion to genres outside the main controlling genre tends to favor the latter, ascribing a degree of stability and autonomy to individual tonal regions against the larger voice leading. If we return for a moment to the Second Ballade we can see how this issue may offer further illumination of the two-key scheme.

Without addressing directly the interesting question of what Chopin meant by *ballade,* I suggest that one of its markers as a host genre is an association with the barcarolle (at times blended with the siciliano) as guest genre. The opening theme of the Second Ballade is especially close to the archetype of the siciliano as traditionally presented, for instance, in pastoral music, and the tonal setting confirms this association. The connotative values are further exemplified in any number of contemporary Italian and French operas, and the Second Ballade is only one of many early-nineteenth-century piano pieces—most obviously the pastoral rondos that were so popular at the time—that respond to these values. The figurative material, on the other hand, is not just etudelike in a general way. It has explicit intertextual links with the so-called Winter Wind Study, op. 25, no. 11, notable for what Bourniquel called its "irresistible unleashing of power." [17]

The opening theme's tonal differentiation from the figurative material might be viewed, then, as part of a more comprehensive differentiation with an underlying generic basis, and the loss of the initial tonic would take on a symbolic meaning. We would speak here not just of a counter-point of genres but of a conflict of genres, adding a further layer of meaning to the alternation of theme and figuration that Chopin derived from the brilliant style.

The discussion of generic referents leads naturally into the second dimension of the early romantic aesthetic to which Chopin responded: the shaping role of extramusical designates of literary origin. That role was already present, albeit trivially, in the pictorial pieces of a popular repertory, several of which have a two-key scheme (a notable example is Challoner's "Battle of Waterloo"). By choosing the title "ballade," Chopin was, of course, immediately connoting literary influences, but we should note that he uses the title "ballade" by itself. Speculation about Mickiewicz is of limited value, since no specific designate is part of the subject or content of the work, unlike the way in which Lamartine's poetry, for example, is part of the subject (because it is part of the title) of Liszt's *Harmonies poétiques*. Mickiewicz may have played a part in the creative process of the ballades, but that is another matter altogether. Chopin's title is indeed a signifier, but it is one that points only to the narrative quality of the music and the referential code created by a network of generic allusions. Popular genres are, after all, grounded in social functions—dance, worship, mourning, procession—and they often refer to specific affective states; indeed, their role can be partly that of socializing the more extreme affective states.

It was partly through this referential code that nineteenth- and early-twentieth-century critics arrived at the descriptive and even programmatic interpretations of Chopin's music that we tend to dismiss today. The problem with such interpretations is that they allow connotative values to congeal into fixed meanings, which is precisely the problem with references to Mickiewicz. I am suggesting that, given the music's referential code, we do not need a Mickiewicz poem to read the Second Ballade's narrative of innocence under threat, a narrative that in turn presents confrontation, mediation, and transformation. The two-key scheme is a part of that narrative. There is an irresistible parallel, incidentally, with the second of the Nocturnes op. 37, whose barcarolle referent is employed in a very similar way, even down to the final, brief, tonally accommodated reminiscence.

I conclude by returning to the issue of history and structure as complementary modes of understanding. It is obvious that an idea will be expressed in its age's mode of thought, and from the midnineteenth century until relatively recently that mode of thought has been predominantly scientific. Holistic music analysis, like reductionist philosophy, was born of scientism. Just as its application to the individual musical work seeks to embrace contradiction in a higher synthesis, so its search for common principles underlying a group of works tends to subordinate constitutive diversity to an identity principle. As a result analytical inquiry often inclines to a reductive view of history. Major changes in the social history of music between Chopin's age and ours have served to reinforce this reductive tendency, notably the consolidation of a normative repertory of masterworks.

An analytical perspective, then, may seek to view a Chopin work as a unified statement to which alternatives to monotonality represent a potential threat. Such a perspective will also seek to draw that work, together with the rest of his output, into the canon of a notionally unified classical style system, and in relation to such a style system, alternatives to monotonality will naturally be viewed as antecedents of the future rather than as consequents of the past. This perspective tells us above all else about our world; specifically, it tells us what Chopin and the classical style mean to our world.

A historical perspective, on the other hand, seeks to explore the relationship between our world and Chopin's world, and this exploration entails recovering something of Chopin's world and restoring to it the complexity, diversity, and contradiction that inhere in any reality, whether an individual musical work or a style-historical period. It investigates causes rather than functions, styles rather than structures. In this chapter I have attempted to take such a perspective on one specific technical feature of Chopin's music. My conclusions would be underpinned by a study of contemporary theoretical and critical writing, which stresses combinative rather than integrative qualities.[18] They would be further underpinned by a sociohistorical study of Chopin's world. By linking musical styles to particular taste-publics, such a study would resist any temptations to assimilate the brilliant style to a more generalized style system or, alternatively, to ignore it altogether as a shaping influence on Chopin's music.

We need both analytical and historical approaches. I believe, however, that we should pursue each with a certain disciplinary integrity, according to its inner logic, before seeking a project of interdisciplinary mediation. Such a project—linking historical constructs with the systematic study of a field—represents a further stage of inquiry, one whose methods and ultimate findings have only been hinted at here.

NOTES

1. Harald Krebs, "Alternatives to Monotonality in Early Nineteenth-Century Music," *Journal of Music Theory* 25, no. 1 (spring 1981): 1–16.

2. See in particular Alfred Schmidt, *History and Structure,* trans. Jeffrey Herf (Cambridge: MIT Press, 1983).

3. The Fétis review is quoted in Peter Anthony Bloom, "François-Joseph Fétis and the 'Revue Musicale' (1827–1835)" (Ph.D. diss., University of Pennsylvania, 1972), 301–3.

4. For a detailed discussion, see Derek Carew, "An Examination of the Composer/Performer Relationship in the Piano Style of J. N. Hummel" (Ph.D. diss., University of Leicester, 1981).

5. See in particular Irena Poniatowska, "Improwizacja fortepianowa w okresie romantyzmu" (Piano improvisation in the romantic period), *Szkice o kulturze muzycznej XIXw* (Profiles of musical culture of the nineteenth century) (Warsaw: Institut Sztuki, 1980), 4:7–26.

6. I have discussed this issue at length in "Chopin and Genre," *Music Analysis* 8, no. 3 (oct. 1989): 213–31.

7. Carl Czerny, *A Systematic Introduction to Improvisation on the Pianoforte,* trans. and ed. Alice L. Mitchell (New York: Longman, 1983), 11.

8. See Carl Schachter, "Chopin's Fantasy op. 49: The Two-Key Scheme," in *Chopin Studies,* ed. Jim Samson, 221–53. (Cambridge: Cambridge University Press, 1988).

9. References to a brilliant manner date back to Brossard's dictionary of 1701. The brilliant style is discussed in Koch's *Lexicon* of 1802 and elsewhere in the late eighteenth and early nineteenth centuries.

10. See Janet Ritterman, "Piano Music and the Public Concert," in *The Cambridge Companion to Chopin,* ed. Jim Samson, 11–31. (Cambridge: Cambridge University Press, 1992).

11. *The Musical World,* 15 July 1836, and *The Athenaeum,* 27 October 1842.

12. John Rink, "The Evolution of Chopin's 'Structural Style' and its Relation to Improvisation" (Ph.D. diss., Cambridge University, 1989).

13. Józef Chominski, *Sonaty Chopina* [Chopin's sonatas]. (Krakow: Polskie wyd-wo muzyczne, 1960).

14. Jim Samson, "The Composition-Draft of the Polonaise-Fantasy: The Issue of Tonality," in *Chopin Studies,* ed. Samson, 41–58; Wojciech Nowik, "Proces twórczy Fryderyka Chopina w swietle jego autografów muzycznych" (The creative process of Frederic Chopin in light of his musical manuscripts) (Ph.D. diss., University of Warsaw, 1978); Jeffrey Kallberg, "Chopin's Last Style," *Journal of the American Musicological Society* 38, no. 2 (summer 1985): 264–315.

15. It may be noted in passing that since the schemes usually involve third-related keys, they offer a historical perspective on the double-tonic complex identified by Robert Bailey and others in Wagner and post-Wagnerian symphonic structures. See, for example, Bailey's "Das Lied von der Erde: Tonal Language and Formal Design," paper read at the Forty-fourth Annual Meeting of the American Musicological Society, Minneapolis, 21 October 1978.

16. Leonard G. Ratner, *Classic Music: Expression, Form and Style* (New York: Schirmer, 1980).

17. Camille Bourniquel, *Chopin,* trans. Sinclair Road (New York: Grove, 1960), 167.

18. See Ratner, *Classic Music.*

Directional Tonality and Intertextuality: Brahms's Quintet op.88 and Chopin's Ballade op.38

KEVIN KORSYN

1

The second movement of Brahms's Quintet op.88, completed in 1882,[1] exemplifies directional tonality; from $C\sharp^{major}_{minor}$ it chooses a new tonal future, closing in A major. The genesis of this work suggests that its tonal plan was not achieved without reflection, since the movement subsumes two earlier pieces by Brahms, both originally monotonal: a saraband in A^{major}_{minor} and a gavotte in A major, both probably composed in 1855 (see exs.1 and 2).[2] It appears that when Brahms decided to embrace these

Example 1. Brahms, Saraband (1855), mm.1–4.

poco forte

two dances within a single design, he chose as his model another experiment in directional tonality: Chopin's Ballade op.38 (composed 1836–39),[3] which begins in F major and ends in A minor.

In the Quintet directional tonality creates a new tonal future within a stratified discourse in which the authority of the past is invoked and contested. In the light of the Ballade, Brahms reshaped his earlier Saraband and Gavotte, which had their own models in Bach's suites.[4] Thus the Quintet records Brahms's struggle with at least three major precursors: his earlier self, Bach, and Chopin. Moreover, these personalized influences are only part of an intertextual space that also includes all the anonymous forces that both sustain and resist the imagination: the legacy of the tonal system; the protocols of the various genres, forms, and styles available to the composer; and so on. Brahms, anxiously choosing

Example 2. Brahms, Gavotte (1855), mm. 1–8.

an orientation among all these discourses, becomes "both the historian and the agent of his own language."[5]

My juxtaposition of the Ballade and the Quintet, then, does more than merely add another layer to our knowledge of Brahms's use of models. It also raises some urgent questions about intertextuality in music. What was Brahms trying to do for himself by modeling a piece on Chopin? Why does this modeling seem to liberate, rather than limit, Brahms's originality? How does Brahms reinterpret his earlier self? How do all these discourses relate to one another?

These questions propel us toward a theory of intertextuality; without a general account of how composers internalize tradition, particular cases will resist explanation. I therefore interpret the relationship of the Quintet to the Ballade by appropriating two paradigms, both drawn from literary criticism: Harold Bloom's theory of poetic influence and Mikhail Bakhtin's concept of dialogism. By invoking two precursors, two models, two critical languages, I hope to capture the tensions of Brahms's stratified discourse.

Arguing from different perspectives, Bloom and Bakhtin insist that works of art are dynamic relationships rather than static entities, events rather than objects. Adopting this dynamic stance may provoke anxiety, for we must abandon the naïve yet cherished belief that compositions are monadic totalities that can be understood in isolation. We may mourn this loss of autonomy, but only such a sacrifice will enable us to inscribe the Ballade and the Quintet in history. Intertextuality also complicates the status of directional tonality in these works. Instead of being an independent system that can be mastered through a neutral inventory of structure, directional tonality involves reinterpreting prior tonal language. The story of directional tonality unfolds in the context of a *historical poetics* of music.

2

Before we can investigate the model relationship, we must establish that Brahms knew the Ballade prior to reworking his Saraband and Gavotte. Although the date of his first hearing of the Ballade is unknown, we can locate a *terminus ad quem:* 1 November 1877. Brahms discussed the Ballade in detail in a letter to Ernst Rudorff bearing that postmark (Rudorff was one of Brahms's coeditors in the Breitkopf and Härtel edition of Chopin's works, a project that occupied Brahms in the late 1870s).[6] This letter establishes Brahms's thorough familiarity with the Ballade. Significantly, he referred to it as the A-Minor Ballade (and not, as one often sees it listed on concert programs, as the F-Major Ballade). Rudorff had sought advice on several textual problems in the piece, and Brahms's reply reveals an intimate knowledge of the score. Brahms urged Rudorff to retain Chopin's rather puzzling triplet sign in m. 45; he cited a subtle parallelism at m. 147 to decide a disputed bass note in m. 53; and he declared himself in favor of the parallel fifths in mm. 113–14. By 1877, then, five years before completing the Quintet, Brahms not only knew the Ballade but had studied it in depth.

A further historical digression may suggest a reason for Brahms's interest in the Ballade. Like the Quintet, the Ballade may have originated as a monotonal piece. Although no manuscript evidence survives to document this hypothesis, considerable historical testimony supports it. Chopin sanctioned playing the opening Andantino (mm. 1–45) by itself; in the copy belonging to Jane Stirling, double crosses in Chopin's hand frame this section, indicating that it could be played separately.[7] Indeed, according to Pauline Viardot-Garcia, Chopin himself often played it this way; she told Saint-Saëns that he often played the Andantino but never the rest.[8] It is possible, then, that this section had once been an independent piece and that by allowing an alternative mode of performance Chopin still acknowledged its original autonomy. (It would have made a lovely prelude.)

There is also evidence that Chopin first sought to expand the Andantino into a monotonal work. In the 1850s A. J. Hipkins heard Princess Marcelline Czartoryska play "an extended version of the first section only, in F major."[9] Presumably she learned this from Chopin. Perhaps this was the version that Robert Schumann heard in 1836; in a review published in 1841, he wrote that "the impassioned episodes seem to have been inserted later; I recall very well that when Chopin played the Ballade here it concluded in F major; now it ends in A minor."[10] Since Brahms knew both Schumann and Pauline Viardot-Garcia, he could have learned about these issues from them, whether through personal contact or by reading Schumann's criticism.

One reason for Brahms's interest in the Ballade, then, may be that he recognized solutions to problems that he also faced: not only the problem of expanding preexisting material but also the more strenuous challenge of form and directional tonality. Remember that classical forms such as the sonata embody monotonality. If, to paraphrase Tovey, form is tonality writ large, then how can one write directional tonality in the large? This must have been a vexing question for many nineteenth-century composers. Wagner's answers to it are fused with his dramatic action. For composers like Schubert and Wolf, directional tonality is often motivated by text setting.[11] How can one adapt nineteenth-century tonal innovations to purely instrumental works? This question engages Brahms in the Quintet, and the Ballade must have been a stimulus to him. Naturally, it is not a question of borrowing an external formal schema. Rather, Chopin's achievement was to dramatize directional tonality into a new kind of narrative pattern, one that subverts traditional formal paradigms.

3

My intertextual reading of the Ballade and the Quintet will proceed in dialectical stages, starting from the (relatively banal) level of influence as continuity and moving toward a more difficult notion of influence as "*dis*continuous relations between past and present . . . texts,"[12] or what Harold Bloom calls "antithetical influence." Conventional source study will largely determine my first comparison; noting a series of formal correspondences, I inscribe the Ballade and the Quintet within a common tradition, showing that they exemplify similar formal types. Later, however, I reinterpret and reevaluate these preliminary observations. One must therefore follow my analysis with a certain caution, for each stage in this dialectic has only provisional truth; to speak in the manner of Paul Ricoeur, each reading will be "surpassed and retained" in the next.[13]

As a first approximation, then, tables 1 and 2 compare the formal and tonal articulations of the two pieces. Both compositions, as I have already noted, exemplify directional tonality; Chopin begins in F major

Table 1 Chopin, Ballade op. 38, sectional divisions.

Theme	A¹	B¹	A²	B²	A³
Key	F major	A minor	F major	A minor	A minor
Tempo	*andantino*	*presto con fuoco*	tempo 1	*presto con fuoco*	tempo 1
mm.	1–45	46–81	82–139	140–96	196½–204

Table 2 Brahms, Quintet op. 88, second movement, sectional divisions.

Theme	A¹	B¹	A²	B²	A³
Key	$C\sharp_{\mathrm{minor}}^{\mathrm{major}}$	A major	$C\sharp_{\mathrm{minor}}^{\mathrm{major}}$	A major	$A_{\mathrm{minor}}^{\mathrm{major}}$
Tempo	*grave ed appassionato*	*allegretto vivace*	tempo 1	*presto*	tempo 1
mm.	1–31	32–79	80–116	117–63	164–208

and ends in A minor, whereas Brahms moves from $C\sharp_{\mathrm{minor}}^{\mathrm{major}}$ to A major. (Note that Brahms reverses Chopin's key relationship, a decision whose consequences will later become clear.) In both works the gap, the distance between tonal origin and destination, is dramatized as an opposition or collision between two strongly contrasted thematic complexes. The polarity between these two themes involves not only tonality but also tempo, texture, and mood. Rather than restore tonal equilibrium, both works end in the original tempo and with the opening thematic material, but in the *second* key. Chopin's conclusion with his opening material is quite brief compared to Brahms's, but Chopin also alludes to his opening theme in the bass of his second Presto section. (Exs. 3–6 show the opening themes and their final recall in both works.)

In his illuminating discussion of the Ballade, Jim Samson emphasizes the "deliberate discontinuities, tonal and other, at the first division in the form. . . . We step from one tonal platform to the next as to another world."[14] Discontinuity also characterizes the first formal juncture in the Quintet. Chopin's contrast is more explosive, to be sure: after the extreme dynamic restraint of the Andantino (sotto voce and *pianissimo* throughout), the *fortissimo* of the Presto brings a shock, while the use of

Example 3. Chopin, Ballade op. 38, mm. 1–8.

Example 4. Chopin, Ballade op. 38, mm. 195–203.

registral extremes and octave doublings is intentionally startling. Brahms does venture a change of time signature ($\frac{3}{4}$ to $\frac{6}{8}$), however, a disruptive effect that Chopin does not attempt, preferring to keep the Ballade in one meter. In both works the second theme follows without any transition or preparation, thus maximizing contrast.

In both pieces the second theme is incomplete and embraces a transition back to the first theme. Both composers thus contrast the relative autonomy of a closed first theme with a tonally open second theme. As tables 1 and 2 confirm, the alternation of these two themes results

Example 5. Brahms, Quintet op. 88, second movement, mm. 1–7.

in a five-part plan (A¹–B¹–A²–B²–A³). The reappearances of these two themes are far from being mere repetitions, however. As I show later, the two themes in both works change in far-reaching ways, undergoing a process of revision and reevaluation and entering thereby into a dialogue in which the themes interact, each changing to accommodate the demands of the other. Examples 7 and 8 show the beginnings of the second themes of both pieces.

Example 6. Brahms, Quintet op. 88, second movement, mm. 164–70.

Significant correspondences occur even in subtle details of compositional technique. Consider, for example, how both composers prepare their second tonality during their opening themes. Chopin twice tonicizes A minor during the opening Andantino, briefly in mm. 17–19 and more extensively in mm. 33–37. The second modulation prepares the ultimate tonic function of A minor all the more dramatically since it occurs

Example 7. Chopin, Ballade
op. 38, mm. 46–48.

within an expanded reprise. Measures 26–45 present an expanded repetition of the opening strain; the cadence expected in m. 33 is postponed until m. 39, so that the piece modulates to A minor at the precise moment when the listener expects a cadence in F major. Brahms prepares his second key by presenting A-major or -minor triads within the context of C#$^{major}_{minor}$. In mm. 10–11 and 24–25 Brahms intensifies the emphasis on A by preceding the VI harmony with a secondary dominant. In m. 15 and again in m. 19 the juxtaposition of the C# and A triads (in both major and minor forms) encapsulates the basic tonal conflict of the movement. The final cadences of the theme also juxtapose a C#-minor triad with an augmented triad on A (mm. 26 and 28). By stressing the Neapolitian harmony in mm. 27 and 29, the final cadences also foreshadow A major, since the D-major triad becomes the subdominant of the new key. In this regard the Neapolitan in m. 12 also prefigures the shift to A major.

Both composers exploit the tonal reinterpretation of pitch motives, in particular the use of $\hat{7}$–$\hat{8}$ in one key as $\hat{5}$–$\hat{6}$ in the other. In the Ballade the F-major and A-minor triads have two common tones, A and C; the tones that differ, F and E, become a crucial semitone motive in the piece. For example, E–F occurs at the apex of the opening theme (m. 3 and parallel passages), whereas F–E occurs at the beginning of the Presto (m. 46). Within the F-major music, E, the leading tone, is an unstable pitch that demands resolution up to F, whereas in the A-minor sections, F ($\hat{6}$) becomes a relatively unstable pitch that resolves down to E ($\hat{5}$).[15] Since Brahms has reversed Chopin's key relationship, this same reinterpretation of pitches works in his piece as well. Thus G#–A functions as $\hat{5}$–$\hat{6}$ in C#$^{major}_{minor}$ and as $\hat{7}$–$\hat{8}$ in A major, so that a single dyad becomes a structural pivot between the two keys. The opening theme repeatedly emphasizes G#–A; the second violin part in mm. 1–2 offers the first of many instances. The second theme reinterprets G#–A as $\hat{7}$–$\hat{8}$; notice, for example, the repeated emphasis on this dyad at the end of the first phrase of the second theme (mm. 35–36).

Cf.
Kenison's
analyses

Example 8. Brahms, Quintet op. 88, second movement, mm. 32–38.

Even as a first approximation, my comparison has revealed certain features that may be unique to these two pieces. There are other movements, of course, that alternate two highly contrasted themes; among Beethoven's works, the slow movements of both the Ninth Symphony and the Quartet op. 132 are of this type. Both pieces alternate two themes that contrast profoundly in key, tempo, meter, character, phrase rhythm, and register. Careful attention to these cases, however, reveals that they differ from the Ballade and the Quintet in at least three crucial respects: (1) they are monotonal, resolving a tonal conflict in favor of the first key; (2) they rely to a large extent on strict variation techniques, so that repetitions of the two themes usually involve complete varied restatements that maintain a bar-by-bar correspondence between theme and variation, something that the Ballade and the Quintet avoid; and (3) the first theme is tonally open, so that there is a transition to the second theme rather than a sudden break.[16] Without denying that other works, including these two Beethoven slow movements, may have had some impact on Brahms, my first intertextual reading suggests that the Ballade is the primary model for the Quintet. No other pair of movements offers a comparable pattern of structural correspondences.

Nonetheless, this model relationship will always remain a productive hypothesis rather than an absolute fact; there is nothing that counts as final evidence here. Rather than lamenting this lack of systematic proof, however, we should recall that "verification, in the sense of logical positivism, is one type of fulfillment among others and not the canonical mode of fulfillment."[17] For my purposes here, fulfillment will entail inscribing the Ballade and the Quintet in a larger context, so that their juxtaposition will invite an ever-richer interpretive process. In search of that context, I interrupt my intertextual reading to consider two theories of intertextuality.

Korsyn, not
B + Chopin

4

In 1973 Harold Bloom published *The Anxiety of Influence,* where he argues that "poetic history is indistinguishable from poetic influence, since strong poets make that history by misreading one another, so as to clear imaginative space for themselves."[18] Bloom's theory—or at least the phrase "the anxiety of influence"—became so widely known that various recent discussions of musical influence have mentioned Bloom.[19] Yet Bloom's thought, to echo Peter de Bolla, deliberately resists appropriation, even by other literary critics, and "strenuously avoids any pressures within it to become a methodology."[20] Musicians, therefore, should be wary of premature attempts to recruit Bloom. As I have shown elsewhere, however, a prolonged engagement with his thought suggests that Bloom relies on a musicalized poetics, so that the possibility of capturing Bloom for music lies in the internal structure of his theory.[21] Rather than repeat my summary of Bloom here, I merely amplify a few points that are easily misunderstood.

The notion of the anxiety of influence is essentially a theory of originality; through his dialectical concept of "antithetical influence," Bloom shows how poets become original by resisting influence. Hence Bloom departs radically from traditional notions of influence as imitation, continuity, benign transmission, or passive reception, and he repeatedly insists that conventional source criticism is not his concern:

We are speaking here of the greatest apparent puzzle in poetic influence, which is that the deepest or most vital instances of influence are almost never phenomena of the poetic surface. Only weak poems, or the weaker elements in strong poems, immediately echo precursor poems, or directly allude to them. The fundamental phenomena of poetic influence have little to do with the borrowings of images or ideas, with sound-patterns, or with other verbal reminders of one poem by another. A poem is a deep misprision of a previous poem when we recognize the later poem as being absent rather than present on the surface of the earlier poem, and yet still being in the earlier poem, implicit or hidden in it, not yet manifest, and yet there.[22]

The idea of one poem being absent rather than present in another will seem less extravagant if we recall Bloom's almost Kierkegaardian desire "to save the authentic individual."[23] The task, the paradox around which this enterprise revolves, can be summarized by Ricoeur's splendid question: "How can I, by starting from another—say from the father—become myself?"[24] Bloom transposes this self/other dialectic into terms of originality and tradition. Neither poems nor people can escape prior models, but an original relationship to the past involves discontinuity as well as continuity. Bloom's strong poet refuses "to accept somebody else's description" of him- or herself, seeking instead "a way to describe the past which the past never knew."[25] Instead of passively imitating the past, strong poets relate to their precursors antithetically. Bloom's subject, then, is repressed influence; his six revisionary ratios chart the paths by which one poem evades or excludes another.

As I have shown elsewhere, this dialectical concept of influence offers powerful advantages over other paradigms for literary history: "Conventional source criticism tends to dissolve a poem into its alleged 'sources' without explaining what constitutes its unique claim on our attention. Formalist criticism treats poems as autonomous entities, leaving poems unconnected to history. By showing how poems repress and exclude other poems, Bloom can show how poems become unique, yet relate to other poems, by defending themselves against influence."[26] Although Bloom's theory has obvious affinities with the widespread notion that one work of art can be an interpretation or critique of another, no other critic has elaborated this insight with such imaginative vision.

To supplement Bloom, I recruit Mikhail Bakhtin (1895–1975), another critic whose work meets the need for a historical poetics. Although Bakhtin's legacy resists any finalizing summary, his insistence on the dialogic character of experience provides a crucial point of orientation for any account of his work. Bakhtin gives the word *dialogue* two distinct senses, one extremely broad and the other more specialized. Dialogue in the broad sense applies to language in general: "Bakhtin understands discourse to be not an individual writer's or speaker's instantiating of a code, but, instead, the product of a complex social situation in which real and potential utterances, habits and 'genres' of speech and writing, and a variety of other complex social factors shape all utterances from the outset. Utterances address an 'already-spoken-about' world and arise out of a socially constituted 'field of answerability.'"[27]

Dialogue in the second sense entails an opposition to monologic discourse. For Bakhtin, monologue is coercive, because it "pretends to be the ultimate word."[28] There is a strong ethical basis to Bakhtin's preference for dialogue. Monologue treats the other as an object, a thing; dialogue treats the other as a subject who retains his or her individuality.[29] Bakhtin sees literary history as a struggle between monologue and dialogue.[30] Dialogism involves a profound shift in cultural orientation and perception in which we surrender the naïve belief that our language is a unique, privileged window on reality:

What is involved here is a very important, in fact, a radical revolution in the destinies of human discourse: the fundamental liberation of cultural-semantic and emotional intentions from the hegemony of a single and unitary language, and consequently the simultaneous loss of a feeling for language as myth, that is, as an absolute form of thought. . . . It is necessary that heteroglossia wash over a culture's awareness of itself and its language, penetrate to its core, relativize the primary language system underlying its ideology and literature and deprive it of its naive absence of conflict.[31]

For Bakhtin, the primary field in which this dialogic consciousness is achieved is the novel. Bakhtin distinguishes between novels and "novelness"; although novelness is a property common to all novels, it exists in varying degrees, and "greater or lesser degrees of novelness can serve as an index of greater or lesser awareness of otherness."[32] This concept of novelness, then, describes a new type of unity, a unity more inclusive than that of monologic genres. Instead of lying on a single plane, novelistic discourse is stratified, incorporating multiple genres: "the language of the novel is a *system* of languages that mutually and ideologically interanimate each other."[33]

By artistically representing a variety of socially and ideologically di-verse languages, the novel creates a dialogue in which each voice represents a distinct way of viewing the world.[34] It is crucial to recognize that these dialogic voices cannot completely be divided among external participants; the boundaries between utterances are often blurred, and the speech of a single character may be double-voiced through the "intense anticipation of another's word."[35] Even a single word may function within two or more ideological and axiological systems, creating a microdialogue. The voices of these various discourses do not merge; they do not lose their identity; they do not collapse into a synthesis. The individuality of different world views is preserved. Rather than present a coercive, monologic unity, novelness heightens our awareness of otherness and difference.

The vast scope of Bakhtin's cultural vision invites appropriation by disciplines outside literary criticism. He believed that authors like Rabelais and Dostoevsky had "modified the nature of perception itself."[36] Instead of belonging exclusively to literary history, the history of novelness belongs to the development of human consciousness.[37] Listening to music with an ear for dialogism, then, seems a logical extension of Bakhtin's enterprise.[38]

Bakhtin's insights seem especially compelling for artists like Chopin and Brahms, who worked during a period of increasing stylistic diversity. In Chopin's case, for example, his exposure to the *Well-Tempered Clavier,* Polish folk music, Italian opera, nineteenth-century composer-pianists, Viennese classicism, and much else certainly liberated him from the authority of any unitary tradition. Brahms's still more acute historical consciousness also intensified his awareness of the relativity and contingency of any musical discourse. Thus instead of passively accepting any absolute style, both composers knew the demands, so lucidly analyzed by Bakhtin, of having to choose an orientation among discourses: "Consciousness finds itself inevitably facing the necessity of *having to choose a language*. With each literary-verbal performance, consciousness must actively orient itself amidst heteroglossia, it must move in and occupy a position for itself within it, it chooses, in other words, a 'language.'"[39] Bakhtin's methods, therefore, may help to explain the interaction of the various musical discourses in the Ballade and the Quintet.

Bakhtin also seems well-suited to supplement Bloom. Their ideas harmonize on several key points. (1) Like Bloom, Bakhtin insists that language is always marked by prior use: "Language is not a neutral medium that passes freely and easily into the private property of the speaker's intentions; it is populated—overpopulated—with the intentions of others."[40] Consequently both see works of art as relationships rather than as static entities. (2) Both stress the need to struggle against prior discourse. Just as Bloom's strong poets struggle against their precursors, for Bakhtin, the "authoritative word" contends with "the internally persuasive word."[41] (3) Both urge us to resist what Bakhtin calls "finalization from without." According to Bakhtin, Dostoevsky's characters "all do furious battle with all such definitions of their personality in the mouths of other people."[42] In this they resemble Bloomian strong poets; like a belated poet, denied the first word, they demand the last, refusing to allow others to utter the ultimate word about them.

These points of intersection permit a dialogue between Bloom and Bakhtin. At the same time, however, obvious differences in ideology guarantee productive disagreement and difference. Like partners in a Bakhtinian dialogue, each will preserve his individuality; there is no need for them to merge or to collapse into a synthesis. This stratified discourse will help to capture the multivoicedness at work in Brahms and Chopin.

5

Returning, then, to music, let me consider tonality in terms of Bakhtin's distinction between monologue and dialogue. Monotonal genres tend to be monologic, submerging tonal difference and otherness within hierarchical narratives in which any resistance to the primary key is ultimately defeated. Monotonality could be described through binary oppositions—primary key/secondary key, closure/nonclosure—in which the first member of each pair is the privileged term.

In the Ballade, however, Chopin deconstructs classical tonality. Deconstruction: for the word to be useful here, we must recover the rigor it has lost through casual appropriation. Here I quote Jonathan Culler: "A deconstruction involves the demonstration that a hierarchical opposition, in which one term is said to be dependent upon another conceived as prior, is in fact a rhetorical or metaphysical imposition and that the hierarchy could well be reversed."[43] or *collapsed*

By ending in A minor Chopin deconstructs the classical tonal hierarchy. The secondary key area becomes primary, reversing traditional expectations that a piece will return to its tonal point of origin; instead of being a detour on the way back to F major, A minor becomes the goal. The result is a chiasmatic pattern, a crossing, in which the two key areas interchange functions (see fig.1; the diagonal lines in the figure represent the chiasmus).[44] This subverts what Paul de Man called the "autotelic, self-contained, or if you will, narcissistic idea of form as a definitional description within certain boundaries."[45] Because the second key asserts

Figure 1

[handwritten margin note: did any of the early listeners report this tension?]

genuine resistance to the authority of the first, tonality is stratified rather than limited to a single plane. Instead of collapsing into the closed unity of a monotonal (and monologic) genre, the two key areas preserve their integrity. A tension remains between them, so that otherness and difference are acknowledged, creating a new type of narrative that we might, following Bakhtin, call dialogic.

From Bloom's perspective Chopin's deconstruction of monotonality is a revisionary strategy, a form of misreading. The new narrative paradigm that organizes the Ballade can be understood only through its historical position; it involves a reinterpretation of the past. Unlike Brahms, who often seems to personify anteriority through allusions to particular precursors, the precursor here is anonymous; Chopin subverts the tonal tradition in general.

Here my intertextual reading reaches a new level: I can suggest deeper reasons for Brahms's modeling. Instead of being a mere appropriation of a formal procedure, the model relationship involves resisting the self-contained unity of monologic genres; through Chopin Brahms learned how to write a dialogic piece. At the same time the Quintet is, in Bloom's terms, a misprision that aims to usurp the precursor's authority, or what I have elsewhere called a "modeling-as-misreading."[46] Chopin becomes one voice in a larger dialogue whose other partners include Bach and Brahms's earlier self.

We can read both pieces, then, in terms of dialogic relationships, to see how the musical discourses within them and between them illuminate each other. We can also read them in terms of Bloom's revisionary ratios. Through these combined strategies we will move beyond formalism, reclaiming the historicity of these works.

Seen through Bloom's revisionary ratios, Chopin's Andantino exemplifies *clinamen,* the initial swerve from the precursor through the trope of irony. Irony is to say one thing and mean another, and that is exactly what Chopin's deconstruction of tonality accomplishes. The Andantino says, in effect, "F major is the tonic," but this claim undergoes an ironic reversal, as F major progressively loses its hegemony.

The Andantino harbors another irony: it seems to offer a relatively self-contained, autonomous structure, as if it were a complete piece in F major. Since it achieves complete melodic and harmonic closure, it exemplifies what Schenker would call a transferred form of the fundamental structure ($\hat{5}$–$\hat{4}$–$\hat{3}$–$\hat{2}$–$\hat{1}$ over the bass arpeggiation I–V–I; see ex. 9).[47] This impression of tonal closure is so strong that it is not surprising that Chopin sanctioned performing the Andantino separately. The repeated cadences in mm. 38–45 provide especially strong closure; even ending this section on a cover tone (a^1) in m. 45 cannot erase this sense of autonomy. (Moreover, it is not unusual for Chopin to end a complete piece on a cover tone, fostering a certain open-ended quality without thereby reducing the piece to a fragment.)

Brahms's modeling process reproduces Chopin's ironizing *clinamen*. The Quintet also begins with a tonal irony, asserting that C#$_{\text{minor}}^{\text{major}}$ is the tonic, a claim contradicted by the A-major ending of the movement. Brahms's theme is also relatively autonomous and self-contained. Here a comparison with the composer's early Saraband is suggestive. In revising this piece Brahms intensified its self-contained quality. The progression VII^{o7}–I that ends the Saraband creates a weaker impression of closure than the V–I cadences in the Quintet. Moreover, the Quintet, after cadencing in mm. 25–26, has a two-measure cadential phrase that is repeated. The Saraband fails to attain melodic closure, ending on an active scale degree ($\hat{3}$), whereas the Quintet achieves complete melodic and harmonic closure; like the first theme in the Ballade, this theme exhibits a transferred form of the fundamental structure ($\hat{3}$–$\hat{2}$–$\hat{1}$ over the bass arpeggiation I–V–I; see ex. 10).

Significantly, the form of the Quintet theme, A^1–B–A^2 with codetta, resembles that of the Andantino in the Ballade. This suggests that in revising his early suite movements, Brahms may have consulted the Ballade; his Saraband has a binary design.

This impression of formal closure dramatizes the tonal conflict in both works. Rather than present a gradual transition to the second key, both composers risk a radical break in continuity, a moment of rupture. This allows the second thematic/tonal region to assert a stronger claim than might occur in more continuous movements. The two themes somewhat resemble two separate movements rather than parts of a single design.[48] This contributes to the stratification of discourse, resisting a unitary, monologic narrative.

In addition to tonal contrast, the use of sharply differentiated genres is crucial in establishing the various strata of discourse. The generic qualities of Chopin's Andantino demand careful scrutiny. It bears striking associations to the pastorale, a genre originally associated with the

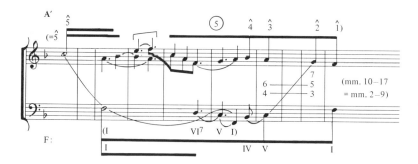

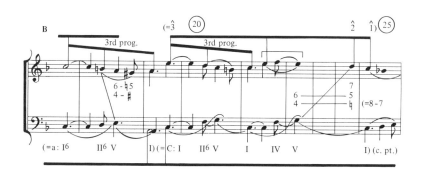

Example 9. Chopin,
Ballade op. 38, mm. 1–45,
voice-leading graph.

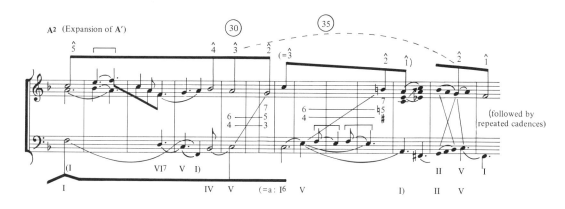

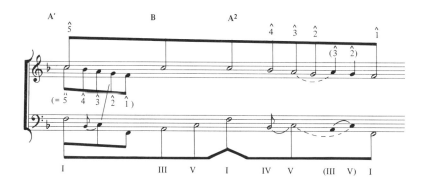

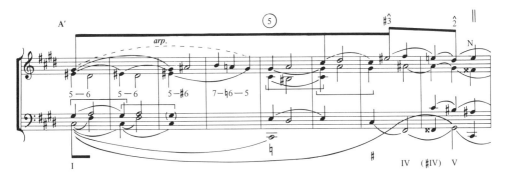

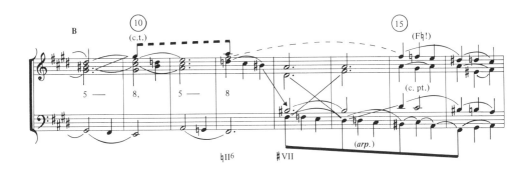

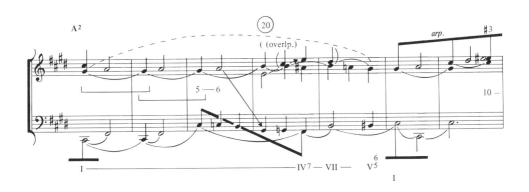

Example 10. Brahms, Quintet op. 88, second movement, mm. 1–31, voice-leading graph. *Continued on next page*

Christmas songs of Italian shepherds. By the seventeenth century this genre was already highly stylized. A related genre, the pastoral mass, was cultivated throughout central Europe and would have been familiar to Chopin.[49]

The generic characteristics of the pastorale include meters such as $\frac{6}{8}$, $\frac{9}{8}$, or $\frac{12}{8}$; major mode; slow or moderate tempo; lilting rhythms with largely diatonic, folklike melodies emphasizing scalar or triadic construction; a homophonic texture; and, typically, pedal points or drones. The Andan-

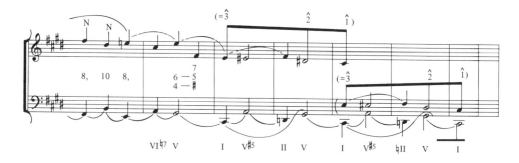

cf. mm. 3-4 and mm. 17-21

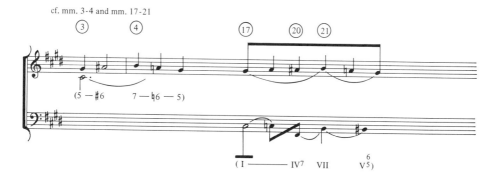

Example 10—*Continued*

tino exemplifies all these qualities (see table 3). Closer study of the genre reveals another common idiom: internal repetitions within phrases, a device also found in the Andantino. For comparison, ex. 11 shows the "Pifa" from Handel's *Messiah* and part of the Ballade. This juxtaposition suggests that both composers were probably drawing on a common vocabulary of pastoral idioms.

This use of genre evokes what Bakhtin calls the "lyric-epic chronotope."[50] According to Bakhtin, there is a fundamental difference between the temporality of the epic and that of the novel. The epic belongs to the "absolute past," a temporal category that is hierarchically valorized, remote, finished, and complete, "closed like a circle," lacking any gradual transitions that might connect it to the present.[51] By combining a relatively self-contained form with the conventions of the pastorale genre, Chopin isolates the Andantino from what follows, establishing it as a distinct layer of discourse with a particular temporal association; it seems to belong to an idyllic past.

Brahms's use of the saraband genre invites a similar interpretation. An archaic genre associated with the baroque suite, it functions to create a certain temporal remoteness. Here one can also see how Brahms stations his precursor Bach in the Quintet. By evoking a great, temporally distant precursor, Brahms summons an epic past that seems immutable, memorialized, isolated from contact with the present.

Table 3 Comparison of Chopin's Andantino and the Pastorale

	Conventions of the pastorale genre	Chopin, Ballade op. 38, Andantino
meter:	$\frac{6}{8}$, $\frac{9}{8}$, or $\frac{12}{8}$	$\frac{6}{8}$
mode:	major	major
tempo:	slow to moderate	Andantino
rhythms:	lilting	primary rhythmic figures: ♩ ♪ ♩♩
melody:	generally diatonic	mm. 1–17 completely diatonic; subsequently limited chromaticism
	scalar or triadic	scalar and triadic
texture:	mostly homophonic	homophonic
pedal or drone:	often found	stationary bass in mm. 2–3, 9–11 and elsewhere

Example 11. (*a*) Handel, *Messiah,* "Pifa," mm. 1–3 (first violin only); (*b*) Chopin, Ballade op. 38, mm. 6–9 (melody only).

At this stage in my intertextual reading, I can begin to demonstrate how the interaction of genre and temporality in the Ballade may have stimulated Brahms, showing him how to incorporate his Saraband material into a more complex context. A telling difference from Chopin's piece, of course, is in mood; whereas the Ballade begins with an idyllic, pastoral tone, the opening of the Quintet has an elegiac quality. Both works, however, observe the protocols of earlier genres to suggest an idealized and distant past. A problem for both pieces is how to assimilate this past, how to establish some authentic continuity with it.

6

Since the Andantino is seemingly complete, Chopin's piece can continue only by an arbitrary act. The second part (Presto con fuoco) begins

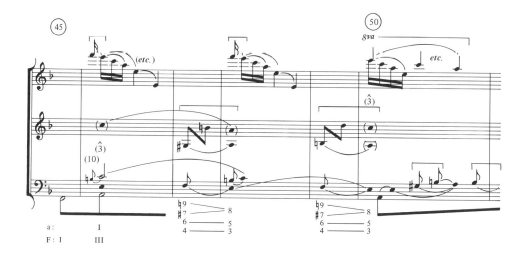

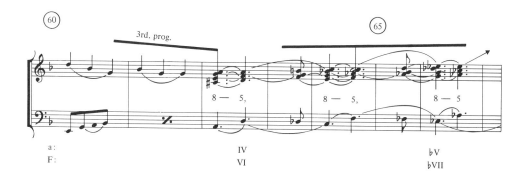

Example 12. Chopin, Ballade op. 38, mm. 46–82, voice-leading graph.

with an eruption, an explosion whose violence must be called arbitrary, since there is nothing in the previous music to prepare or motivate it. This sort of drastic shift suggests many parallels in romantic poetry. As Bloom has shown, romantic poems often experience moments of crisis and catastrophe, changing suddenly rather than gradually.[52] In Bloom's

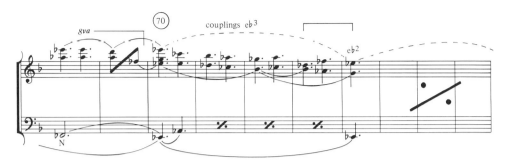

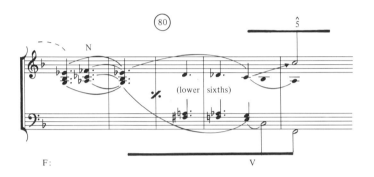

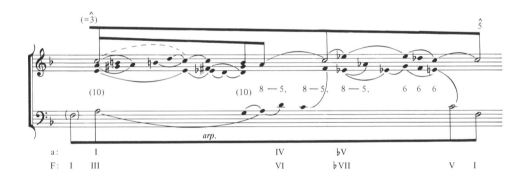

terms Chopin's reversal into the opposite could be called a *tessera*, or antithetical completion.[53]

I have already noted the radical changes in tempo, tonality, texture, and mood here; more important than any single source of contrast, however, is the complete reversal of the previous structural pattern. Whereas the Andantino has a tonally closed form, with a three-part symmetrical design, the Presto is tonally open and formally incomplete. Instead of the decisive closure of the F-major music, cadences in A minor are avoided here (see ex. 12). As Krebs has observed, Chopin withholds the dominant of A minor. The dominant could have been introduced in m. 66, but Chopin uses an E♭ seventh chord instead, a harmony calculated to undermine the stability of A minor.[54]

This highly chromatic, tonally unstable, formally open music over-turns the diatonic, stable, closed environment of the Andantino. Chopin takes a totally new stance toward his own text, giving the music a radi-cally new temporal orientation. Tonal closure is a way of arresting move-ment toward the future; by remaining tonally open and unfinished, the Presto identifies with the present and faces the future. Thus the opposi-tion between the Andantino and the Presto involves more than contrasts of key, tempo, texture, mood, or register: the dichotomy involves two conflicting temporal models of the world, creating two discursive zones: the absolute past versus a mode of experiencing time that is oriented toward the present and open to the future.

To differentiate these opposing positions, I must enlist Bakhtin, whose lucid analysis captures the tension between these two worldviews:

The present . . . is in essence and in principle inconclusive; by its very nature it demands continuation, it moves into the future, and the more actively and consciously it moves into the future the more tangible and indispensable its in-conclusiveness becomes. Therefore, when the present becomes the center of human orientation in time and in the world, time and world lose their completedness as a whole as well as in each of their parts. The temporal model of the world changes radically: it becomes a world where there is no first word (no ideal word), and the final word has not yet been spoken. . . . Every event, every phe-nomenon, every thing, every object of artistic representation loses its completed-ness, its hopelessly finished quality and its immutability that had been essential to it in the world of the epic "absolute past," walled off by an unapproachable boundary from the continuing and unfinished present.[55]

In Brahms's piece we find the same contrast between a tonally closed first theme and a tonally open second theme. Example 13 shows the voice leading of mm. 32–79. Here Brahms's revisions of his early Gavotte are fascinating, although we must rely on Pascall's reconstruction of the ending, since the only extant manuscript of the piece is incomplete. In revising this material Brahms did exactly the opposite of what he had done with the Saraband. Where Brahms had enhanced the closure of the Saraband, strengthening its cadences and generally increasing its au-tonomy, he abandoned the closed form of the Gavotte. Instead of closing in A major, he supplied a long transition back to the first theme, end-ing on a seventh chord that functions as both V^7/IV in A major and as a German sixth chord leading back to $C\sharp^{\text{major}}_{\text{minor}}$.

[handwritten margin note: recovering "jouissance"]

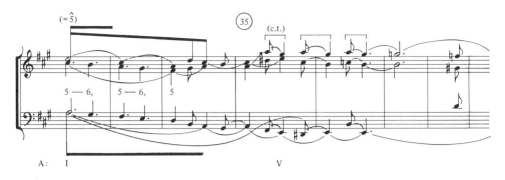

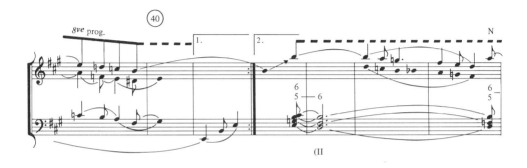

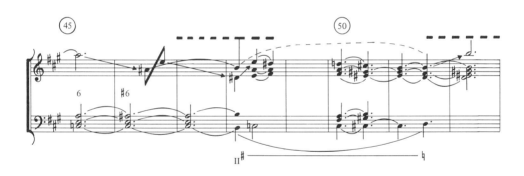

Example 13. Brahms, Quintet op. 88, second movement, mm. 32–79, voice-leading graph. *Continued on next page*

Significantly, Brahms's revision also alters the gavotte-like character of the original, changing the meter from common time to $\frac{6}{8}$. The phrasing scheme becomes much more complex, because Brahms extends many four-measure groups to five measures; many rhythmic and registral displacements make the texture far less fluid; and various chromatic inflections are introduced. Thus this section, unlike the Gavotte on which it is based, does not project the character of a baroque suite movement.

The contrast between the two themes in the Quintet, then, suggests a shift in temporal orientation comparable to that in the Ballade. In both

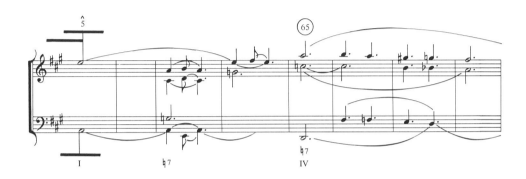

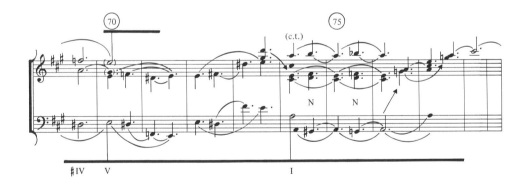

Example 13—*Continued*

pieces the first theme belongs to the absolute past, whereas the second theme identifies with the continuing and unfinished present.

7

As Chopin and Brahms return to their two themes, both avoid literal repetition. We therefore need to understand not only how these themes change but, more important, the motivations for these changes. Indeed, in romantic music in general, we need new paradigms to explain why compositions change as they revisit earlier material. Here Bloom's theory offers us some imaginative possibilities, because Bloom accounts for both *inter*textual and *intra*textual influence. That is, he considers not only the influence of one poet on another but also how the poet alters his or her stance toward the poem he or she is writing.

In Bloom's terms Chopin's return to his Andantino theme (m. 82) falls under the ratio of *kenosis,* the movement of discontinuity with the precursor and with one's own text. In m. 82 Chopin resumes his opening theme but finds that, after the events of mm. 46–81, the epic-idyllic past cannot be recovered; its naïve simplicity and diatonic innocence are lost. This anxious awareness, then, seems to be at work when Chopin interrupts his reprise with silence in m. 87. When Chopin picks up the theme again, he compresses it violently. Between m. 87 and m. 88 Chopin omits twenty-six bars of the Andantino (mm. 82–87 = mm. 2–7; mm. 88–94 = mm. 34–40). Bloom would associate this sort of disruption of temporal continuity with the Freudian defense of isolation. In m. 95 Chopin substitutes a diminished-seventh chord on F♯ for the expected F-major triad, thus undoing the cadence. Thus m. 93 is the last F-major cadence in the piece; Chopin's *kenosis* begins to phase out his first key (see ex. 14).

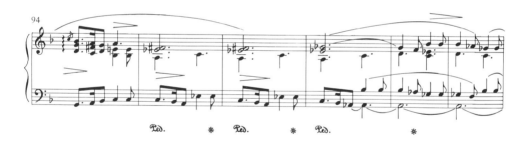

Example 14. Chopin, Ballade op. 38, mm. 94–99.

The music begins to surrender some of its original formal completeness and tonal stability; the chromatic instability and formal openness of the Presto begin to infiltrate this section. This infiltration becomes evident even in the dynamics, which sometimes rise to *fortissimo,* and in the texture, which begins to explore registral extremes not found in the opening Andantino.

Brahms also avoids merely restating his first theme. After its opening phrase he interrupts his reprise, first echoing the phrase ending (mm. 84–85) and then continuing with an imitative dialogue (see ex. 15). Brahms's reprise includes not only this lengthy expansion but also phrase contrac-

Example 15. Brahms, Quintet op. 88, second movement, mm. 80–86.

tions in which the cadences of mm. 26–27 and 28–29 are compressed from two measures into one (ex. 16)

Chopin's second Presto section can be read through Bloom's ratio of *daemonization,* the "movement towards a personalized counter-sublime, in reaction to the precursor's Sublime."[56] This sublime moment depends on repression; the text elevates the sublime, but only through an "unconsciously purposeful forgetting" of a prior text.[57]

Example 16. Brahms, Quintet op. 88, second movement, mm. 109–16.

forgets or "fixes," submits?

Here I suggest that the second Presto forgets its original instability, its disruptive and ambiguous chromaticism. Whereas the first Presto avoids the dominant of A minor, the dominant now comes into its own. There is still local chromaticism, but it is integrated within a tonic-dominant axis. This appears most strikingly in mm. 176–78 and 180–82 of Chopin's coda. This series of chromatic descending $^6_3$ chords recalls a similar progression in mm. 78–82 that forms a transition back to the Andantino.[58] In

Figure 2

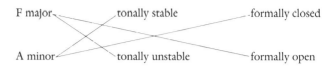

the later passage, however, the chromatic chords prolong a motion from tonic to dominant in A minor. Remarkably, even the E♭ triad, which undermines A minor in mm. 68–78, is now heard within an A-minor context.

There seems to be a reciprocal relationship between the *kenosis* of mm. 82–139 and the *daemonization* that begins in m. 140. The Andantino is wounded into incompleteness through Chopin's undoing of his own text. By surrendering its original autonomy, its formal and tonal closure, it acquires some of the chromatic instability and incompleteness that characterize the second theme. This seems to allow the A-minor music to achieve its daemonic climax; liberated from the control of F major, the dominant of A minor, long suppressed, now appears, making possible the eventual closure of the piece in A minor. The F-major music had been sealed off from the Presto, isolated through an epic-idyllic distance. Now this barrier between the themes breaks down, permitting a zone of dialogic contact and establishing a genuine relationship between the two themes. Figure 2 shows this reciprocity. The present-oriented discourse is now seen from a new dialogic angle, so that the A-minor music can finally attain closure at the end of the composition.

Something similar happens when Brahms resumes his second theme (m. 117). Again, variation here is not merely local but involves larger issues. The local changes include tempo, meter, and dynamics: the tempo is *presto* rather than *allegretto vivace; alla breve* replaces $\frac{6}{8}$; dynamic levels, which previously had reached only *mezzo forte,* now attain *fortissimo* climaxes. The larger changes involve phrase expansions; compare, for example, mm. 53–57 with the corresponding passage in this section (mm. 143–49), where a five-measure phrase is expanded into seven measures. There are also significant harmonic alterations in this section, so that rather than having a transition to $C\sharp_{\text{minor}}^{\text{major}}$, the music remains in A major, thus setting up the reprise of the first theme in $A_{\text{minor}}^{\text{major}}$

The conclusion of the Ballade suggests Bloom's final ratio *apophrades,* or the return of the dead. This is a poem's final defense against the anxiety of influence, its ultimate internalization of tradition, associated with the trope of metalepsis. Metalepsis is the trope that reverses prior tropes;

romantic poems often end with schemes of metaleptic reversals, troping on prior tropes and raising them to a higher level, often by introjecting (identifying with) futurity. That is precisely what happens at the end of the Ballade. Chopin returns to his Andantino theme, but now it appears in A minor (ex. 4). It identifies, therefore, with a new tonal future, entering the tonal region of the Presto theme, as if to suggest that an authentic connection had been formed between them. The original epic-idyllic past of the Andantino is given up, but some aspect of it survives and continues in the present.

Brahms also negotiates the *apophrades* at the end of his piece. Since the first theme now appears in A_{minor}^{major}, it identifies with a new tonal future, entering the tonal region of the second theme (ex. 8). The music seems to acknowledge that the idealized past represented by the Saraband cannot be wholly reconstituted, but this awareness brings consolation.

8

So far, my intertextual reading has stressed Brahms's continuity with Chopin, showing how the model relationship allowed Brahms to write a dialogic piece. The issue of discontinuity, however, can now finally be addressed. The question that confronted Brahms in modeling a piece on Chopin was a variation on Ricoeur's question quoted earlier: How can I, by starting from another—say, from Chopin—become myself?

Brahms's originality can best be captured through Bloom's ratio *tessera,* or antithetical completion. I have already considered *tessera* as one stage in both the Ballade and the Quintet. In a larger sense, however, *tessera* is the Quintet's predominant revisionary gesture, the basic strategy by which Brahms attempts to subvert Chopin. Recall Bloom's definition:

A poet antithetically "completes" his precursor, by so reading the parent-poem as to retain its terms, but to mean them in another sense, as if the precursor had failed to go far enough. . . . In the tessera, *the later poet provides what his imagination tells him would complete the otherwise "truncated" precursor poem and poet. . . . The* tessera *represents any later poet's attempt to persuade himself (and us) that the precursor's Word would be worn out if not redeemed as a newly fulfilled and enlarged Word of the ephebe.*[59]

Let us now try to discover how Brahms antithetically "completes" Chopin, retaining the terms of the Ballade by using similar compositional processes but using them in a different sense, as if Chopin had failed to go far enough. Both composers conclude their pieces by recalling an earlier cadence. Chopin ends with the cadence of mm. 33–37,

Example 17. Chopin,
Ballade op. 38, mm. 34–37.

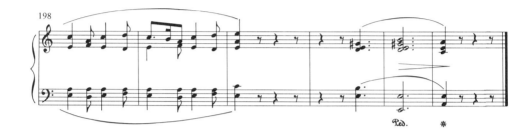

Example 18. Chopin,
Ballade op. 38, mm. 198–203.

raising it to a higher level by making an internal cadence into a final cadence (exs. 17 and 18). Brahms invokes the cadence of mm. 26–30 (exs. 19 and 20).

But the same device yields antithetical effects. Chopin's cadence serves to clinch A minor; what had been merely an internal cadence within a larger prolongation of F major is elevated to the status of a final cadence, signaling that F major has been replaced as tonic. (Note that Chopin cancels the flat sign in his key signature for this final section.)

Brahms, on the other hand, uses his cadential material to heighten tonal uncertainty. Is the A-major ending a transition to the finale or a structural ending in A major? Brahms declines to choose between these alternatives. The reprise of the first theme in A^{major}_{minor} (m. 164) certainly strengthens the impression that A is the tonal center, yet Brahms refuses to relinquish C♯ entirely, since he creates significant V–I cadences in that key in mm. 175–76, 188–89, 197–98, and 199–200. (Note that the key signature of four sharps remains in effect, as if to suggest that C♯ has not been completely eclipsed by A.)

Throughout their respective compositions, we can see that whereas Chopin gradually phases out F major, Brahms allows A major to assert its claims without undermining C♯$^{major}_{minor}$. This becomes clear if we compare the third sections of both pieces. As I have shown, both composers interrupt their respective reprises with an imitative dialogue. Chopin withholds the F-major cadence expected in m. 95, beginning a process of undermining F major. Brahms, however, far from demolishing C♯$^{major}_{minor}$,

Example 19. Brahms, Quintet op. 88, second movement, mm. 24–31.

leads the music to a strong arrival on its dominant in m. 90, and his reprise, although expanded, still concludes in C♯.

If Chopin deconstructs classical tonality, Brahms deconstructs Chopin's deconstruction. As I have shown, Chopin reverses the hierarchy between primary and secondary tonalities; A minor, originally a secondary key subordinate to F major, becomes the primary key. Although this

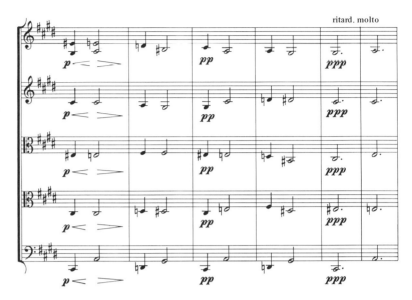

Example 20. Brahms,
Quintet op. 88, second
movement, mm. 196–208.

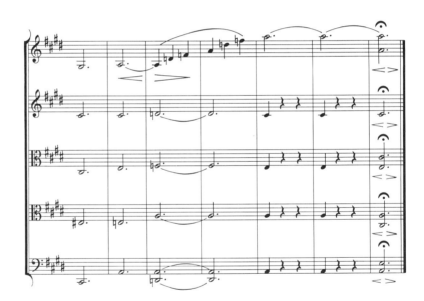

overturns the tonal hierarchy, it establishes a new hierarchy in which
A minor usurps the role of tonic. Brahms, on the other hand, by allowing C#$_{minor}^{major}$ to remain an important key in the last section, leaves the
respective hierarchical positions of his two keys in question. This intensifies the dialogic character of the piece, because the two tonal regions
remain equal partners. Thus Brahms antithetically "completes" Chopin,

using Chopin's procedures to explore a different, and in some ways a more radical, alternative to monotonality.[60]

NOTES

1. Margit L. McCorkle, *Johannes Brahms. Thematisch-Bibliographisches Werkverzeichnis* (Thematic: bibliographical catalogue of works) (from preliminary work in collaboration with Donald M. McCorkle), ed. Ernst Herttrich (Munich: G. Henle Verlag, 1984), 363.

2. Experts disagree on the precise dating of the Saraband. Some authorities identify it with the Saraband mentioned by Joseph Joachim in a letter to Brahms dated 27 June 1854 (*Johannes Brahms im Briefwechsel mit Joseph Joachim* [Brahms's correspondence with Joachim], ed. Andreas Moser, 2 vols. [Berlin: Deutsche Brahms Gesellschaft, 1908], 1:47). Thus Robert Pascall accepts the 1854 date ("Unknown Gavottes by Brahms," *Music and Letters* 57 [1976]: 406), as does Kurt Hofmann (*Johannes Brahms. Zeittafel zu Leben und Werk* [Timeline for his life and work; Tutzing: Hans Schneider, 1983], 406). William Horne, however, uses Clara Schumann's diary entries to argue that this Saraband was composed early in 1855 ("Brahms's Düsseldorf Suite Study and His Intermezzo, Opus 116, No. 2," *Musical Quarterly* 73, no. 2 [1989]: 260). The Saraband, along with another one in B minor, was first published in 1917 by Max Friedländer (Johannes Brahms, *Zwei Sarabanden für Klavier* [Berlin, 1917]) and later appeared in the Brahms Gesamtausgabe (*Johannes Brahms: Sämtliche Werke*, ed. E. Mandyczewski and H. Gal, 26 vols. [Leipzig: Breitkopf and Härtel, 1926–28], 15:57). The Gavotte was composed in 1855 and was first published by Robert Pascall in his 1976 article. Both the Saraband and the Gavotte belonged to a suite that is now lost. Horne believes that "Brahms had decided that these movements were the most successful ones in the suite" (254). In 1855 and 1856 both Brahms and Clara Schumann performed a saraband and gavotte by Brahms, most likely this pair. A summary of how Brahms adapted the Saraband material in the Quintet is provided by Hans Gal .n *Johannes Brahms: His Work and Personality,* trans. Joseph Stein (New York: Knopf, 1963), 163–68. Pascall comments briefly on the relationship between the Gavotte and the Quintet.

3. According to Maurice J. E. Brown, the first version of the Ballade was composed in 1836; the final version was completed at Majorca in 1839. See his *Chopin: An Index of His Works in Chronological Order,* 2d ed. (London: Macmillan, 1972), 104.

4. Brahms's early suite compositions were connected with his intensive study of the Bach suite literature. See Horne, "Brahms's Düsseldorf Suite Study."

5. Paul de Man, *Blindness and Insight: Essays in the Rhetoric of Contemporary Criticism,* 2d ed. (Minneapolis: University of Minnesota Press, 1983), 152.

6. Johannes Brahms, *Briefwechsel* (Correspondence), ed. Wilhelm Altmann, 2d ed., 16 vols. (Berlin: Deutsche Brahms Gesellschaft, 1907; reprint Tutzing: Hans Schneider, 1974), 3:171–73.

7. Jean-Jacques Eigeldinger, *Chopin: Pianist and Teacher as Seen by His Pupils,* trans. Naomi Shohet with Krysia Osostowicz and Roy Howat, ed. Roy Howat (Cambridge: Cambridge University Press, 1986), 207.

8. Camille Saint-Saëns, "A Chopin M.S.: The F Major Ballade in the Making," in *Outspoken Essays on Music,* trans. Fred Rothwell, 97–105 (London: Kegan Paul, Trench, Trubner, 1922), 102.

9. Arthur Hedley, *Chopin,* 4th ed. (London: Dent, 1957), 174.

10. Robert Schumann, "Kürzere Stücke für Pianoforte" (shorter piano pieces), *Neue Zeitschrift für Musik* 15 (1841): 142. "Die leidenschaftlichen Zwischensätze scheinen

erst später hinzugekommen zu sein; ich erinnere mich sehr gut, als Chopin die Ballade hier spielte und in F-Dur schloß; jetzt schließt sie in A-Moll."

11. Harald Krebs has shown how text setting often motivates departures from monotonality in Schubert's songs. See "Alternatives to Monotonality in Early Nineteenth-Century Music," *Journal of Music Theory* 25, no.1 (spring 1981): 1–16.

12. Louis A. Renza, "Influence," in *Critical Terms for Literary Study,* ed. Frank Lentricchia and Thomas McLaughlin, 186–202 (Chicago: University of Chicago Press, 1989), 187.

13. Paul Ricoeur, *Freud and Philosophy: An Essay on Interpretation,* trans. Denis Savage (New Haven: Yale University Press, 1970), 61.

14. Jim Samson, *The Music of Chopin* (London: Routledge and Kegan Paul, 1985), 180.

15. Harald Krebs discusses this motive in his dissertation "Third Relation and Dominant in Late Eighteenth- and Early Nineteenth-Century Music" (Ph.D. diss., Yale University, 1980), 150 and 166; see also William Kinderman, "Directional tonality in Chopin," in *Chopin Studies,* ed. Jim Samson, 59–75 (Cambridge: Cambridge University Press, 1988), 73–74.

16. Both of these Beethoven slow movements are discussed in my dissertation, "Integration in Works of Beethoven's Final Period" (Ph.D diss., Yale University, 1983), 122–68. See also my article "J. W. N. Sullivan and the *Heiliger Dankgesang:* Questions of Meaning in Late Beethoven," *Beethoven Forum 2* (1993), 133–74.

17. Ricoeur, *Freud and Philosophy,* 30.

18. Harold Bloom, *The Anxiety of Influence: A Theory of Poetry* (London: Oxford University Press, 1973), 5.

19. John Hollander, a poet and critic, was perhaps the first to relate Bloomian notions of poetic influence to music. In *The Figure of Echo: A Mode of Allusion in Milton and After* (Berkeley: University of California Press, 1981) he briefly discusses Benjamin Britten's Serenade op.24, showing how Britten's music responds to and intensifies intertextual echoes in poems by Tennyson, Keats, and Blake. More recently, Bloom has been mentioned in various musical studies, notably David Lewin, "Music Theory, Phenomenology, and Modes of Perception," *Music Perception* 3 (1986): 381–82; Joseph N. Straus, *Remaking the Past: Musical Modernism and the Influence of the Tonal Tradition* (Cambridge: Harvard University Press, 1990); Reinhold Brinkmann, *Musik-Konzepte 70: Johannes Brahms, die Zweite Symphonie: Späte Idylle,* ed. Heinz-Karl Metzger and Rainer Riehn (Munich: edition text + kritik, 1990), 24–25, 78; Elaine Sisman, "Brahms's Slow Movements: Reinventing the 'Closed Forms,'" in *Brahms Studies: Analytical and Historical Perspectives,* ed. George S. Bozarth, 79–103 (Oxford: Clarendon, 1990), 80–81; and in an unpublished paper by Michael Cherlin, "Musical Imagination and Other Fictions: Rhetorical Trope as Musical Process," which he kindly made available to me in January 1992. Cherlin's study displays insights stemming from familiarity not only with Bloom's theory but also with the works of Bloom's precursors. See also the review article by Richard Taruskin, "Revising Revision," *Journal of the American Musicological Society* 46 (1993): 114–38.

20. Peter de Bolla, *Harold Bloom: Towards Historical Rhetorics* (London: Routledge, 1988), 73.

21. Kevin Korsyn, "Towards a New Poetics of Musical Influence," *Music Analysis* 10, nos.1–2 (March–July 1991): 12–14.

22. Bloom, *Kabbalah and Criticism* (New York: Continuum, 1975), 66–67.

23. Christopher Norris, *The Deconstructive Turn: Essays in the Rhetoric of Philosophy* (London: Methuen, 1983), 90.

24. Ricoeur, *Freud and Philosophy,* 186.

25. Richard Rorty, *Contingency, Irony, and Solidarity* (Cambridge: Cambridge University Press, 1989), 28–29.

26. Korsyn, "Towards a New Poetics," 13.

27. Gary Saul Morson, "Dialogue, Monologue, and the Social: A Reply to Ken Hirschkop," in *Bakhtin: Essays and Dialogues on His Work,* ed. Gary Saul Morson (Chicago: University of Chicago Press, 1986), 83.

28. Mikhail Bahktin, "Toward a Reworking of the Dostoevsky Book," in *Problems of Dostoevsky's Poetics,* ed. and trans. Caryl Emerson, 283–301 (Minneapolis: University of Minnesota Press, 1984), 293.

29. Wayne C. Booth, "Freedom of Interpretation: Bakhtin and the Challenge of Feminist Criticism," in *Bakhtin: Essays and Dialogues on His Work,* ed. Gary Saul Morson, 145–76 (Chicago: University of Chicago Press, 1986), 152.

30. Michael Holquist, *Dialogism: Bakhtin and His World* (London: Routledge, 1990), 75.

31. Mikhail Bakhtin, *The Dialogic Imagination: Four Essays,* ed. Michael Holquist, trans. Caryl Emerson and Michael Holquist (Austin: University of Texas Press, 1981), 367–68.

32. Holquist, *Dialogism,* 73.

33. Bakhtin, *The Dialogic Imagination,* 47.

34. Ibid., 73.

35. Bakhtin, *Problems of Dostoevsky's Poetics,* 205.

36. Holquist, *Dialogism,* 76.

37. Ibid., 73.

38. Recently several writers on music have cited Bakhtin, most often in reference to his concept of the "Carnivalesque." See George S. Lipsitz, "Cruising around the Historical Block: Postmodernism and Popular Music in East Los Angeles," *Cultural Critique* 5 (winter 1986–87): 157–78; Lipsitz, "Mardi Gras Indians: Carnival and Counter-Narrative in Black New Orleans," *Cultural Critique* 10 (fall 1988): 99–122; Lawrence Kramer, *Music as Cultural Practice, 1800–1900* (Berkeley: University of California Press, 1990); Susan McClary, *Feminine Endings: Music, Gender, and Sexuality* (Minneapolis: University of Minnesota Press, 1991).

39. Bakhtin, *The Dialogic Imagination,* 295.

40. Ibid., 294.

41. Ibid., 342.

42. Bakhtin, *Problems of Dostoevsky's Poetics,* 59.

43. Jonathan Culler, *The Pursuit of Signs: Semiotics, Literature, Deconstruction* (Ithaca, NY: Cornell University Press, 1981), 183.

44. The graphic representation of the chiasmatic reversal in figure 1 is derived from similar figures in Paul de Man's essay "Pascal's Allegory of Persuasion," in *Allegory and Representation,* ed. Stephen J. Greenblatt, 1–25 (Baltimore: Johns Hopkins University Press, 1981).

45. Paul de Man, *The Resistance to Theory* (Minneapolis: University of Minnesota Press, 1986), 109.

46. Korsyn, "Towards a New Poetics," 28.

47. My analysis of Chopin's theme differs somewhat from that offered by Harald Krebs in "Alternatives to Monotonality." We both read a fifth-progression from C5 to F4 in mm.1–17, but where I hear a second fifth-progression in mm.26–41, he hears a descending third, C5 to A4, thus ending the section with $\frac{3}{1}$. This contradicts his reading of the beginning, since the end of the Andantino is actually an expanded repetition of the first idea. Chopin repeats the first theme almost intact, but instead of descending directly to $\hat{1}$ in m.33, he expands his repetition to accommodate a tonicization of A minor. So $\frac{2}{V}$ already appears in m.32, and there is no difficulty reading a fifth-progression ending on F4 in m.39. The arrival on $\hat{1}$ is reconfirmed by the repeated cadences in mm.40–45; the A5 in m.45 is a cover tone.

48. Significantly, Brahms's Quintet has only three movements because the second

movement functions as both slow movement and Scherzo. Of course, Brahms's early Saraband and Gavotte were originally two separate pieces.

49. Familiar examples of the Christmas pastorale include the "Pifa," or Pastoral Symphony, from Handel's *Messiah,* the Pastoral Symphony from Bach's *Christmas Oratorio,* and the last part of Corelli's "Christmas" Concerto, op.6, no.8. For more information on the pastoral mass, consult Peter Wagner, *Geschichte der Messe* (Leipzig: Breitkopf and Härtel, 1913; reprint 1972), 219–24. [Editor's note: compare Jim Samson's discussion of the role of pastoral music in the Ballade in the previous chapter.]

50. Bakhtin, *The Dialogic Imagination,* 103.

51. Ibid., 15–19.

52. Harold Bloom, *Agon: Towards a Theory of Revisionism* (Oxford: Oxford University Press, 1982), 224. If Chopin found inspiration in the poetry of Mickiewicz, as Schumann believed, it may have involved this matter of the rhythm of psychological development. Like many romantic poets, Mickiewicz favored certain patterns of crisis and rhetorical disjunctions.

53. Readers may consult my "Towards a New Poetics of Musical Influence" for a fuller exposition of Bloom's ideas and their application to music.

54. Harald Krebs, "Alternatives to Monotonality," 11. My interpretation of Chopin's voice leading differs from that proposed by Krebs, who hypothesizes two primary tones in the Ballade, reading C ($\hat{5}$) as the *Kopfton* of the F-major sections but E ($\hat{5}$) as the *Kopfton* of the A-minor sections. His reading is a provocative departure from Schenkerian norms, but disregards the distribution of thematic material between the left and right hands. In mm.46, 48, and 50–53 the right-hand figuration, although motivically significant, is subordinate to the main idea in the left hand. In these measures the right hand functions somewhat as in the Etude op.25, no.11, whereas the left hand works as it does in the B-Minor Prelude. Thus in mm.46 and 48, for example, I read the left hand as embodying both the actual bass *and* the structural upper voice, while the right hand plays cover tones. In mm.47 and 49 the right hand takes over, responding to and continuing the idea from the previous measures. If this is acknowledged, there is no difficulty in reading C ($\hat{3}$) as the primary tone of the A-minor music, giving the whole piece a connected melodic structure. Krebs still hears $\hat{5}$ active at the end of the Ballade—an unresolved tension that I do not hear. My reading has the advantage of motivic economy. In m.47 I hear the motive G♯–B resolving to an implied A, whereas m.49 adds a parallelism B–D resolving to an implied C, thus regaining the primary tone.

Such arguments over primary tones may seem like theological debates concerning angelic pin dancing. Actually, however, *Kopfton* disputes are discussions of how the music is heard.

55. Bakhtin, *The Dialogic Imagination,* 30.

56. Bloom, *The Anxiety of Influence,* 15.

57. Bloom, *Poetry and Repression: Revisionism from Blake to Stevens* (New Haven: Yale University Press, 1976), 236.

58. Cf. William Kinderman, "Directional Tonality in Chopin," 74–75.

59. Bloom, *The Anxiety of Influence,* 14, 66–67.

60. One might object, of course, that the Ballade is a more radical critique of monotonality because it is a complete composition, whereas Brahms's piece belongs to a larger cyclical whole that is tonally complete. This objection, however, might be vulnerable to the question of whether the tonal ambiguity of Brahms's slow movement affects the rest of the piece. If the slow movement is tonally unstable, then the context into which it fits might also be rendered unstable. Fuller consideration of these issues, however, would demand a detailed analysis of the whole Quintet, a project exceeding the scope of this chapter.

Some critics have compared the end of the second movement of the Quintet to the baroque procedure of ending a movement on a triad that stands in a mediant relationship to the following movement. This comparison, however, is relatively superficial. In baroque examples the listener's tonal orientation is seldom in doubt; by ending on a triad other than the tonic, the piece will seem tonally incomplete, but it does not become tonally ambiguous. This is different from the situation in Brahms's op. 88, where the interplay between the two keys throughout the piece renders the ending tonally uncertain.

Part 2: The Second Practice of Nineteenth-Century Tonality

An Evolutionary Perspective on Nineteenth-Century Semitonal Relations

PATRICK McCRELESS

familiar feature of nineteenth-century tonality is its incorporation, at relatively deep harmonic levels, of semitone relationships outside the diatonic system of closely related keys. Semitone relationships of this sort provide a window through which we can view the evolution of tonal practice through the nineteenth century and into the twentieth. Although other tonal relationships—those by whole tone or by thirds, for example—might provide an equally illuminating view of the development of nineteenth-century tonality, semitone relationships provide a particularly perspicuous example, since they are abundant throughout the century and theorists have devised a variety of explanations for their behavior. Such an investigation can also shed light on a broader question: are there two tonal systems in the nineteenth century—a classic diatonic system and a nineteenth-century chromatic system—as Gregory Proctor has suggested, or is there but one, as suggested by Matthew Brown?[1]

My strategy in approaching this question is first to adduce examples of deeper structural semitone relations in the repertory, from early Beethoven through Wagner, Schoenberg, and even Shostakovich. Second, I introduce the concept of chromatic tonal space and view the examples in terms of how they make compositional use of that space. Third, I import an interdisciplinary analogy from the work of paleontologist, evolutionary biologist, and historian of science Stephen Jay Gould, in hopes of further illuminating the historical process that seems to be at work in the examples and of suggesting, if not an answer to the question that generated the study, at least a criterion for answering it.

FROM BEETHOVEN TO WAGNER, SCHOENBERG,
AND SHOSTAKOVICH

Example 1. Beethoven,
Piano Trio in C Minor,
op. 1, no. 3, fourth
movement, mm. 343–84.

The juxtaposition of tonicizations of scale degrees a semitone apart at relatively deep structural levels is an extreme rarity in the music of the baroque era and, for the most part, in tonal music in general until around 1800. Inasmuch as tonal pieces of this period normally tonicize only diatonic degrees, and broad tonal motion tends to be by the interval of the fifth rather than by that of seconds or thirds, such adjacent tonicizations occur infrequently. When they do, they are readily explained as subsidiary motions within a more global linear and harmonic context. Such is the case, for example, in brief tonicizations of the flatted second scale degree, which generally return smoothly through the dominant to the tonic. Only in radical and experimental works are we forced to come to grips with semitone relations that penetrate to deeper levels of harmonic structure. The prolonged tonicization of C♯ minor in the D-minor context of J. S. Bach's Chromatic Fantasy comes to mind, as do similar examples from the fantasies and rondos of C. P. E. Bach. Even these instances lend themselves easily enough to a linear approach, and we can often legitimately claim, as Schenker so often did, that the lines generate the harmonies rather than vice versa. The same can be said for Haydn's and Mozart's experiments in a similar vein, such as Haydn's Fantasia from the String Quartet in E♭ Major, op. 76, no. 6, and the slow movement of Mozart's Piano Concerto in B♭ Major, K. 456.

A classic example of the kind of semitone relation that I discuss in this chapter—and one far less complex than those found in the fantasies of J. S. and C. P. E. Bach, Haydn, and Mozart—occurs in an early work of Beethoven, at the end of the final movement of the Piano Trio in C Minor, op. 1, no. 3. The principal theme, having already returned in the tonic, is suddenly and without harmonic preparation brought back a semitone below the tonic, in B minor (see ex. 1). Now, we may disagree about how structurally "deep" the tonicization of B minor is. It is short-lived and probably to some ears rather clumsy, although I show later that it can easily be rationalized motivically and linearly in terms of the piece as a whole. In any case, however we might wish to rationalize it, the event's effectiveness surely arises from the work's landing suddenly and without warning in a harmonically distant region a semitone below the tonic. The ploy is, of course, one of Beethoven's favorites, and Douglas Johnson cites digressions into distant keys at the ends of rondo finales as a "stylistic fingerprint" of the composer's works of 1795.[2] Johnson does not discuss this general phenomenon in theoretical terms but simply

points out what he perceives to be its "humorous" quality, and he adduces other examples, including the finales of the Piano Concertos op. 15 and op. 19 and the Sonata op. 2, no. 3. Although the date of composition of op. 1, no. 3, is probably before 1795, and although Johnson does not cite it specifically, its jarring move to B minor, while hardly "humorous," like the digressions in the other pieces, clearly relates it to other finales composed around the same time.

Ernst Kurth discusses the same passage as follows: at m. 361 there is a "sudden turn from C minor to B minor, which is immediately articulated by a return to pianissimo in the dynamics. One can already recognize clearly that the basic process here involves a purely chromatic, unmediated type of movement, in spite of the simple tonal connection to the dominant of C minor, and in spite of the fact that, in a more typically encountered manner, a modulatory, closed return leads back into the main key and thus reestablishes the [tonal] relationship that the chromatic movement itself destroyed."[3] Kurth articulates a specific harmonic mechanism by which the B-minor tonicization is led back to C minor, yet he also conceives of the matter metaphorically, in terms of "color" and "surprise" rather than technique. And rightly so: if anything characterizes many nineteenth-century composers' attempts to introduce distant tonal regions into their music, it is the tendency to articulate and dramatize the leap out of the diatonic sphere with techniques from the arsenal of rhetoric and gesture: changes of dynamics, orchestration, texture, and rhythmic flow; pregnant silences; and the like. The tendency is particularly evident in cases such as this one, where the threat to diatonic stability is localized in a single passage and thus remains relatively foregrounded with respect to the entire movement or work.

From a theoretical point of view the Beethoven example involves an early and strictly circumscribed instance of what Gregory Proctor has called the "transposition operation": the exact, rather than diatonically adjusted, transposition of a passage by any interval other than the perfect fifth or fourth, producing a diatonic scale relatively distant from the original one.[4] The transposition operation is a central component of Proctor's nineteenth-century chromatic tonality, and he offers numerous examples of its use in works of composers ranging from Schubert to Liszt, Wagner, Grieg, and Tchaikovsky. He notes, however, that transposition by major or minor third and by major second is far more common in the period than transposition by semitone. Of semitone transposition, which is my concern here, he gives but a single example, from Berlioz's *Symphonie Fantastique*.[5] The example involves a chromatic stream of parallel sixth chords that might be strictly construed as involving the transposition operation. Such an interpretation is trivial, however, given the tempo of the excerpt and the fact that only a single chord, not a larger unit, is transposed. Here there is no question whatsoever of the transposition operation's penetrating deeper than the surface of the piece.

A better example is supplied by a passage from the exposition of the Finale of Schubert's Fourth Symphony in C Minor, D.417 (ex.2). Here (mm.147–63) a chromaticized simple voice-leading pattern brings a flurry of evanescent tonicizations of C♭, C, D♭, D, and E♭. To be sure, the succession of tonicizations is effected by the conventional voice-leading paradigm $\hat{5}$–$\hat{6}$–$\hat{5}$–$\hat{6}$–$\hat{5}$ (ex.3). The listener's perception of a sequence of keys is no less real, however. Schubert in a sense multiplies the procedure of the Beethoven Trio by four and reverses direction, moving four semitones up rather than one down.

Proctor's transposition operation suggests again the work of Ernst Kurth, who unquestionably recognized and described the same phenomenon, even though he was hardly inclined to formalize it or develop its theoretical ramifications thoroughly. In the section of *Romantische Harmonik* dealing with what he calls *außertonale Sequenzen* [extratonal sequences], he writes:

Whenever a particular melodic fragment is repeated in this way [i.e., without diatonic adjustment], a sequence arises, such that each time it is displaced by a particular interval higher or lower. When these displacements no longer follow [one another] in the manner of a tonal sequence—that is, so that the individual repetitions of the figure maintain the same key—the harmonic connection is broken and an exact repetition of particular chords by a given interval takes place; thus arises the außertonale Sequenz. *One might even call it "mechanical," because both melody and chords, completely unchanged, simply experience a transposition, whereas in the tonal sequence the particular intervallic relations must undergo alterations, in order to accommodate the same key.*[6]

Example 2. Schubert,
Symphony No. 4 in
C Minor, fourth movement,
mm. 139–66.

Example 3. Sketch of
$\hat{5}$–$\hat{6}$–$\hat{5}$–$\hat{6}$–$\hat{5}$ pattern in
example 2.

Kurth apparently would have agreed with Proctor on the matter of what transposition levels were most frequently used: most of his examples—at least those of a length comparable to those of Proctor's examples—involve the operation by major or minor third, with only a few by whole tone and even fewer by semitone. As an instance of the operation in which semitone transposition is used, he invokes from the first movement of Bruckner's Seventh Symphony the passage leading into the recapitulation.[7] Here the tonal goal of E minor is prepared by successive tonicizations of C and D, with a semitonal motion through a passing area of E♭ connecting the D to E minor (see mm. 249–81).

The technique that Kurth identifies here has been dubbed by Robert Bailey the "expressive" use of tonality in the music of Wagner.[8] Like Kurth, Bailey conceives of the practice in terms of "expressive intensification" (Kurth's term is *Steigerung*). He cites examples such as Tannhäuser's "Hymn to Venus" (*Tannhäuser,* act 1), which has successive strophes in D♭, D, and E♭; "Elsa's Dream," in act 1 of *Lohengrin,* which moves from A♭ to A; and the juxtaposition of the D♭ of the end of *Das Rheingold* and the D of the beginning of *Die Walküre* in the *Ring*. Both Bailey and Kurth invoke instances in which such tonal intensification is immediate and sequential (since it involves repetition of thematic material, as in the Bruckner symphony and *Tannhäuser*) and examples in which such repetition is lacking (as in Bailey's example of the end of *Das Rheingold* to the beginning of *Die Walküre*). Kurth considers widely separated semitonal tonal relations of this sort to apply the principle of the sequence at a much higher level and to determine broader aspects of structure: "In this way is developed the harmonic organization of large structures, which in Wagner's dramatic music is often connected quite clearly with a poetic idea."[9] In any case, both writers emphasize the technique's poetic and dramatic import, and both classify it as a central element of late-nineteenth-century, but not classical, tonal practice.

Christopher Lewis offers an example of a different kind of semitone relation in his analysis of Schoenberg's song "Traumleben," op. 6, no. 8. Lewis's analysis demonstrates a situation that involves neither a brief digression to a semitone-related area, a sequentially based motion connecting a number of such areas, nor a large-scale intensification by semitone motion. Rather, it involves the projection—or at least the implication—of two keys a semitone apart, one overlaid on the other, in the manner of Bailey's double-tonic complex.[10] The song begins in E but moves up a semitone to F by mm. 20–23 before returning to E at the end, yet it does so in such a way that *both* keys are projected at the beginning. The seeds of F are embedded in the opening measures of the song, and it emerges uncontested at m. 20.[11]

A different and rather more complex type of semitone relation is introduced in David Lewin's analysis of the tonal structure of *Parsifal*.[12] Lewin points out passages in the D-minor music of Amfortas's Prayer to Titurel toward the end of act 3 where D♯ minor substitutes momentarily for D minor (*Stollen* 1), and where D♭ major substitutes for D minor or major (*Stollen* 2 and *Abgesang*).[13] Later he extends the idea of substitution to the tonal structure of the entire opera, to the point that he interprets the D of Amfortas's Prayer as substituting for an unheard but implied subdominant D♭. Although I cannot enter into the details of Lewin's analysis here, its relevance to my study of harmonic semitone relations is clear enough, since his claim that an explicit tonal area can substitute for a deeper, "unheard" one unquestionably goes a step beyond examples like those of Kurth and Bailey, which involve juxtaposition of real tonal areas, not substitution for unreal ones.

A twentieth-century reincarnation of the idea of substitution occurs in the music of Prokofiev and Shostakovich, who frequently displace a prevailing key by one a semitone lower or higher. A classic example occurs in Shostakovich's March from *Six Children's Pieces* (ex. 4). Richard Bass has devised an analytical terminology and a Schenkerian graphing technique for dealing with this phenomenon.[14] In his analysis of the March he refers to the displaced tonic key, C, as a "shadow" of the displacing key of D♭. He then demonstrates in his analytical sketches the possibility of hearing such passages in three different ways: (1) entirely in the original key of C, with the displacing passages in D♭ normalized as though they were actually in C; (2) entirely in the displacing key of D♭, with the passages in C normalized up a semitone; and (3) as the music appears in the score (see ex. 5).[15] Even though the Shostakovich example is far removed from the nineteenth-century practice that I examine here, it is valuable because it shows the extent to which twentieth-century listeners easily accept semitone substitutions in tonal music: the D♭ in the March is not only a neighboring tone *to* C; it is also a substitution *for* C, just as D♭ and D♯ are substitutions for D in the *Parsifal* example.

Example 4. Shostakovich, March from *Six Children's Pieces,* © copyright 1965 by MCA Music Publishing, a division of MCA Inc., 1755 Broadway, New York NY 10019. International copyright secured. All rights reserved. Used by permission.

A THEORETICAL AND HISTORICAL PERSPECTIVE

We are faced with a number of examples all ostensibly instantiating the same phenomenon, the harmonic use of semitone relations. The examples include a brief tonicization in a fundamentally diatonic context; chromatic sequences or instances of the transposition operation; two keys functioning together in a double-tonic complex; and semitone substitution. But what do the examples say about the underlying tonal system or systems? What is the relation, say, between the tonal system that supports the Beethoven example and that which supports the Wagner? Is it the same tonal system, or do the uses of structural semitones in the examples point to underlying complexes of harmonic relations that are really quite different?

One avenue through which we may productively approach the ques-

Example 5. Richard Bass, analysis of Shostakovich, March, mm. 21–24.

tion of whether there is one tonal system or two in the nineteenth century is a distinction introduced by J. J. Bharucha, a cognitive psychologist of music, and further developed by Fred Lerdahl: the distinction between *event space* and *tonal space*.[16] Event space involves our ability to hear, comprehend, abstract, and imagine ordered musical events in real time. It is the ordered musical structure inferred by listeners from performed pieces. Tonal space, on the other hand, is atemporal; it is the mental pitch or pitch-class schema through which we interpret the music that we hear. It is the atemporal tonal and harmonic mental set—the filter, as it were—that enables us to process tonal music and make sense of it. Event space and tonal space are interdependent. As Lerdahl points out, listeners cannot develop the atemporal mental schema of tonal space without extensive experience in hearing pieces in event space, yet understanding the event space of particular pieces presupposes that the interpretive grid of tonal space functions in the listener.

The classic representation of event space in a tonal piece is Schenkerian linear analysis, but we often forget that our ability to construct such analyses depends entirely on an already encoded interpretive strategy, one that involves intuitively comprehending tonal space's hierarchical nature. Constructing a Schenkerian analysis requires that we have in our brains an a priori atemporal diatonic space with a hierarchical ordering of scale degrees and harmonic functions. It was the historical stability of this underlying tonal space that enabled Schenker to concentrate on musically interesting aspects of tonal music such as linear and motivic structure.

Given the thoroughgoing linear orientation of his later theories, it is easy to overlook the fact that Schenker carefully separated tonal and event hierarchies in his early work. Thus he writes in the introduction to volume 1 of *Counterpoint,* "I have already presented the theory of scale degrees in *Harmony,* without adding any voice-leading theory."[17] Elsewhere in this introduction he speaks of the "purely abstract" nature of the harmonic scale degree, and he suggests its separation from the real world of voice leading.[18] He thus implicitly recognizes the essence of what I am calling tonal space: its "*a priori* nature"[19] and its independence from counterpoint and thus from event space. As his interests leaned more and more toward analysis, however, he tended progressively to conflate tonal and event space, to the point where in *Free Composition* he writes, "The combination of the fundamental line and the bass arpeggiation constitutes a *unity.*"[20] To be sure, the prolonged tonic triad still represents tonal space, but as William Benjamin has pointed out, the *Ursatz* itself is more a contrapuntal than a harmonic event.[21]

What does the concept of tonal space have to do with structural semitone relationships and for the previously posed question concerning the existence of one or two tonal systems in the nineteenth century? Two recent theorists, both writing about Schenker and Schoenberg, provide a hint. Fred Lerdahl has noted that "Schenker was primarily interested in event hierarchies and Schoenberg in the tonal hierarchy."[22] And Christopher Lewis, in the previously cited article, points out the appropriateness of Schoenbergian theory, which can deal with simultaneous implications of more than one key, and the inappropriateness of Schenkerian theory, which is limited to a monotonal framework, for much late-nineteenth-century music. Looking back at my examples of semitone relations from the theoretical perspective of Schenker and Schoenberg, one might hypothesize that these examples trace the evolution in the nineteenth century of the concept of a *harmonically based* chromatic tonal space, a space in which the guiding harmonic point of reference is not a single tonic triad to which all other sonorities are necessarily related but an entire twelve-key system of potentially tonic triads, any two or more of which may be invoked over time to control the large-scale harmonic structure of a given piece. My examples thus trace a process whereby listeners learned to filter pieces not just through a single diatonic space but through a more variegated chromatic space as well and to shift back and forth between chromatic and diatonic space as context might require.

The previously adduced examples of semitone relations follow a single but telling evolutionary branch in the history of the chromaticization of tonal space and the development of compositional techniques for distributing this chromatic tonal space in event space. I can paint this evolutionary picture by discussing each of my examples in terms of how it invokes tonal and event space and what sort of relations it establishes between the two, but before I do so, it will be helpful to have some notion of the relation between the two spaces in the essentially diatonic music of the eighteenth and early nineteenth centuries. In this music a stable diatonic space functions as the framework for the event space of musical surfaces. The tonal space in which listeners interpret individual pieces is limited to the diatonic melodic and harmonic scale degrees, including possible local tonicizations of the latter. The event space of such pieces unfolds essentially according to the prolongational constraints defined by Schenker and involves a variety of passing, neighboring, and arpeggiating motions within the confines of a stable harmonic system. Only rarely—and usually in exceptional pieces such as fantasies and toccatas—is the interpretive mental set of diatonicism ever seriously threatened.

In the late eighteenth and early nineteenth centuries composers began to seek ways of incorporating more distant tonal areas. At this time the twenty-four-key, complete chromatic circle of fifths was already a theoretical reality; it remained for nineteenth-century composers to make this twenty-four-key system (or as Schoenberg would later have it, simply the twelve-key chromatic system)[23] a practical and musical reality. Interestingly, early experiments in this vein—at least the successful ones—tended to adopt the linear techniques of diatonic event space to rationalize their tonal flights and make them comprehensible. Thus, as we have seen, the more chromatic passages in the fantasies of both J. S. and C. P. E. Bach are frequently grounded on a clear linear progression, usually in the bass, that connects diatonic scale degrees. Another linear technique that emerged both to generate and to rationalize chromaticism was motivic development, not so much in the conventional sense as in the Schenkerian sense of motivic expansion.

Here we can benefit from another look at the example from the Beethoven C-Minor Piano Trio (ex.1). Kurth's analysis of the passage from the end of the Finale emphasizes the shock of the turn to B minor. This aggressive intrusion of chromatic space into diatonic space, with no immediately apparent means to make diatonic sense of it, is surely responsible for his affective interpretation. If we listen more closely, however, we note that the B-minor statement of the theme can make rational sense to us because it can be heard as an expansion of the C–B–C motive in the bass of the opening theme itself (see m.1 [C]–m.7 [B]–m.9 [C]). This motive is ubiquitous in the final movement and is central to the opening theme of the first movement (for example, note the bass of m.1 [C]–m.3 [B]–m.5 [C]). The new element of tonal space introduced here (B minor in the context of C minor, or the raised seventh scale degree) is made palatable by a technique derived from event space.

This rationale underlies most of Schenker's later explanations of chromaticism. By explaining events that evoke chromatic tonal space in terms of the techniques of diatonic event space, he makes them more comprehensible and less threatening. Furthermore, I suspect, he really does capture the essence of what makes chromaticism work in the music of composers such as Haydn, Mozart, Beethoven, and Chopin, for the better composers between, say, 1775 and 1850 did everything in their power to clarify and justify their chromatic adventures. Not only did they bring all their gestural and rhetorical resources into play to dramatize chromatic events and give the listener time to absorb them, but they also appropriated line and motive in the service of rendering chromaticism—however daring—coherent and comprehensible. Schenker is right to adduce these elements in support of his claims for the artistic superiority of these "masters" over many of their contemporaries.

Nonetheless, the time was soon to come when leaps into chromatic space would take on a different expressive character and suggest a different analytical meaning. Consider, for example, the passage from Schubert's Fourth Symphony quoted in ex.2. I have shown that a voice-leading paradigm underlies the ascending motion in semitones. I might also claim that Schubert is using a linear-motivic means here to ratio-

Example 6. Schubert,
Symphony No. 4 in
C Minor, fourth movement,
mm. 1–20.

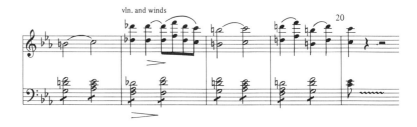

nalize the chromaticism; the melodic succession C (m. 5)–D (m. 9)–E♭
(m. 14), or $\hat{1}$–$\hat{2}$–$\hat{3}$, is explicit in the opening theme (ex. 6), and the harmonic succession C♭–C–D♭–D–E♭ in ex. 2 might be considered an ex-
pansion of the same motive, although it begins on C♭ rather than C. The
Schubert example is palpably different from the Beethoven, however. It
does not invoke expressive or gestural rhetoric to call attention to the
chromaticism. Furthermore, unlike the Beethoven passage, it traverses
a succession of semitone-related keys rather than just one. Kurth might
say of the example that it is more mechanical, both in terms of expressive gesture and in terms of the chromatic keys' remaining diatonically
unmediated. There thus arises the significant question: is it sufficient, in
the analysis of such passages, simply to show how the radical chromatic

sequences arise linearly and how they fit motivically into the controlling diatonic framework? Perhaps it is; in this sense all of Schubert's most daring chromatic sequences, such as those noted by Richard Taruskin in his well-known article on nineteenth-century precedents of Stravinsky's harmony,[24] can be rationalized linearly. Yet I cannot help but feel that such sequences are different from earlier chromatic tonicizations: they are ungrounded in the diatonic space that surrounds them, and they call out to be heard in different terms, even though we can explain them in traditional terms if we like.

Another reason for considering such sequences as fundamentally different from tonicizations of the sort that occur in the Beethoven piano trio is suggested by many of the middle and late works of Schubert that employ equal interval cycles as a means of structuring development sections. Usually, as in the first movements of the Piano Sonatas in E♭ Major, D. 568, and in D Major, D. 850, such cycles are by major or minor third, although occasionally, as in the development section of the first movement of the Piano Trio in E♭ Major, D. 929, semitone relations are involved as well.[25] In D. 568 and D. 850 Schubert abandons yet another tried-and-true means of justifying extensive chromatic tonal areas: preparing for a foreign tonicization by introducing the appropriate chromatic scale degree as a detail early on and by establishing it as a harmonic area later. Douglas Johnson adduces the first movement of Beethoven's op. 10, no. 3, as an example of this familiar technique, and Edward T. Cone's classic analysis of Schubert's Moment Musical no. 6 in A♭ Major provides another.[26] The equal-interval key cycles of development sections such as those of D. 568 and D. 929, however, emerge totally unprepared; the expositions of the movements give no hint whatsoever as to what is to come in the development. We are thus encouraged to hear the chromatically related keys not as temporary tonicizations prepared by pitch-class association from the beginning of the piece but rather as keys in themselves and thus as independent paths through the chromatic tonal space instead of, or at least as well as, broad inflections of a stable diatonic space.

Kurth and Proctor are right to point out the radical character of such tonal procedures. Kurth's sequences and Proctor's transposition operations, whether by semitone, whole tone, or thirds, always invoke chromatic space. From the point of view of chromatic theory, the issue here is not whether we can subsume these operations linearly into the diatonic event space of a given piece and ultimately to abstract diatonic tonal space; in Schubert, at least, we always can. The real issue that such passages force us to consider is whether the transposition operation necessarily takes us out of our governing diatonic mind-set, even if ever so briefly, and into a chromatic one. I believe that it does and that its doing so raises an even more interesting question: when, historically speaking, does deeper-level chromaticism of this sort become sufficiently pervasive to penetrate to the core of our diatonic mind-set and begin to orient that mind-set toward a Schoenbergian, twelve-note set of harmonic possibilities? Stated more radically, and with a view toward Wagner, Mahler, and Strauss, at what point do such procedures predominate to the extent that we experience diatonicism as a subset of the chromatic spatial universe rather than chromaticism as an inflection of the diatonic one?

Such questions have provocative implications for historical and evolutionary views of the development of chromatic tonality. Too often we understand this historical process only in terms of the musical surface, of local chromatic saturation and harmonic ambiguity. These features are important, to be sure, but the interaction of diatonic hearing and chromatic hearing in passages such as Kurth's chromatic sequences is equally significant, if not more so. A Schenkerian point of view might be that at the most surface level, removed from the larger tonal context, each individual reiteration of a sequential unit such as that from the Schubert Fourth Symphony is locally diatonic in a particular key; that at a more middleground level the sequence itself is chromatic because it passes through equal-interval cycles and invokes the associated foreign keys along the way; and that at a deeper middleground level the passage is diatonic, because it is ultimately incorporated into the diatonic structure of the whole. Interpreted according to a diatonic mind-set, such a point of view accurately depicts our perception. Nevertheless, we could adopt a different vantage point: we could say that with such sequences we approach a situation in which the controlling perceptual space through which the music—or at least some of it—moves is the chromatic space of twelve diatonic keys, not the diatonic space of a single governing key. In support of such an interpretation we could argue that, because of our strong intuition to hear diatonically in a key, the unrelated keys of a chromatic sequence leap out at us and force us to hear them as things in themselves. Ironically, it is our diatonic mind-set itself that, at least for the moment, jerks us out of a piece's diatonic space into chromatic space. Given our inclination to hear in diatonic space, our desire for diatonic stability at every moment in an example such as the Schubert symphony temporarily overrides even the broad context of E♭ major and leads us to grasp separate moments of C♭, C, D♭, D, and E♭.

The crux of my argument here is that the historical development of chromatic space in the nineteenth century involved a gradual and almost imperceptible progression from a state of affairs where such leaps into chromatic space catered to the inculturated security of global diatonic space by adopting conventional linear-motivic means to rationalize them and by limiting their absolute duration to a state of affairs where the demand to hear in chromatic space is so pervasive that we must hear on its terms rather than on the terms of diatonic space. In Wagner's works from the *Ring* on, the historical process becomes complete, and our concept of structural levels is turned upside down with respect to diatonic and chromatic space. The deepest harmonic space, through which we process whole operas or post-Wagnerian symphonies, is Schoenbergian twelve-tone space. Of course, this space can and must be expressed locally, even in long stretches of music, through the prolongation of diatonic space. I might even suggest that, say, at the beginning of a Wagner opera, our internal programming leads us to hear in diatonic space, but only until such time as that space is threatened by chromatic space, thus shifting us into a perceptual mode whereby we hear individual diatonic prolongations in the context of a broader chromatic context. Accordingly, our diatonic space is necessarily foreground with respect to the chromatic space demanded by the whole, which accordingly must be viewed as background. The background is no longer *given* but *chosen:* the background is that scheme of ordered harmonic relations that the composer chooses to shape a particular piece. Each such background is, to quote Benjamin Boretz, a "hypothesis of what can be learned to be heard";[27] each piece is a composer's hypothesis (and I use this positivistic term fully realizing that nineteenth-century composers probably thought more in terms of expression and originality than in terms of experiment) of how chromatic tonal space can be distributed coherently in event space. Whereas Schenker rationalizes forays into chromatic space by showing how they function in terms of diatonic prolongation, the theory of late-nineteenth-century music must rationalize diatonic prolongation by showing how it fits into the larger context of chromatic space. Sitting on the cusp between the two mind-sets are Schubert's chromatic sequences, which evolved naturally out of earlier practice but introduced, almost unnoticed, a new premise that had enormous implications for tonal hearing.

In the examples of the transposition operation that Bailey adduces from *Lohengrin* and the *Ring,* Wagner entices us even more than does Schubert to hear in terms of chromatic space, since he expands it in time and adds to the abstract operation itself a dramatic association that in a sense articulates and justifies it (although he would argue that the tonal operation articulates and justifies the dramatic structure, rather than vice versa). Surely one musical factor that influenced his dramatic theories, and thus the *Ring* itself, was his intuition of the insecurity induced in midnineteenth-century listeners by excessive adventures into chromatic space. Drama was a new, nonmusical means of rationalizing that space. Thus he writes in *Opera and Drama:*

The capacity extends (as a result of harmonic modulation) to such an inconceivable degree of variety that we can set up alliances between the principal key and those even which are most removed from it. . . .

Music had suddenly upraised itself from the ground-tone of harmony. It had extended itself to such colossal and varied dimensions that at last the absolute musician could only lose courage upon finding himself wafting restlessly about with no object in view. Nothing could he see before him but an infinite waving sea of possibilities, whilst in himself he was conscious of no object capable of putting them to a definite use. . . .

Accordingly the musician was necessarily brought to the verge of repenting his extraordinary swimming power. . . . Strictly speaking, therefore, it amounted to his confessing himself possessed of a capability which he did not know how to use; it amounted in short to his longing for the poet.[28]

For Wagner, apparently, abstract semitone relations such as A♭ to A in *Lohengrin* (which was of course written before *Opera and Drama*) and D♭ to D in the *Ring* are rendered more comprehensible if they are grounded by dramatic associations—to Elsa and Lohengrin, respectively, in the former case, and to Valhalla and the storm that opens *Die Walküre* in the latter.

We can understand the tonal structure of Wagner's later operas, and the works of composers such as Bruckner, Mahler, Strauss, and the early Schoenberg, only if we hear them in terms of a mental schema of chromatic pitch space and only if we understand their background tonal structures as a means of appropriating this tonal space to real-time event space. Otherwise we could never cope with either the thoroughgoing chromatic nature of their large-scale key relationships or the directional component whereby single acts and whole operas, or even short pieces, begin in one key and end in another.

Perhaps the most interesting example of all is *Parsifal,* for it forces us to deal directly with the notion of substitution. Although *Parsifal* is the first of the examples that makes this notion explicit, it is in fact implicit in all of them. For instance, it is possible to claim that the startling effect of the Beethoven Trio's B-minor tonicization arises from the fact that B minor suddenly erases, displaces, and indeed *substitutes* for C minor. To be sure, the effect is justified and rationalized by linear-motivic means: it makes more sense in the context of the piece to slide briefly into B minor than into, say, F♯ or E, but the effect itself depends on the erasure of our C-minor world and its replacement by another world a semitone removed. Similarly, in the Berlioz, Schubert, and Bruckner examples, our ties to the global tonal world in which we are oriented are suddenly severed, and we are displaced into new worlds, however briefly. What *Parsifal* does is to create a world that globally seems to be in diatonic space but is in fact full of warps and seams that posit the coexistence of a chromatic space. What the opera is about, tonally speaking—and here I rely extensively on Lewin's analysis—is the relation of diatonic space and chromatic space (which Lewin calls "Riemannian space") at the deepest of harmonic levels. Specifically, following Lewin's argument, what enables the tonal magic of *Parsifal* to work is the interaction between diatonic space and chromatic space: the first act in the diatonic world of the Grail; the journey in act 2 through the magic, enharmonic, chromatic world of Klingsor; and finally, the reconciliation of the Riemannian world and the diatonic one by the end of act 3.[29] That is why the tonal world of *Parsifal* necessarily had to follow the tonal worlds of the *Ring, Tristan,* and *Die Meistersinger.* Although the opera as a whole begins and ends in the same key, as does act 2 by itself, we cannot construe these beginnings and endings in the same key in any sense as representing conventional prolongational monotonality. Rather, we must understand the broad diatonic tonal space of *Parsifal* as interacting profoundly with the chromatic tonal space through which we have learned to perceive Wagner's other later operas and through which we perceive this last opera itself. We hear its diatonic world less as a traditional diatonic world than as a place from which we can enter into and to which we can return from a fundamentally different, chromatic world. Indeed, it is only because, by the time of *Parsifal,* we are so familiar with *both* worlds that we can make the mental leaps that the opera requires: to hear, for example, the tonal areas of D♯ and D♭ not as neighboring tones to D but as substitutes for it. If we did not have both diatonic space and chromatic space deeply embedded in our brains, we could not perform such leaps. That we can perceive such substitutions in *Parsifal* shows us that chromatic space is now reified to the extent that it requires neither linear-motivic rationalization nor sequential patterning to justify it. Furthermore, such substitutions show how profoundly our chromatic and diatonic mind-sets interact, for we cannot understand *Parsifal* unless we process it through both the chromatic and the diatonic mental frameworks.

All of which brings me to Shostakovich, whom I can dispatch with two brief comments. First, although his little March is, to say the least,

far removed from *Parsifal* and the Germanic tradition that has primarily
concerned me here, there can be little doubt that his "angle," like Stravinsky's, ultimately stems from Germanic roots, since it is at least in part the
chromatic sequence, the transposition operation, on which his sleights
of hand are based. Second, the nonchalance with which he slides into
and out of tonal areas a semitone apart, from substance into shadow and
back, suggests that we twentieth-century listeners live comfortably in
both conventional diatonic space and chromatic space. If we did not, we
would not so breezily accept "Barry Manilow" tonality, which places the
final verse of a popular song a semitone (or in recent years, a whole tone)
above the key in which it began. In both Shostakovich and contemporary popular music, however, the shifts are immediate, automatic, and
mechanical. That they are so facile not only shows us how thoroughly we
have assimilated chromatic and diatonic space but also reflects tellingly
back on the nineteenth century, where, from Beethoven to *Parsifal*, expressive and gestural rhetoric and linear-motivic techniques were often,
although not always, deemed necessary to coax listeners into accepting
the unfamiliar.

My examples, considered in toto, raise one final significant issue that
merits a brief exegesis before my interdisciplinary analogy: the issue of
tonal memory and its relation to the idea of chromatic tonal space that
I have adopted for late-nineteenth-century music. It should be clear
enough that much recent analysis, not only of Wagner, Mahler, and
Strauss, but also of Verdi, relies implicitly on what I refer to here as the
mental schema of chromatic space. A number of years ago Joseph Kerman, in a thoughtful essay responding to an article by Siegmund Levarie
on key relations in Verdi's *Un ballo in maschera,* addressed the issue of
tonal perception and memory.[30] Kerman juxtaposes what he calls a conservative, "contextualist" view of tonal relations, as exemplified by the
work of Donald Francis Tovey, and the more radical, "absolutist" view,
as exemplified by Levarie. Tovey articulates the contextualist view on the
first page of his book on Beethoven's piano sonatas: "In classical music
no two keys are related through the medium of a third tonic, and . . .
no sense of key-relation arises except between keys that are in immediate juxtaposition."[31] Against Tovey, Kerman posits analyses of Levarie,
for whom, he claims, "keys are regarded as absolutes, independent both
of their modulatory surroundings and also of any sense of time," and
for whom tonality is "a sort of non-temporal spatial field generated by a
timeless tonic."[32] Kerman attacks the absolutist position on the grounds
that most listeners lack the long-term pitch memory required to make

tonal relations of the sort described by Levarie perceptible, and he argues that most listeners hear in terms of immediate harmonic context rather than abstract key relations.

One can hardly fail to note the striking parallel between Kerman's contextualist and absolutist positions and the concepts of event space and tonal space adopted here. Nonetheless, from premises similar to his I arrive at quite different conclusions. Unlike Kerman, I do not find an atemporal concept of key relations intrinsically unsatisfactory; it is neither unmusical nor perceptually invalid to suggest an atemporal mental schema through which we process tonal music. I have already noted that such an atemporal diatonic scheme underlies Schenker's conception of diatonic tonal music, and I hope that I have adequately argued the claim that an equally atemporal chromatic scheme is necessary to comprehend fully the tonal relations in the later examples that I have cited. The real questions that Kerman addresses involve, first, how this atemporal tonal space, whether diatonic or chromatic (and usually both), is distributed coherently in event space (a question that I have barely touched on here), and second, the extent to which tonal memory enables us to keep our place in real time. In music that is fundamentally diatonic, our place-finding sense is secured by the asymmetrical diatonic system, which is in fact precisely what Kerman calls a nontemporal spatial field generated by a timeless tonic. In more chromatic nineteenth-century music, however, this diatonic space often unfolds in the context of a still deeper chromatic space, a space that not only is utterly symmetrical but usually also lacks a "timeless tonic." Kerman's questions, then, concern how capable we are of keeping ourselves oriented in this space. Such concerns involve issues of perception far beyond the scope of this chapter, but the late-nineteenth-century works that I have adduced here certainly may be regarded as hypotheses that we can learn to hear relationships of this sort.

These questions are interesting even when we ask them of relatively conventional diatonic works that happen to involve distant tonal regions. I have deliberately limited the discussion here to works involving structural semitone relations that are directly juxtaposed. But what about examples such as the dramatic E-major tonicization in the middle of the development of Haydn's Eb-Major Piano Sonata, Hob. XVI/52, or the F♯ tonicization that begins the development of Mozart's G-Minor Symphony, K.550? Are we to believe, with Tovey, that such tonicizations are related only to what immediately precedes and follows them? I argue that they are not, that they establish coherent and audible semitone relations with the global tonic in each case. That is, even in the late eighteenth century, certain works lend themselves to a hearing in a global chromatic space, even though that space is not the primary space of the piece. Works of this sort, although fundamentally diatonic and explicable by means of diatonic theories such as Schenker's, nevertheless introduce chromatic premises that, once they are loosened from the diatonic bonds that hold them, will require of listeners a remarkably different mental schema for their perception.

AN EVOLUTIONARY ANALOGY

How many tonal systems operated in the nineteenth century? The question is not an easy one, and perhaps I can answer it better through an interdisciplinary analogy than through a purely music-theoretical exposition. The examples that I have cited implicitly suggest an evolutionary point of view. I now make that point of view explicit by adducing an example from an essay by Stephen Jay Gould, the Harvard evolutionary biologist, paleontologist, and historian of science. In this essay Gould discusses a theoretical problem that Darwin himself saw as a difficulty for his theory and that has been a thorn in the side of Darwinian evolutionists in their ongoing battle with creationists and Lamarckians. The issue concerns what Gould calls the problem of "truly exquisite design" and turns on physiological organs that are highly specialized and complex, such as the eye. Creationists ask, "How could creatures without eyes evolve into creatures with eyes? Are not such organs incontrovertible evidence of the plan of the Creator?" Lamarckians, who believe in evolution but see it as an ordered and rational progression of simple to complex, with our own species at the top of the evolutionary ladder, ask, "How could creatures without eyes evolve into creatures with eyes unless there were a larger plan, a linear purpose to evolution?" The problem facing Darwinians responding to such arguments is that they must explain the early stages of the evolution of an organ like the eye *solely* in terms of natural selection, with no recourse to theology or to a controlling master plan in evolution. "What good," asks Gould, "is 5 percent of an eye?"[33] That is, how could a creature evolve gradually, through natural selection, an organ that would be useless until it was fully developed?

Gould, a strict Darwinian, counters that organs like the eye were originally features that served another purpose entirely. He argues that evolution works slowly, developing a series of sequential steps between a rudimentary organ and one of exquisite design. The problem is to reconstruct the various evolutionary stages and show that each stage was functional for the organism, even though—and this is a crucial point—the use of the organ in the early stages may have been entirely different from its use later. Evolutionists refer to this process as "preadaptation," of which the following can serve as an illustration:

To invoke a standard example, the first fishes did not have jaws. How could such an intricate device, consisting of several interlocking bones, ever evolve from scratch? "From scratch" turns out to be a red herring. The bones were present in ancestors, but they were doing something else—they were supporting a gill arch located just behind the mouth. They were well designed for their respiratory role; they had been selected for this alone and "knew" nothing of any future function. In hindsight, the bones were admirably preadapted to become jaws. The intricate device was already assembled, but it was being used for breathing, not eating.[34]

A comparable instance is provided by Gould's example of the lowly dung beetle. Although Gould does not develop the example in detail, it is easy enough to construct a Gouldian preadaptive scenario for the creature's evolution. Creationists would have it that God in his wisdom created the dung beetle, and that was that. Lamarckians would have it that a series of purposeful evolutionary stages led to the development of the full-fledged dung beetle from its less distinctive progenitors. For Gould the problem is more complex. How could nature evolve a dung beetle out of non-dung-beetledom? Obviously the dung beetle evolved from some ordinary beetle that did not employ a survival strategy whereby it was protected from its enemies by looking like dung. How can we explain the fact that this evolution occurred without resorting to the attribution of purpose to the dung beetle itself? Gould's explanation would be that, as is typical of speciation, some population of ordinary beetles must have become separated geographically or environmentally from the rest of their species and began to develop environmentally induced characteristics of color or shape that might enable us to identify them as proto–dung beetles, beetles that were still members of the original species but already had developed some characteristics of dung beetles without employing these characteristics behaviorally as dung beetles do. For example, due to differences in environment this population may have experienced changes in color and shape that made them, purely by chance, look more like dung than the members of the larger population. But, asks Gould, "can there be any [evolutionary] edge in looking only 5 percent like a turd?"[35] Obviously, there is none, yet at some point in evolutionary time, given that these processes of change continued, the proto–dung beetle could reach a point where other creatures—specifically, its enemies—would see it as looking more like dung than like a beetle. At this point characteristics that had evolved purely environmentally could suddenly take on an entirely new meaning. This watershed in the beetle's evolutionary history would enable natural selection to encourage further the survival of beetles that looked more like dung and less like their beetle relatives and thus promote the development of a new species. As Gould notes: "In short, the principle of preadaptation simply asserts that a structure can change its function radically without altering its form as much. We can bridge the limbo of intermediate stages by arguing for a retention of old functions while new ones are still developing."[36]

There is a profound music-historical lesson here, for in music history as in natural history, an entity can begin as one thing but over time reach a critical point where it is possible for it to become something else entirely. This is precisely what happens in the chromaticization of the tonal system in general and in the development of structural semitone harmonic relations in particular. As long as such relations were confined to brief tonicizations of the Neapolitan and linearly and motivically rationalized chromaticism that were easily reconciled to diatonicism, the diatonic tonal space of earlier tonal music was never threatened. When composers saw that the same semitone relations, or whole tone or third relations for that matter, could be multiplied, and that they could function perfectly well without linear or motivic justification, they wrote music that required listeners to adjust their sense of the tonal schema through which they processed the music that they heard. Because such procedures involved changing from one diatonic key to another abruptly and without preparation, the listener was forced to interpret such passages in chromatic rather than diatonic tonal space—to hear, even though Schenker has long encouraged us not to do so, a succession of keys rather than a prolongation of a single key through contrapuntal lines. The dramatic and associative import attributed to such tonal relations by composers such as Weber and Wagner could only hasten the development of a more harmonically oriented, twelve-key chromatic tonal space.

If I were to specify that point in tonal history that served as a watershed parallel to the point in time when the dung beetle began to look more like dung than like a beetle, I would locate it in the discovery, probably by Schubert and then Liszt independently, of the transposition operation. It is this operation more than any other chromatic procedure that forces us out of diatonic space and into chromatic space. It is the transposition operation, particularly when it occurs on relatively deep levels, as it does in Wagner, that makes us hear a background in terms of keys and to subsume individual prolongations of single keys, no matter how extensive, into the larger, chromatically based harmonic framework.

In the end, perhaps the question of whether there is one system or two or more should be conceived more in historical and evolutionary terms. To carry my biological analogy a bit further, I might say that, in the case of the beetles, we certainly end up with two species rather than one. So should I say that we end up with two tonal systems rather than one? Perhaps so, but we must also remember that just as the dung beetle carries with it much of the structure and genetic information of its forebears, so does late-nineteenth-century tonal practice incorporate at its very core much of the earlier practice that made it possible in the first place. It is difficult to separate the later practice based on chromatic space from the earlier one based on diatonic space, simply because late-nineteenth-century music preserves at its essence the central features of more diatonic music. Thus, whether we choose to recognize two systems or one depends on criteria rather like the criteria that biologists use for differentiating species in the natural world. Biologists differentiate two populations as separate species if they do not interbreed. Accordingly, our choice of two systems or one must ultimately rest on our musical sense of how much diatonic space and chromatic space interpenetrate. Since there can be no intersubjectively verifiable test of the type that interbreeding between biological species offers, we are left with a choice that depends on the structural depth at which we opt to hear chromatic relations in a music about which we care: whether we hear all the music of the nineteenth century as involving, at one level or another, the prolongational techniques of diatonic space, and thus all of a single tonal system, or whether we feel that the evolution of chromatic space in this music so fundamentally altered the framework through which we perceive it that there are two systems rather than one.

NOTES

1. Gregory Proctor, "Technical Bases of Nineteenth-Century Chromatic Tonality: A Study in Chromaticism" (Ph.D. diss., Princeton University, 1978); Matthew Brown, "The Diatonic and the Chromatic in Schenker's Theory of Harmonic Relations," *Journal of Music Theory* 30, no.1 (Spring 1986): 1–34.

2. Douglas Johnson, "1794–1795: Decisive Years in Beethoven's Early Development," in *Beethoven Studies 3,* ed. Alan Tyson, 1–28 (Cambridge: Cambridge University Press, 1982), 25.

3. Ernst Kurth, *Romantische Harmonik und ihre Krise in Wagners Tristan und Isolde* (The crisis of romantic harmony in Wagner's *Tristan*), 2d ed. (Berlin: Max Hesses Verlag, 1923), 293–94.

4. Proctor, "Technical Bases," 159–62.

5. Ibid., 182.

6. Kurth, *Romantische Harmonik,* 334.

7. Ibid., 355.

8. Robert Bailey, "The Structure of the *Ring* and Its Evolution," *19th-Century Music* 1, no.1 (1977): 51.

9. Kurth, *Romantische Harmonik,* 353–54.

10. Christopher Lewis, "Mirrors and Metaphors: Reflections on Schoenberg and Nineteenth-Century Tonality," *19th-Century Music* 11, no.1 (Summer 1987): 26–42; reprinted as "Mirrors and Metaphors: On Schoenberg and Nineteenth-Century Tonality," in *Music at the Turn of Century,* ed. Joseph Kerman, 15–31 (Berkeley: University of California Press, 1990). For a discussion of the double-tonic complex, see Robert Bailey, "An Analytical Study of the Sketches and Drafts," in *Wagner: Prelude and Transfiguration from "Tristan und Isolde,"* ed. Bailey, 113–46 (New York: Norton, 1985), 117–24.

11. For the example and Lewis's discussion of it, see "Mirrors and Metaphors," *Music at the Turn of Century,* 21–26.

12. David Lewin, "Amfortas's Prayer to Titurel and the Role of D in *Parsifal:* The Tonal Spaces of the Drama and the Enharmonic C♭/B," *19th-Century Music* 7, no.3 (April 1984): 336–49.

13. For the example, see ibid., 338.

14. Richard Bass, "Prokofiev's Technique of Chromatic Displacement," *Music Analysis* 7, no.2 (July 1988): 197–214.

15. Ibid., 207.

16. J. J. Bharucha, "Event Hierarchies, Tonal Hierarchies, and Assimilation: A Reply to Deutsch and Dowling," *Journal of Experimental Psychology, General* 113, no.3 (1984): 421–25; Fred Lerdahl, "Tonal Pitch Space," *Music Perception* 5, no.3 (Spring 1988): 315–49.

17. Heinrich Schenker, *Counterpoint,* trans. John Rothgeb and Jürgen Thym, 2 vols. (New York: Schirmer, 1987), 1: xxx.

18. Ibid., 1: xxxi.

19. Ibid.

20. Heinrich Schenker, *Free Composition,* 2d ed., trans. Ernst Oster, 2 vols. (New York: Longman, 1979), 1: 11. William Benjamin has discussed the evolution in Schenker's thought from a harmonic to a contrapuntal orientation in an insightful essay on what he calls "pitch-class counterpoint." See William Benjamin, "Pitch-Class Counterpoint in Tonal Music," in *Music Theory: Special Topics,* ed. Richmond Browne, 1–32 (New York: Academic, 1981).

21. Benjamin, "Pitch-Class Counterpoint," 31.

22. Lerdahl, "Tonal Pitch Space," 344.

23. Arnold Schoenberg, *Theory of Harmony,* trans. Roy E. Carter (Berkeley: University of California Press, 1978), 387.

24. Richard Taruskin, "Chernomor to Kashchei: Harmonic Sorcery; or Stravinsky's 'Angle'," *Journal of the American Musicological Society* 38, no.1 (Summer 1985): 72–142.

25. For a detailed study of third relations in the music of Schubert and his contemporaries, see Harald Krebs, "Third Relation and Dominant in Late Eighteenth- and Early Nineteenth-Century Music" (Ph.D. diss., Yale University, 1980), chap.2.

26. Johnson, "1794–1795," 27; Edward T. Cone, "Schubert's Promissory Note: An Essay in Musical Hermeneutics," *19th-Century Music* 5, no.3 (Spring 1982): 233–41.

27. Benjamin Boretz, "Meta-Variations: Studies in the Foundations of Musical Thought (1)," *Perspectives of New Music* 8, no.1 (Fall/Winter 1969): 6

28. Richard Wagner, *Opera and Drama,* trans. Edwin Evans, 2 vols. (London: Associated Board of the Royal Schools of Music, n.d.), 2: 513–15.

29. Lewin's article suggests, in a way sufficiently complex that I cannot explicate here, that diatonic space and chromatic space—*Stufen* space and Riemannian space—are incompatible, even though they may occupy the same musical surface.

30. Joseph Kerman, "Viewpoint," *19th-Century Music* 2, no. 2 (Nov. 1978): 186–91.

31. Donald Francis Tovey, *A Companion to Beethoven's Pianoforte Sonatas* (London: Associated Board of the Royal Schools of Music, 1931), 1.

32. Kerman, "Viewpoint," 187.

33. Stephen Jay Gould, *Ever Since Darwin: Reflections in Natural History* (New York: Norton, 1973), 107.

34. Ibid., 107–8.

35. Ibid., 104.

36. Ibid., 108.

The Mind's Chronology: Narrative Times and Harmonic Disruption in Postromantic Music

For Eileen

CHRISTOPHER LEWIS

The statue is concentrated in one moment of perfection. The image stained upon the canvas possesses no spiritual element of growth or change. If they know nothing of death, it is because they know nothing of life, for the secrets of life and death belong to those, and those only, whom the sequence of time affects, and who possess not merely the present but the future, and can rise or fall from a past of glory or of shame. Movement, that problem of the visible arts, can be truly realized by Literature alone. It is Literature that shows us the body in its swiftness and the soul in its unrest. — Oscar Wilde.

Oscar Wilde regarded literature as the greatest of the arts because he thought that only literature could portray the essence of life, the passage of time.[1] It is unfortunate that he had little critical understanding of music, for the times of literature and of music are in many respects similar. As Jonathan Kramer has pointed out, music unfolds in time and time unfolds in music.[2] Such a truism can be nothing less than profound, and like all profound truisms it raises more questions than it answers. Moreover, its truth is not diminished in the following variants: "Life unfolds in time and time unfolds in life," or "Narrative unfolds in time and time unfolds in narrative," and so on. As I read a novel or a poem or view a painting, I can do so at my own pace, so that the unfolding of my time and the work's time may well be different. Music, however, shares with drama the peculiarity of removing observational time from the physical control of the audience. As I listen to a piece of music, I can exercise control over its time only in the mind—in my powers of memory and in my anticipation of events not yet sounded. Because memory and expectation are the primitive basis for distinguishing between what we call past and what we call present,[3] they form the foundation not only for our experience of music but also for our understanding of literary narrative. The essence of narrativity, like that of tonal harmony, is process.[4] Comprehension of narrative requires the recognition and constant reassessment of narrative contingencies that are no more than fragments of fictional history.[5] We reconstruct the process that underlies narrative by making its discontinuous fragments continuous, and although we may do so at our own speed, we must do so under the direction of the chronological order of the narrative itself. The reader's apparent freedom from the constraints of time is only a chimera, and the similarities between the conceptual bases of narrative and those of tonal harmonic progression are striking.

Paradoxically, it is often in music and literature in which chronicity seems to be abandoned that the reconstruction of the narrative sequence is most illuminating. In the closing moments of Verdi's *Otello*, as Otello slowly expires in E major, he offers Desdemona one last kiss, over a C-major triad (see ex.1a). That extraordinary chord, so foreign to the

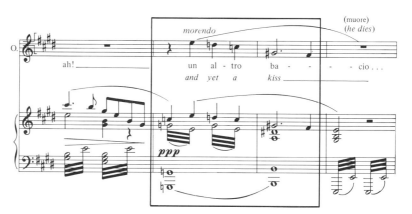

Example 1a. Verdi, *Otello*, act 4, vocal score, 363–64.

serene E major that surrounds it, can be read as a peculiar chromatic divider between the tonic and dominant, but both the sonority itself and the sense of dislocation it creates recall at least four similar events in the act (see exs.1b–e) and thus give it a contextual meaning that transcends its voice-leading function. By stimulating a conscious musical memory, the C-major chord makes itself known as the last in a series of widely separated C-major events, each of which interrupts or otherwise prolongs an E-major or -minor chord, and the harmony draws the listener's attention to a similarity of the dramatic situations at these precise points.

David Lawton finds that Verdi has imbued E and C with associative meanings, pitting C major, which symbolizes Iago's intrigues and Otello's downfall, against E major, which symbolizes both the greatness

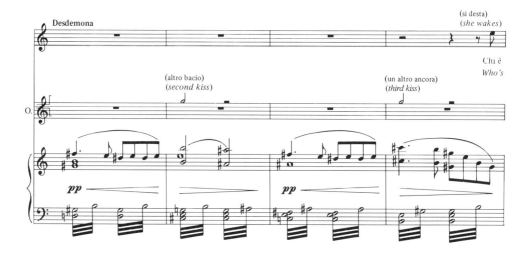

Example 1b. *Otello,* act 4, 343–44.

and the tragic potential of Otello's character.[6] Example 1b gives the version of the "*bacio* [kiss]" theme played as Otello kisses the sleeping Desdemona. In the fifth measure the E-major cadence that is the apparent goal of the passage is simply displaced by a C-major chord in second inversion. At Desdemona's question "*Chi è là* [who's there]?" the harmony tells us that it is Otello—but he is there under Iago's malevolent influence. In the next excerpt (see ex. 1c) a C-major chord accompanies the accusation that Iago has planted in Otello's mind. As Desdemona denies her guilt, the music plunges directly to E minor. Later, as Otello gazes at the strangled body from which the last breath is escaping, he whispers her epitaph in C major (see ex. 1d). Finally, when Otello realizes what he has done, and that he, too, must die, a C-major chord under his outburst "*O! Gloria!* [Ah! Glory!]" interrupts the E-major context (see ex. 1e).

Example 1c. *Otello,* act 4, 347–48.

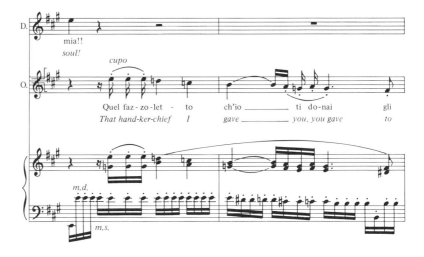

In each earlier case, as with the final kiss, the C-major triad appears as an interpolation, a parenthetic disruption of normal tonal syntax. Only by understanding that all these events are linked in spite of their temporal displacement, that they form a disjunct series of C-major events that ties together certain aspects of the dramatic structure, can we understand that the illogicalities they create in the musical foreground are merely signposts to a much deeper and more significant tonal coherence and that we accept the harmonic discontinuity easily because the dramatic logic is so clear. These harmonic phenomena are not the musical equivalent of narrative but merely a musical reflection of aspects of the drama; nonetheless, they suggest the possibility that similar harmonic aberrations might have a purely musical meaning and that tonality might be so directly analogous to narrative as to work similarly on its own. An ex-

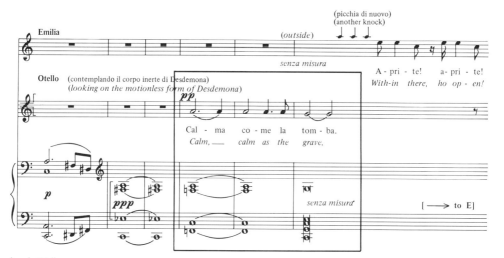

Example 1d. *Otello*, act 4,
352.

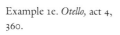

Example 1e. *Otello*, act 4,
360.

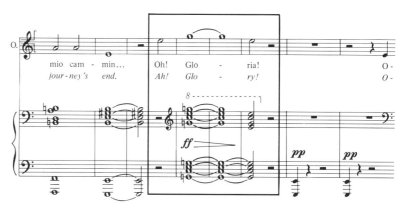

amination of two seemingly incongruent works, one narrative and the other musical, shows that this is indeed the case.

Some time ago, while I was thinking about the tonal language of the Adagio of Bruckner's Seventh Symphony, I happened to see Maurizio Nichetti's film *The Icicle Thief* (*Ladri di saponette*). I immediately realized that the movie manipulates its narrative and temporal elements precisely as the Adagio manipulates its tonal strata. The correspondence is so powerful as to stimulate a number of ideas about how musical times and narrative times may be similar and how postromantic harmony may owe much of its chromatic surface not to a fundamental scalar chromaticism but rather to the juxtapositions of disparate events created by a disrupted and distorted chronological sequence.

The film plays off three interconnected narrative threads, which also represent three different periods of time and three different kinds of reality (see table 1). The first thread portrays the situation of director Nichetti (playing himself) as a sincere artist trying desperately to get a crass and unthinking world to listen to what he has to say. Nichetti shows up at a television studio to be interviewed in connection with a broadcast of his neorealist film *The Icicle Thief*. Almost immediately he is faced with an ignorant program host, uncaring producers, and the artistic butchery of a commercial operation. The second thread is the double strand of events in TV-land: on the one hand, the loud, obnoxious commercials that constantly interrupt the showing of Nichetti's film, and on the other, a family of couch potatoes who mindlessly watch television, unmoved by Nichetti's art but fascinated by the commercials, which constantly blare out promises of a better way of living. Finally, the third narrative thread is *The Icicle Thief*, Nichetti's film-within-a-film, set about forty years in the past. It tells the story of Antonio, also played by Nichetti, and his wife, Maria. They and their two children live in abject, mind-numbing poverty, and the plot turns on Antonio's great luck in finding a job at a glass factory.

The three streams are distinguished not only by their characters and narrative contents but also by simple technical devices. Nichetti's reality is filmed largely in close-ups, often with an apparently hand-held camera to give a sense of news-reel immediacy, and the colors are subdued; there is no background music except what comes over the studio monitors. In stark contrast, TV-land is bright, slick, and glitzy; the blaring music for the commercials is synthesized electro-pop. Finally, the film-within-the-film is photographed in gritty black and white; the sound track is mostly in an early-fifties cabaret style, with an anguished string orchestra accompanying the more tense moments.

Table 1. Structure of Maurizio Nichetti's film *The Icicle Thief*

	#1	#2	#3	#4	#5
A. Nichetti's "Reality" · Color, no music · **The present**	Nichetti arrives at TV studio for screening of his film.		Nichetti introduced; his films contain "quotes & reminiscences of a glorious past."		*The Icicle Thief* is introduced: "only through images can the film-maker explain the past and the present."
B TV-land · Color · 1. Commercials Loud electro-pop music · 2. Couch-potato TV family. TV sound track as background · **The future** according to TV		Family in their living room to watch the Nichetti program. The parents ignore their son Francesco playing with a Lego set. We see Nichetti on the screen of the TV.		Family watches TV with sound off; they each talk about the program but ignore one another.	
C *The Icicle Thief* The film-within-the-film · Black and white · Sound track mostly subdued early fifties cabaret style · **The past**					

The structural premise at first seems simple: what we assume to be the main story line is interrupted abruptly as the film cuts back and forth, initially between the first two streams and then among all three. We see Nichetti at the studio being interviewed, watching his own film as it is broadcast, and being offended by the interrupting commercials. We are reminded that his films contain "quotations and reminiscences of a

Table 1 (*Continued*)

	#6	#7	#8	#9	#10
A. Nichetti's "Reality" • Color, no music • **The present**				As music from the advertisements interrupts the film, the film cuts to the studio, where Nichetti protests that the ads are butchering his film.	
B TV-land • Color • 1. Commercials Loud electro- pop music • 2. Couch-potato TV family. TV sound track as background • **The future** according to TV			Advertisements interrupt film: a naked woman is selling soap; a blond in a bathing suit sells "Splash" soft drink; children sell "Big-Big" chocolate bar.		"Big-Big" ad. TV family watches it. The mother discusses the ad with *her* mother on the phone. *The Icicle Thief* starts again on the TV. Bruno in the film sees Francesco eating a Big-Big, and asks for one. He starts singing the Big-Big jingle.
C *The Icicle Thief* The film-within- the-film • Black and white • Sound track mostly subdued early fifties cabaret style • **The past**		The film starts. Antonio, unemployed, is married to Maria, who has ambitions to be a cabaret singer. Blinded by their troubles, they ignore children Bruno & Paolo. The parallel with the brain-dead TV couple is obvious.	In church of priest Dom Italo, Maria sings her part in the choir in cabaret style. Bruno tells the priest that his father is to become a black marketeer. Priest finds Ant. a job in glass factory. Maria dreams of an icicle-like chandelier, an image she has seen in the cinema.		Antonio & Maria are dumbfounded.

glorious past" and that "only through images can the filmmaker explain the past and the present." We quickly become aware that, although the three streams influence one another, each has a narrative thread independent of the story lines of the other two. In spite of our sympathy for Nichetti, we soon wonder just what is interrupting what. Then, the reality of one stream subtly begins to affect that of the others. First, in

Table 1 (*Continued*)

	#11	#12	#13	#14	#15
A. Nichetti's "Reality" · Color, no music · **The present**					Nichetti complains at finding Heidi in his film, and is told that it's just a "misunderstanding." He protests that Ant. should be killed accidentally on his way home, Maria become a prostitute, and the children be sent to an orphanage. The studio says the problem is in Rome. He rushes out to take a train.
B TV-land · Color · 1. Commercials Loud electro-pop music · 2. Couch-potato TV family. TV sound track as background · **The future** according to TV		Another commercial. Heidi, a tall blonde in a bathing suit, dives into a pool as a power blackout shuts down the TV broadcast. Power is restored. The TV family still ignores the son, who is building a model of the Kremlin in Lego.		A blue Super-man is selling "Vial-Blue"; Maria drops into his commer-cial.	
C *The Icicle Thief* The film-within-the-film · Black and white · Sound track mostly subdued early fifties cabaret style · **The past**	We are now full-frame back in the movie. Antonio leaves for work, and Maria leaves for the cabaret. At the factory, Ant. decides to steal a chan-delier for Maria. After work he starts to carry it home on the handle-bars of his bike.		As Antonio cycles along the river bank, he finds Heidi in the water. He hauls her out; she is in color, her sound track crosses, too. He dries her off and her color rubs off. He takes her home, forgetting his chandelier. While he and Maria argue, she looks after Bruno. The parents leave to look for the chandelier; they cannot find it. In despair, Maria walks into the water; Ant. finds one "icicle," but Maria is gone.		

segment 10 Antonio's son Bruno looks out of the film *into* TV-land, hears a chocolate-bar jingle, and starts to sing it. Two segments later, after a brief power blackout, wholesale transference among streams begins, as characters from the commercials float into poor Nichetti's movie and disrupt the scripted plot. He is distraught and leaves the studio; he catches a train to Rome in color but gets off it in black and white as a charac-

Table 1 (*Continued*)

	#16	#17	#18	#19	#20	#21
A. Nichetti's "Reality" • Color, no music • **The present**						
B TV-land • Color • 1. Commercials Loud electro-pop music • 2. Couch-potato TV family. TV sound track as background • **The future** according to TV		A commercial for floorwax starring Maria, dancing to the music of *Carmen*.		An apéritif ad, then the Big-Big commercial, now starring Bruno. Commercials interrupt one another. Nichetti tries to get the characters back where they belong. The TV family is utterly confused, unable to sort out the "real" from the "unreal."		Francesco, his Lego feat unnoticed, goes to bed. On the TV, Nichetti is now trapped behind the shopping carts in what used to be his film. He pounds on the TV screen, but he is now just one more unreal image in TV-land. The mother turns off the set; we see goldfish in a bowl by the TV, then a fade out.
C *The Icicle Thief* The film-within-the-film • Black and white • Sound track mostly subdued early fifties cabaret style • **The past**	The police drag the river for Maria; Ant. is accused of her murder. Nichetti now finds himself in black and white, getting off the train into his own movie. He goes to the glass factory to try to sort things out but is tossed out as a friend of "that thief" Antonio. He then goes to Dom Italo to get Antonio's address.		Nichetti arrives at Antonio's house and tells Bruno that he should be in an orphanage. Heidi enters, but Nichetti fails to get rid of her; he goes to the police to explain Ant.'s innocence. Bruno, to avoid the orphanage, frames Nichetti, who is arrested and put in a cell with Ant.; Ant. is released. All escape, and a mad chase ensues.		Antonio is consoled for the loss of his wife by Dom Italo. At the apartment they are met by Heidi, who has decided she wants to go back. Maria and Nichetti arrive with about a dozen laden shopping carts: Maria's Nirvana!	

ter in *The Icicle Thief*. His attempts to restore the plot lead only to more confusion, as first Maria and then Bruno flee from the bleakness of their movie lives into the cheery consumerism of the commercials. They then return to their flat with dozens of heavily laden shopping carts. In the final scene, viewed on the television in the couch potatoes' living room, Nichetti is trapped behind the shopping carts in what used to be his film.

In despair he pounds on the television screen for help but is ignored, as always—he is just one more unreal character in TV-land. The television set is turned off, and Nichetti's image fades to black. His reality is destroyed; his film is destroyed; he has lost his past and his present, and the blank television screen shows that he has no future. The three streams have fused into one, and ironically, what was in the beginning the interruptive stream now appears as the main thread.

The Adagio of Bruckner's Seventh Symphony is similarly constructed around three interwoven and mutually interruptive threads. Instead of having plot lines, we have three tonal streams that are both independent and interdependent. The movement is cast in a simple rondo form, ABA′B′A, with conventional principal tonal relations underlying the design: the initial tonalities of the parts are C♯ minor, F♯ minor, C♯ minor, G♯ minor (enharmonically notated as A♭), and finally, C♯ minor again.[7] Stephen Parkany observes that an important aspect of the larger formal strategy is "the avoidance, subversion, and increasingly directed reconfirmation of the tonic C♯."[8] That is so: in part 1 of the movement three interwoven tonal threads complement and interrupt one another, creating together the sense of a subverted C♯, while at the same time each establishes an intrinsic coherence that transcends its function as a part of the whole. That is, the tonal strata are manipulated precisely as are the narrative threads in Nichetti's film.

Bruckner's Adagio is not simply in C♯ but is founded on a principal tonal pairing of C♯ and E enunciated in the opening four measures. Curiously, almost none of the music in the remaining two dozen measures of part 1 is concerned directly with those areas. Instead, three separate threads are developed and interwoven (see ex. 2). The first (stream B) leans toward the sharp side of C♯, tonicizing V and V/V of that key; the second (stream C) tends toward the flat side of E, tonicizing in turn IV, IV/IV, and IV/IV/IV; and the third (stream A) is concerned almost exclusively with F♯ as a means of bridging the tonal distance between the other two: at the beginning of the excerpt F♯ is heard as IV of C♯, and by m. 19 it is V/V of E. Each stream is foreshadowed in the introductory four measures, and if we allow ourselves to suspend our traditional understanding of chords as a progression unfolding through time, subsumed by the deeper-level event encompassed by the whole span, then as discrete events, the introductory chords link up—sometimes across a gulf of many measures—with other events. At the end of the Adagio, as at the end of the movie, the contrasting streams reach a point of confluence and resolve to C♯.

The separation of the tonal streams is far from arbitrary. My princi-

Example 2. Tonal strata in the Adagio of Bruckner's Seventh Symphony, mm. 1–27.

to Section III, m. 100ff.

transition
to Sect. II[F♯]

pal thesis is that temporal disruptions and displacements allow complex chromatic passages to be formed from the combination of two or more independently coherent progressions.[9] That is precisely the case here if we allow ourselves to hear the excerpt as we see *The Icicle Thief*, through a kind of time filter exercised by the memory that instantaneously bridges the gaps. Just as Nichetti's three narratives are distinguished by color, sound track, and camera technique, so too are the main points of disjuncture of Bruckner's constituent streams carefully demarcated (see ex. 2). At mm. 7–8 the reference to stream C is articulated by the entry of the trombones for those two measures only, by the dynamic terracing, and by the register differential, which in turn creates a disjunction in the voice leading. The entry of stream B at m. 9 is marked by an articulative silence, by a change in the expressive manner (to *zart* [delicate]), and by the generally brighter register. Again, at m. 12 silence and a strong dynamic contrast set off the reentry of stream B, and at m. 14 the single-measure interruption by stream A is reinforced by the entry of high woodwinds for those chords only. Finally, the last segment, representing stream B, is isolated by dynamic contrast, articulative silence, and the commencement of an orchestrated crescendo.

More to the point, however, is the degree to which the music exhibits perfectly coherent and smooth voice leading *across* the interruptions. In the F♯ stream (stream A) each of the gaps save one is bridged by a simple change of chord position. In the G♯ stream (stream B) the first gap is bridged by a change of position, the second by an elision of the tonic (V_5^6 to V_2^4/IV) and the last by a progression from IV6 to a cadential $_4^6$. Stream C, the most disjunct and unstable, is left unresolved in the first section of the Adagio, only to be resumed and carried one step farther in the middle of the movement, at m. 101. Each of the two main streams constitutes a fully coherent tonal passage in its own right when the temporal displacements are rectified; the third stream is part of an equally coherent single gesture whose completion occurs only after an interruption of some dozens of measures, but the remoteness of the harmony at the final point of disjuncture in m. 17 and the powerful articulation of the resumption in m. 101 help to bridge that long gap. We have, then, three sets of events that together provide a sense of the movement's middle- and background tonal reliance on references to the C♯/E principal complex and to secondary areas related to G♯ and F♯.

The relationship of tonal technique in Bruckner's Adagio to narrative structure in Nichetti's film is more than a striking coincidence; it is evidence of a powerful analogue between the very essences of tonality and narrative and suggests that not only musical design and gesture but also foreground-level harmony can be linked to narrative temporalities. There are in literary narrative four fundamental ways of shaping the reader's perception of time. In any given work all four time shapes may obtain at various points, but usually one of them dominates.[10] The first, "process time," maintains a natural chronological sequence.[11] Process time is not identical with "real time" (which I suspect does not obtain in any art form, including the Wildean drama), for proportions and other aspects of relative duration may be freely manipulated: a moment may appear to last an age, and years may seem to flash by, but they will flash in the correct order. Although our perception of the speed at which time passes is highly subjective,[12] our perception of the order of events normally is not. What matters, then, is that the sense of process time depends on the presentation of a succession of events in a certain order, so that the sequence continually unfolds and develops through successive stages until it culminates in a specific result, thus stressing a process and its underlying causality.[13] In musical terms, that is common-practice tonal time. A given event evolves directly from the immediately preceding event at the same level. The linkage of chronology and causality is fundamental to the basic laws of tonal syntax:[14] to put it very simplistically, I–II–V–I and I–I–V–II are not equivalent tonal statements.

Although apparent chromatic anomalies are the key to unraveling the strands of interwoven tonalities in Bruckner's Adagio, it would be a mistake to regard *every* harmonic anomaly as evidence of distorted chronological sequence. For example, extended chromatic interjections are normal, perhaps even normative, in the music of Chopin. Gerald Abraham described such passages as "harmonic parentheses,"[15] ascribing to some of them a "temporary suspension of the principle of tonality."[16] We now understand these chromatic excursions very differently, finding them fully compatible with the principles of common-practice tonality. In Chopin's Polonaise in C♯ Minor a parenthesis initiates a self-contained progression apparently tonicizing the Neapolitan (see ex. 3). The domi-

Example 3. Chopin, Polonaise in C♯, op. 26, no. 1, mm. 59–61.

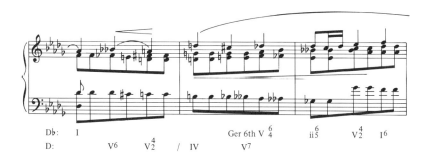

nant seventh of D, however, is an enharmonic German sixth of D♭; the passage actually serves to affirm D♭ major, and the chromaticisms are fully subsumed by that key. They have only a local influence and seem unrelated to any earlier or later event of the piece. That is to say, the linear and harmonic successions are entirely logical on their own terms and function in a purely local context. The rule of monotonality has not been violated by the parenthesis, and the tonal-harmonic time sense is the monolinear causality of process time.

The second kind of narrative time, "retrospective time," illustrates Kierkegaard's comment that "life can only be lived forward and understood backward."[17] Narrative retrospective time folds the time line on itself[18] and focuses either on two juxtaposed states of being or on the change that occurs as the character looks back.[19] At its simplest it involves the interweaving of two streams of memory—the author's memory of the narrative present and the character's memory of the narrative past— that interrupt each other and disturb the normal sense of causality. Ironically, the disruptions themselves contribute to the ultimate causality, the character's reconciliation of the two streams. More complex manifestations interweave two or more streams that not only represent different time periods but may also relate to entirely different plot lines or characters. In either case the structure turns on some transcendental, even epiphanic moment that reveals the dismembered causality of the flow from past to present or of connection between disconnected threads. Italo Calvino's *If on a Winter's Night a Traveller*[20] is a prime example: Calvino interjects a set of incomplete novels into a separate, complete story. Part of the structure's irony is that each fragment begins as a real novel, whereas the real novel begins as commentary on the fragments. The roles of the two structural elements are first reversed and then finally reconciled. Retrospective time is also the time shape of both Nichetti's *The Icicle Thief* and the Adagio of Bruckner's Seventh.[21] In both works the disparate streams eventually tend toward the reconciliation of a common goal.

Retrospective time creates many of the chromatic anomalies of postromantic music. In Pfitzner's early song "Kuriose Geschichte," an entirely conventional and even simple-minded progression in D is rudely interrupted by a chromatic excursion at m. 14 (see ex. 4). It is possible to read the chromaticism in terms similar to those applied to the previous Chopin excerpts. Example 4b shows the prolonged F major as a chromatic mediant acting as a divider between I and V and the prolonged B♭ as a chromatic submediant acting as a neighbor to V. In the context of the song, however, that reading is not convincing. The second half of the

Example 4a. Pfitzner, "Kuriose Geschichte," mm. 10–22. Courtesy of Ries and Erler, Berlin.

Example 4b. "Kuriose Geschichte," linear sketch.

Example 4c. "Kuriose Geschichte," interacting tonal streams.

binary-form stanza begins with the tonicization of F, and the ritardandi and the cadential formulas in mm. 17 and 21 provide a sense of temporary closure on the flat side. The A^7 of mm. 18 and 19 sounds interruptive rather than interrupted—prolongational rather than structural. I therefore suggest a reading that ignores the common-practice distinctions of structural and prolongational events. The F of mm. 16 and 17 is the dominant of the B♭ triad sounded in mm. 20–21, as well as a divider between I and V of D. That B♭ chord not only prolongs A but is itself a structural event in a conflicting tonal stream, resolving the F chord from two measures earlier. To put it simply: there are two parallel harmonic progressions, one in D (I–V/ii–ii–V–I) and one in B♭ (V/V–V–IV/V–V–I–IV–I) (see ex. 4c). These two streams interrupt each other, and we must, as it were, reconstruct each of them after the event by remembering back over the interruptions, just as in act 4 of *Otello* we recall all the invoca-

tions of C major. We have then not one but three harmonic threads to follow: one in D, one in B♭, and the complex juxtapositional combination formed by the folding back of the two single streams on each other.

In Hugo Wolf's *Michelangelo Lieder* retrospective time shapes not only the design of the individual songs but also the set of three songs as a cycle. The close of the first song, "Wohl denk' ich oft," dramatically illustrates the technique. The principal tonic of the song is G, but the harmonic causality is twice disrupted in the final ten measures of the song. At m. 13 the tonic chord is altered to become V^7/IV, but at m. 15 that extended V^7 of C is succeeded by a prolonged E-major triad. That in turn progresses by successive fifths to V of G, and then the final authentic cadential progression in G is interrupted by a very powerfully articulated subdominant. One way of reading the penultimate chord is as a plagal prolongation of the tonic,[22] but another way is to understand it as a disruptive reference back to, and a resolution of, the V^7/IV from mm. 13 and 14. Example 5 reconstructs two coherent progressions in the piece that are folded back on each other only to be united at last by the common goal. The logic of the individual harmonic streams created when we

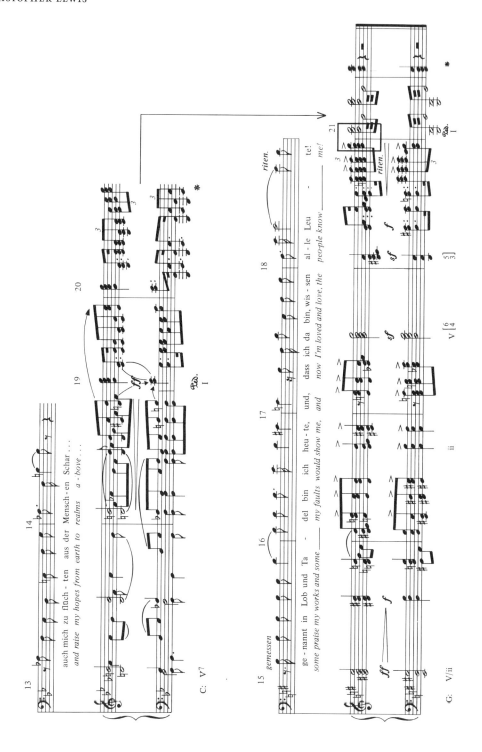

Example 5. Tonal streams in Hugo Wolf, "Wohl denk' ich oft," mm. 11–22.

decompose the compound progression is strengthened by registral and voice-leading connections across the interruptions. For example, in the dominant chord of m. 14 the stepwise ascent in the upper voice proceeds to E^5 in m. 19, the seventh in the middle voice resolves to E^4 in m. 18, and the tenor voice resolves its stepwise ascent to C^4 in m. 19. Even more striking is the anticipation in m. 18 of the B^5 of mm. 21–22.

The harmonic disjunctions in the Pfitzner and Wolf songs, if not explicitly narrative, are nonetheless linked to the texts. Pfitzner's tonal shifts underscore the changes in poetic voice of a dialogue. Wolf's song is about alienation; the first disruption occurs at the line *auch mich zu flüchten aus der Menschen Schar* [also for me to flee from humankind], and the abandoned stream returns right after the line *dass ich da bin, wissen alle Leute!* [everyone knows I'm there!]. In both songs, therefore, the tonalities are partly associative, like the C-major chords in *Otello*, but they differ from Verdi's usage in that they create their own syntactic tonal context, however short; moreover, like Bruckner's Adagio, they differ from the tonal parentheses of Chopin and his contemporaries in that the successive interjections are linked to one another to form a comprehensible tonal context that transcends their interruptive function. To put it another way, it becomes less clear in the later music which is the primary, structural tonal context and which is the interruptive, prolongational event.[23]

Hearing in retrospective time often allows for rehabilitation of a lost tonal causality. Many years ago Paul Henry Lang wrote that Debussy's music stands at "the frontiers of logical consciousness," that it lacks a sense of "causal continuity."[24] Although Lang was primarily referring not to what we now call the harmonic foreground but to the succession of compositional ideas, Debussy's harmony often does seem to abandon logical causality. The final section of the *Prélude à "L'après-midi d'un faune"* is a varied reprise of the piece's opening, and the intervening tonal motions are directed in several ways to the extended dominant of C♯ that immediately precedes it. After all, the first four statements of the opening theme begin on C♯, the principal thematic contrast—the big tune at m. 55—is in C♯ (notated D♭), and an extended G♯ chord enters at m. 90 supporting a melodic reference to the opening theme: all the signs point to an eventual reprise in C♯. Instead, the big dominant of C♯ resolves to an E^9 chord in an apparent disruption of tonal logic (see ex. 6). John Crotty, following the double-tonic theory of Robert Bailey, has shown some of the ways in which E and C♯ are paired as alternate tonics in the *Prélude*.[25] Reading the tonic of E as a substitute resolution of the dominant of C♯ legitimates Debussy's resolution, which I do not dispute, but

Example 6. Debussy,
*Prélude à "L'après-midi d'un
faune,"* mm. 93–110.

the G$\sharp^7$ also resolves in another way that is fully conventional in every respect except one. That one unconventional aspect is the *time* of resolution, which is actually seven measures too late (m. 100). The C$\sharp$ chord thus reached, as the V^7 of F$\sharp$ (that is, V^7/ii of E), is sustained through m. 102 and then resolves normally in m. 104—one measure too late. The C dominant-seventh chord sounded in m. 103 is a German sixth in E, prepared for in m. 99 and resolved in m. 105. Although the B^7 chord in m. 105 is the ultimate common goal of both harmonic streams, each stream is fully coherent on its own terms, and the apparent disruptions of logical causality occur only when the confluence of the two displaces consequent events from their proper time of occurrence immediately following the antecedent. In a way the time frame of each stream has been distorted, and the listener must exercise a considerable effort to set it right in his or her mind.

The third narrative time shape, "barrier time," breaks off fragments of the narrative and rearranges the order.[26] The most strikingly characteristic use of barrier time in prose composition is to begin a novel with an event that apparently has no context; the broken-off fragment establishes at the beginning of the work the goal toward which the ensuing—or, read a different way, the preceding—events are directed. Perhaps the most familiar example is Emily Brontë's *Wuthering Heights.* The narrator, Lockwood, and the reader enter the picture well after the main events of the narrative have run their course, and they always know the outcome of a given sequence of events before they know their precise nature or order. Similarly, Timothy Findley's *Famous Last Words*[27] begins with Hugh Mauberley leaving Ezra Pound to go into hiding at the end of the Second World War. What had he to do with Pound? From whom was he hiding? Why did he take all his notebooks? What was in them? All these questions are answered in the course of a virtuoso narrative shaped by barrier time. Here the narrative analogy to tonality is even more direct; we know how things come out because the principal events of the plot and many of the characters are historical: we know how the war ended and what happened to Pound, Hitler, and the Duke of Windsor, and because of that we have at the outset some sense of what happened, or will happen, to Mauberley. *Famous Last Words* is a concrete illustration of the "hermeneutic circle," the "insight that human perception and understanding always proceed from foreknowledge of a (however dimly apprehended) totality."[28] Because fragments of the narrative are continually displaced, linking them in a comprehensible sequence requires an exercise both of memory and of intuitive and logical prediction. In hearing disjointed tonality, as in reading *Famous Last Words,* the call on memory is twofold: we have constant recourse both to our memory of previous segments of a particular narrative or tonal stream and to our memory of the historical fact or the tonal paradigm that underlies the particularities of the specific work. The more disembodied and numerous the fragments become, the greater is the exercise of memory needed to straighten out the chronological sense of causality—to cure the mnemonic plague.

I have observed that the opening chords of Bruckner's Adagio foreshadow the three tonal streams of the ensuing section; they *merely* foreshadow, however, since their foreground sense in C♯ is perfectly conventional, and they are not themselves heard as disruptive interjections. A different and far more subtle preliminary announcement is made by the opening chords of Schoenberg's orchestral song "Voll jener Süsse," op. 8, no. 3 (see ex. 7a).

The song's nine measures of orchestral introduction expose two successive half-diminished-seventh chords, each prolonged through a repeated series of voice exchanges. In m. 10, on the entry of the voice, the bass rises diatonically to B, supporting an authentic resolution to a B-major triad, and the next three measures confirm that tonic. As Schoenberg tells us in *Harmonielehre,*[29] and as the song itself quickly confirms, "Voll jener Süsse" wavers between B and C♯. There are strong harmonic resolutions to C♯ in mm. 30–31, 74, 83, and 97–98; B is tonicized not only at m. 11 but also at mm. 24, 37, 65, 71, and 89. In fact, the tonal function of the introduction is to present two chords that have no real connection with each other in a single context but that juxtapose implications of the two tonal centers of the song: mm. 1–3 refer to C♯, and mm. 4–9 to B. Only at the very end of the song, in the orchestral postlude, is the correct succession from both chords established and the disjuncture put right. Example 7b shows a reduction of the introduction and postlude. In m. 82 the opening chord of the song returns and identifies itself by resolving to C♯; in m. 87 the second chord also returns, and it too resolves as a dominant, but to B. Then, at m. 96, when it seems as if B really is the song's ultimate goal, the upper voices resolve to D♯ and

Example 7a. Schoenberg, "Voll jener Süsse," mm.1–10 and 79–98. Copyright 1911 by Universal Edition. Copyright renewed. All rights reserved. Used by permission of European American Music Distributors Corporation, sole Canadian agent for Universal Edition; and Belmont Music Publishers, Pacific Palisades CA 90272.

F♯, which immediately become the fifth and seventh of V⁷ of C♯, and a C♯ chord then ends the song. The final chord reaches back across the preceding ninety measures to link up with, and provide a resolution for, that enigmatic opening chord, the fragmentary splinter of C♯ broken off and imbedded in another context.

The phrase structure of Pfitzner's "Wie glänzt der helle Mond" is characterized by large-scale disruptions caused by the interaction of two pairs of tonics: the song turns both on the opposition of these two tonal complexes and on third-motion within each complex—from C♯ to E on the one hand and from C to E♭ on the other. Example 8a shows the first half of the song, with the C/E♭ interjections indicated by brackets.

Example 7b. "Voll jener Süsse," reduction of introduction, mm.1–10, and postlude, mm.82–98.

Example 8a. Pfitzner, "Wie glänzt der helle Mond," mm.1–18. Courtesy of Boosey and Hawkes, London.

doch wei-ter-hin liegt mei - ner Ju - gend Land.
But fur-ther far has van-ished Youth's ___ fair home.

Gemächlich (quasi Andantino) (etwa ♩ = ♪ vorher)
Quietly   (about ♩ = ♪ before)

Ohn' Rad und Deich-sel gibt's ein Wä - ge - lein,
A cha - riot with-out wheels or shafts___ I know,

rit.

Wieder sehr langsam (Anfangstempo, quasi Adagio)
Again very slow (tempo of the beginning)

drin fahr' ich bald zum Pa-ra - dies hin-ein. ___   Dort sitzt die Mut - ter Got -
In that one day to Pa-ra - dise I'll go, ___   There sits en - throned God's mo -

rit.

The C♯-minor chord of m.3 is continued in m.5, as is that of m.8 in m.11. The C-minor chord of m.4 is continued in m.9 and progresses to V⁷ of B♭ in m.10; following the interruptive C♯-minor chord, the B♭ chord enters in m.12 and continues to E♭.

Examples 8b–e show four parallel passages founded on the C♯/E complex; in each passage disembodied references to the other complex are superimposed. In exs.8b and 8c the rhythmic articulation makes the first

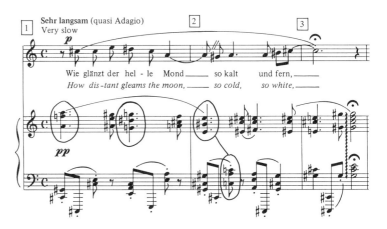

Example 8b. "Wie glänzt der helle Mond," mm.1–3.

Example 8c "Wie glänzt der helle Mond," mm.6–8.

five chords in the treble part sound like the harmonization of a descending scale in C. The opening sonority thus prepares not only the cadential side-slip to C♯ in m.11 but also the precadential V⁷ of B♭, the resolution of which starts the new phrase in m.12. In ex.8d the C♯/E and C/E♭ threads are intertwined, and in ex.8e C♯ is again interrupted with scat-

Example 8d. "Wie glänzt
der helle Mond," m.18.

Example 8e. "Wie glänzt
der helle Mond,"
mm. 27–28.

tered references to C. Although the various interruptions may not constitute a clearly coherent progression, they are related to one another by virtue of their affiliation with one or the other of the clearly established tonal rivals that constitute the song's background. The chronological succession of harmonic events is interrupted and delayed to such an extent that the sense of causality at the surface is all but destroyed. Here, far more than it is in a tonality ordered in process time, reference to the background is absolutely essential for comprehension of the splintered foreground.

The fourth kind of narrative time, "polytemporal time," is a significant technical development of twentieth-century literature[30] that is carried over to twentieth-century music. Chronology is rejected, the "clock hands run berserk,"[31] and the reader often loses all sense of before-and-after connections.[32] In Kurt Vonnegut's *Slaughterhouse Five* Billy Pilgrim learns about this time shape from a disembodied Tralfamadorian voice:

Each clump of symbols is a brief urgent message—describing a situation, a scene. We Tralfamadorians read them all at once, not one after the other. There isn't any particular relationship between all the messages, except that the author has chosen them carefully, so that, when seen all at once, they produce an image of life that is beautiful and surprising and deep. There is no beginning, no middle, no end, no suspense, no moral, no causes, no effects. What we love in our books are the depths of many marvellous moments seen all at one time.[33]

Even the most advanced of tonal excursions can be no more than a preparation for polytemporal time: polytemporality is perhaps the harmonic time sense of atonal music;[34] it is certainly the time sense of aleatory music, and "loose-leaf" composition. The musical difficulty lies not in suspending cause and effect but in hearing the music all at once.

In music, as in literature, the manipulation of chronology can be more than a technical device; it can be the essence of what the piece is about. If ever there were a piece of music whose subjective matter has to do with time and memory, surely that piece is the Adagio of Mahler's Tenth Symphony, which has in the last decade or so been the subject of four distinguished analyses.[35] Richard Kaplan establishes very convincingly the Adagio's primary structural dependence on the paired tonics of F♯ and B♭.[36] V. Kofi Agawu follows up on that line of thought, also drawing attention to certain strategic structural and gestural disjunctions in the work. Nevertheless, he finds the movement highly recursive, exhibiting a static tonal-harmonic structure[37] that derives its essential tonal drama from the alternation of the major and minor modes of F♯.[38] Such apparent tonal stasis is not in the least unusual in variation-like designs, for which there is historical precedent for making the tonal drama internal to each variation while gestural and textural direction creates the principal drama of the movement as a whole. In any case, it is partly because of the lack of tonal motion among the large structural subdivisions and partly because of the constant recurrence of motives and gestures that Agawu finds in the movement an extraordinary sense of reminiscence that refers not only to earlier events in the piece but also to external sources.[39] Invoking the hermeneutic circle, I take this further and suggest that Mahler's later music drives us to remember precisely because it so deliberately requires us to draw on our foreknowledge of the music's "dimly apprehended totality." To this end the final section of this Adagio, like the close of the last movement of the Ninth, carefully alludes to past events—events that have shaped both foreground and background—and

Table 2. Complex of Tonal Relations in Adagio of Mahler's Tenth Symphony

F♯	B♭	B	D	G	D♯
Principal Tonic	Principal Tonic				
		Neapolitan/B♭		Neapolitan/F♯	
German 6/B♭	German 6/D		German 6/F♯	German 6/B	German 6/G
V/B	V/D♯		V/G		

allows us both space and time to make the connections and bring our memories of them into the present.

Although the broad tonal planes of the movement do indeed make constant references to F♯ in either or both of its modes, the tonal design is not static; on the contrary it is predicated on a constant peregrination among a complex of intricately interconnected tonal centers. It is the intensive use of barrier time to shape the foreground that obscures the motion. I have noted Kaplan's demonstration of the centrality of the paired F♯ and B♭; important subsidiary points are their Neapolitan degrees and the dominants of the Neapolitans, which also function as German sixths (see table 2).

The final section of the Adagio unfolds as a slow winding down of tonal, rhythmic, textural, and registral tensions after the climactic explosion of the famous double-dominant chord in mm. 204–8. Although the F♯ tonal stream moves steadily to its final cadence, its surface is not unruffled. Four chromatic interjections interrupt the tonal causality of F♯; these splintered remnants of disembodied tonal contrast, each set off from the principal context by tempo, register, thematic gesture, or orchestration, link themselves in our memory with passages and processes that have saturated the earlier parts of the Adagio. Example 9a shows the fourth and longest of the coda's parentheses, which interrupts the bass-register V of F♯ at m. 238 and again at 241. The dominant is finally resumed at m. 253. The harmonic implications of the intervening passage seem at first glance to be random—an ambiguous reference to a German sixth of B, then a B-major triad followed by a suggestion of V of B♭ and an immediate retreat to four measures of E♭, with a final brief allusion to B and B♭—and they *are* random insofar as they derive no sense of causality from the straightforward successions of process time. Freed from the bonds of chronology, these harmonic shards relate directly back to the viola solo that opens the movement (see ex. 9b); not

incidentally, Mahler makes the back-reference explicit in mm. 246–52, which, although the harmonic shards are assigned to the violins instead of the violas, should be thought of as the fifth and final occurrence of the viola refrain. The back-reference makes a harmonic point: both the tonal excursion in the coda and the opening viola refrain refer to the same tonal materials, one in anticipation and the other in retrospect; the order is of course irrelevant. The refrain opens with an extended arpeggiation of the German sixth of B. That arpeggiation is followed by the dominant of B, which in turn acts as the German sixth of B♭; an implication of motion toward E♭ is then followed by a return to B♭.

I do not for a moment suggest that these implications are perfectly

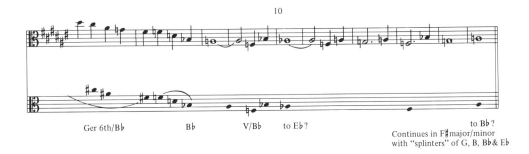

understood as one hears the opening refrain; it is in the nature of barrier time that their meaning becomes clear in memory only in the context of what follows, just as the meaning of the tonal interjections in the coda—which are part of the dissolution of the tensions of the whole movement's principal tonal argument—becomes clear only in our memory of preceding passages. The climactic double-dominant chord[40] is the epiphanic event that brings about the eventual reconciliation of the tonal drama's elements.

That the movement's complex plot is played out in such a way that the causalities of the foreground successions are established in barrier time rather than process time and the tonal contrasts are subsumed by a middleground F♯, rather than a background F♯, does not mean that the tonal drama does not exist. In many passages of the Tenth we come close to the Tralfamadorian ideal of messages heard all at once and producing "an image of life that is beautiful and surprising and deep. There is no beginning, no middle, no end, no suspense, no moral, no causes, no effects." Mahler approaches the chronological freedom of the polytemporal time shape and in so doing destroys the antecedent-consequent relationship of his principal and secondary tonal areas.

In thinking about common-practice music, we often take it for granted (as analysts, although not as composers) that the middleground derives from the foreground and the background derives not so much from the composer's choices as from the syntax of the foreground itself. Lawrence Kramer refers to the contextual background of tonality as the "tonal horizon" and suggests that in much late-nineteenth-century music, the horizon conflicts with the presentation—that is, with the details of the actual piece.[41] That is necessarily so, of course, *only* if the postromantic tonal horizon delimits the same musical landscape as does the horizon of common-practice idiom. The previously discussed music suggests to me, however, that horizon and presentation—background and foreground, if you like—are congruent and derive from a double or triple tonal source. Literary critic Joseph Frank has pointed out that to include more than one image in a poem, it is necessary to "undermine the inherent consecutiveness of language, frustrating the reader's normal expectation of a sequence and forcing him to perceive the elements of the poem as juxtapositions rather than an unrolling in time."[42] This becomes possible in musical terms because one of the radical innovations of the postromantic idiom is that the background can no longer be taken for granted and that foreground events derive from deeper levels that must be worked out in some terms before the foreground is constructed. To put it baldly: Beethoven did not have to work out his deep background, but Debussy and Mahler did.[43]

Harmonic disjunctions arising from the manipulation of chronological causality are not merely evidence of an evolving musical syntax; they are the flower of a far-broader artistic imperative. It is not accidental that radical reconceptions of tonal time are roughly contemporaneous with the abandonment of traditional topology in the plastic arts[44] and with extraordinary reconceptions of the meaning of narrative time in prose and poetry. Whether it is in the flowing watches of Dali's *Persistence of Memory,* Eliot's obsession with time in the *Four Quartets,* Joyce's temporal gymnastics in *Ulysses,* or Mahler's dismemberment of tonal chronicity, the arts near the beginning of this century all demonstrate a "violent pressure" to embody new concepts of time.[45]

Music is not only *of* time and *in* time; frequently it is *about* time. Tonal music in particular is organized in such a way that its syntax is wedded to chronological succession. By altering its conception of tonal time, by deliberately disrupting the harmonic successions of process time, postromantic music joins the other arts in expressing the spirit of its times, in mirroring the uncertainties and paradoxes of our individual one-way passages through time, in allowing us to hear the "subtle variations of the mind's chronology—in dreams and sleep and waking; in illusions and hallucinations; in pain and joy and fear and hope and sorrow; in waiting; and in the marvellous fields of memory."[46]

NOTES

1. Wilde went so far as to call life and literature the two supreme arts in "The Critic as Artist," in *Intentions,* vol. 5 of *The Complete Works of Oscar Wilde,* 12 vols. (Garden City, NY: Doubleday, Page, 1923), 125.

2. Jonathan D. Kramer, *The Time of Music: New Meanings, New Temporalities, New Listening Strategies* (New York: Schirmer, 1988), 1. Kramer's work is an indispensable resource for anyone who thinks about musical time.

3. Hans Meyerhoff, *Time in Literature* (Berkeley: University of California Press, 1955), 18. Such ideas are to a large extent the result of acculturation.

4. See, for example, Kramer's discussion of linearity in tonal music (*The Time of Music,* 25–26). Paul Ricoeur says, "Narrativity [is] the language structure that has temporality as its ultimate referent" ("Narrative Time," in *On Narrative,* ed. W. J. T. Mitchell, 165–86 [Chicago: University of Chicago Press, 1981], 165; cited in Fred Everett Maus, "*Tempus Imperfectum,*" *19th-Century Music* 9, no. 3 [spring 1986]: 235.)

5. W. Wolfgang Holdheim, *The Hermeneutic Mode* (Ithaca NY: Cornell University Press, 1984), 238.

6. David Lawton, "On the 'Bacio' Theme in *Otello,*" *19th-Century Music* 1, no. 3 (Mar. 1978): 215–16.

7. For an intriguing discussion of the dynamic processes of the movement, see Stephen Parkany, "Kurth's *Bruckner* and the Adagio of the Seventh Symphony," *19th-Century Music* 11, no. 3 (spring 1988): 262–81.

8. Ibid., 269.

9. For very important earlier work along these lines, see William Benjamin, "Interlocking Diatonic Collections as a Source of Chromaticism in Late Nineteenth-Century Music," *In Theory Only* 1, nos. 11–12 (Feb.–Mar. 1975): 31–51.

10. David Leon Higdon, *Time and English Fiction* (London: Macmillan, 1977), 4.

11. Ibid., 16–17.

12. A useful discussion of temporal perception as it relates to music, among other things, is given in Laverne Annie Martin, "The Experience of Time" (Master's thesis, University of Alberta, 1986).

13. Higdon, *Time,* 4.

14. As Kramer says, "Tonal motion is always goal-directed" (*The Time of Music,* 25).

15. Gerald Abraham, *Chopin's Musical Style* (London: Oxford University Press, 1939), viii.

16. Ibid., 19–20.

17. Cited in Higdon, *Time,* 6.

18. Ibid., 106.

19. Ibid., 45.

20. Italo Calvino, *If on a Winter's Night a Traveller,* trans. William Weaver (Toronto: Lester & Orpen Denys, 1981).

21. Kevin Korsyn discusses the interaction of two temporal streams in Chopin's Ballade No. 2, albeit from a different perspective, in chapter 3 of this volume.

22. See Deborah Stein's discussion of similar progressions in other Wolf songs in *Hugo Wolf's Lieder and Extensions of Tonality* (Ann Arbor: UMI Research Press, 1985), 26–28.

23. I do not think that my gross generalization about "later" music is invalidated by the respective dates of *Otello* and Bruckner's Seventh Symphony.

24. Paul Henry Lang, *Music in Western Civilization* (New York: Norton, 1941), 1018–19.

25. John Crotty, "Symbolist Influences in Debussy's *Prelude to the Afternoon of a Faun,*" *In Theory Only* 6, no. 2 (Feb. 1982): 17–30.

26. Higdon, *Time,* 106.

27. Timothy Findley. *Famous Last Words* (Toronto: Clarke, Irwin, 1981).

28. Holdheim, *Hermeneutic Mode,* 241.

29. Arnold Schoenberg, *Harmonielehre,* 3d ed. (Leipzig & Vienna: Universal Edition, 1922), 460.

30. Higdon, *Time,* 106.

31. Ibid., 11.

32. The result sometimes approaches the stasis of what Kramer calls "vertical time," the "static, unchanging, frozen eternity of certain contemporary music" (*The Time of Music,* 7). Polytemporal time is not truly static, however, since there are inherent motions that can be reconstructed if the disrupted threads are untangled.

33. Cited in Higdon, *Time,* 106.

34. Of particular interest is Christopher Hasty's work on process in atonal music. See, for example, his essays "On the Problem of Succession and Continuity in Twentieth-Century Music," *Music Theory Spectrum* 8 (1986): 58–74, and "Segmentation and Process in Post-Tonal Music," *Music Theory Spectrum* 3 (1981): 54–73.

35. Peter Bergquist, "The First Movement of Mahler's Tenth Symphony: An Analysis and an Examination of the Sketches," *Music Forum* 5 (1980): 335–94; Richard Kaplan, "Interpreting Surface Harmonic Connections in the Adagio of Mahler's Tenth Symphony," *In Theory Only* 4, no.12 (May–June 1978): 32–44, and "The Interaction of Diatonic Collections in the Adagio of Mahler's Tenth Symphony," *In Theory Only* 6, no.1 (Nov. 1981): 29–39; and V. Kofi Agawu, "Tonal Strategy in the First Movement of Mahler's Tenth Symphony," *19th-Century Music* 9, no.3 (spring 1986): 222–33.

36. Kaplan, "The Interaction of Diatonic Collections."

37. Agawu, "Tonal Strategy," 224.

38. Kaplan disagrees, hearing A♯ (B♭) as an important subsidiary tonality in the movement ("The Interaction of Diatonic Collections," 37). Although Agawu reads F♯ minor and F♯ major as contrasting keys rather than inflections of the same chromatic key, he draws attention ("Tonal Strategy," 227 n.12) to Guido Adler's assertion in *Gustav Mahler* (Vienna, 1916) that "major and minor are associated as though in one and the same basic key." As Robert Bailey and others have pointed out (see Robert Bailey, ed., *Wagner: Prelude and Transfiguration from* Tristan and Isolde [New York: Norton, 1985], 116 n.3), Schoenberg anticipated Adler by several years with statements that go beyond Adler's rather tentative acknowledgement of the chromatic scale (and it is of course possible that both Adler and Schoenberg owe their views to a common, still-earlier source—perhaps even Mahler himself). In the first edition of *Harmonielehre* (Leipzig & Vienna: Universal Edition, 1911), Schoenberg refers several times to the emergence of an independent chromatic scale—see, for example, pp.434, 250, and 273. Not having been fully understood, in the third edition (466) Schoenberg states explicitly that the transition from twelve major and twelve minor keys to twelve chromatic keys greatly antedated his own music. Schoenberg's ideas about fundamental chromaticism seem to me to be more relevant to Mahler's late music than is Adler's characterization of Mahler's style as based "more or less on a diatonic foundation," with "the introduction of chromatic passages as a coloristic means of intensifying sound" (Adler, "Gustav Mahler," trans. Edward R. Reilly, in *Gustav Mahler and Guido Adler: Records of a Friendship,* ed. Reilly, 15–73 [Cambridge: Cambridge University Press, 1982]). In any case, Agawu is certainly correct in later (231) distancing himself from a "coloristic" view of the chromatic chord at the climax of the movement and in agreeing with Kaplan's analysis of the sonority ("Interaction of Diatonic Collections," 38) as comprising the superposed dominants of F♯ and B♭.

39. Agawu, "Tonal Strategy," 228.

40. First identified as such by Richard Kaplan; see note 38.

41. Lawrence Kramer, "The Mirror of Tonality: Transitional Features of Nineteenth-Century Harmony," *19th-Century Music* 4 no. 3 (spring 1981): 191–208.

42. Cited in Monroe K. Spears, *Space against Time in Modern Poetry* (Fort Worth: Texas Christian University Press, 1972), 9.

43. Brenda Dalen has pointed out to me that this may well account for the increased incidence of form sketches and drafts by composers of this century.

44. See, for example, Linda Dalrymple Henderson's brilliant study *The Fourth Dimension and Non-Euclidian Geometry in Modern Art* (Princeton: Princeton University Press, 1983).

45. Spears, *Space against Time,* 3.

46. Alfred Garvin Engstrom, *Darkness and Light* (University, Miss.: Romance Monographs, 1975), 130.

Part 3: Studies of Works

Franz Liszt, Carl Friedrich Weitzmann, and the Augmented Triad

R. LARRY TODD

1

The evolution of Liszt's musical style, from his virtuosic pianistic *Glanz-periode* of the 1830s and 1840s to the boldest experimental essays of his last years, reflects a gradually deepened assimilation of harmonic dissonance into the tonal language. This tendency is nowhere more clearly manifested than in his treatment of the augmented triad, the orphan of traditional music theory that found a secure place in the music of Liszt and of many who followed him. Liszt enriched this singular sonority by testing it in an ever-expanding compass of uses. Although in his earlier years the augmented triad appears primarily as an agent of harmonic color, a more innovative treatment of the sonority emerges during the years approaching the Weimar period. During the 1850s at Weimar Liszt used the augmented triad in increasingly deeper levels of musical structure. Finally, in the experimental idiom of his late period, Liszt explored its use as a means of generating whole compositions, thereby reaching (and breaching) the outskirts of atonality. Liszt may well have been the first composer to establish the augmented triad as a truly independent sonority, to consider its implications for modern dissonance treatment, and to ponder its meaning for the future course of tonality. Liszt's accomplishments in these areas were considerable and support in no small way his position, in Busoni's phrase, as the "master of freedom."[1]

In an earlier study I examined Liszt's treatment of the augmented triad beginning in the 1830s and 1840s in such pieces as *Harmonies poétiques et religieuses, Lyon,* the setting of Petrarch's Sonnet no.104 ("Pace non trovo"), and *Funérailles,* Liszt's homage to Chopin in the year of his death, 1849.[2] The latter work is noteworthy for its association of the augmented triad with the topic of death and mourning, just one example in an extended series that includes the later works *Via crucis,* "La lugubre gondola," "Am Grabe Richard Wagners," and "Nuages gris." By the time he moved to Weimar in 1848, Liszt had shown a pioneering advance-ment of this sonority, but his major contributions were yet to come. In this chapter I examine Liszt's innovative treatment of the augmented triad beginning in the 1850s and also consider the important theoreti-cal recognition given to the sonority around this time in the writings of Carl Friedrich Weitzmann (1808–80). Weitzmann, like Felix Draeseke, was an advocate of the so-called Music of the Future (*Zukunftsmusik*), a movement that provoked aesthetic controversies that are best evalu-ated in a historical context. For that reason, I first briefly review the way in which earlier theorists viewed the augmented triad before examining Weitzmann's reassessment of the chord and Liszt's resourceful artistic treatment of the sonority, developments that were regarded with dismay by some musicians. Looking back at his efforts for the augmented triad, Liszt once recalled: "That later brought me many reproaches, and I was judged poorly for it. But I didn't trouble myself about the issue."[3]

Before the nineteenth century the augmented fifth was typically viewed as a passing dissonance that enjoyed only a limited number of applications.[4] Not until the eighteenth century did theorists begin to at-tach harmonic significance to chords with augmented fifths, and they did so at first with reluctance, if not considerable misgiving. Whereas Jean-Philippe Rameau had recognized as a license the "accord de la quinte-superflüe" constructed on the mediant degree of the minor scale (1722),[5] Johann David Heinichen had viewed the augmented fifth as a false inter-val that causes an extraordinary harshness ("*ausserordentliche Härtigkeit*") (1728); the "*Accord der quintae superfluae*," Heinichen recommended, should be used only in the free style of composition, and then only on rare occasions when harshness was desired.[6] Taking an extreme position, Johann Philipp Kirnberger, whose work in many ways represented the culmination of the figured-bass tradition, had argued that, because of its dissonant qualities, the augmented triad is a "totally useless" con-struct (1776).[7]

Others were comparatively generous to the sonority. Georg Andreas Sorge actually admitted the *trias superflua* as a consonant triad classified among the pungent musical spices ("*scharfen musikalischen Gewürze*") (1747); susceptible to inversion, it could be used effectively to express topics of death, doubt, and suffering.[8] And in the nineteenth century Daniel Gottlob Türk treated the augmented triad in a chapter devoted to dissonant triads and their inversions, with detailed rules about dou-blings in four-part harmony (1824).[9]

Nevertheless, rather than grant the augmented triad status as an au-tonomous harmony, other nineteenth-century theorists continued to explain it as a passing sonority. Thus, Gottfried Weber argued that the raised fifth is an astringent passing tone ("*herber Durchgang*") (1830). There was no need to recognize the triad as a basic harmony (*Grund-harmonie*); such recognition, he warned, would open a Pandora's box, releasing a rash of dangerous new harmonies on the world.[10]

By 1847 Adolf Bernhard Marx was still viewing the "*übermässiger Dreiklang*" as a "*Durchgangs-Akkord,*" or passing chord; in fact, it was the only such chord honored with its own name. Nonetheless, he conceded that in modern practice the augmented triad often appeared in other contexts: it was freely treated in inversion and inserted into novel progressions ("*neue Akkordgänge*)."[11] In 1850 Marx again considered the potential of the triad; this time, however, he engaged in a kind of harmonic brinksmanship:

If we return to the major triad and raise the fifth, the shrill sound of the augmented triad *confronts us. A sequence of such triads has never (at least up to the present) been dared—and we would not presume to motivate someone to undertake it. Such a sequence could be represented only in this bitter manner:*[12]

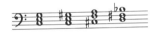

In fact, just this kind of sequential treatment of the triad was dared by Liszt in his *Pensée des morts* (1853) and in the celebrated opening of the "Faust" Symphony (1857), to which I return later. In 1850, however, Marx was at best a reluctant prophet, hinting at a daring new use of the sonority only to recoil from his own suggestion. The lid of the box was raised enough for him to peer at its disquieting contents and then decisively lowered.

In short, at midcentury the augmented triad still posed an enigma for theorists. It was, in Carl Friedrich Weitzmann's metaphor, an unwelcome "sinister guest [ein unheimlicher Gast]," a fledgling harmony whose use was not yet fully understood. The cautionary tone of Marx's comments continued to inform the writings of many theorists who sought to decipher the meaning of the triad and to explicate its proper use. Even as late as 1903, for example, the English theorist Ebenezer Prout let stand the skeptical assessment that "the augmented triad . . . is not very frequently employed, the effect of the dissonance being rather harsh."[13] Prout simply chose to ignore developments in the second half of the nineteenth century, to turn deaf ears to the musical reality around him. There were others in his company, as we learn in this amusing anecdote recorded by Schoenberg in his *Harmonielehre* of 1911: "In Vienna there used to be an old composition teacher who was employed to administer teacher-certification examinations. Year in and year out he is supposed to have asked the candidate the following question: 'What can you say about the augmented triad?' If the examinee was to escape this trap safely, he had to answer: 'The augmented triad is a favorite device of recent German music.'"[14]

2

Although little known today, during his lifetime Carl Friedrich Weitzmann distinguished himself as an effective spokesperson for the music of Liszt and Wagner, earning both praise and criticism from the adherents and detractors of the *Zukunftsmusiker*. Today his theoretical writings have fallen into neglect, and a formal study of his life and work remains unwritten.[15] His early career gave little hint of what was to come: he studied violin with Ludwig Spohr and composition with Moritz Hauptmann, two musicians of a distinctly conservative bent. Hauptmann in particular remained irreconcilably opposed to the musical innovations of the day and took comfort in knowing that he would not live to experience the full effects of the music of the future.[16] Hauptmann was no less critical when he compared Weitzmann's embrace of *Zukunftsmusik* to a retrogressive conversion of Paul to Saul, and continuing in the same metaphorical vein, Hauptmann rejected Liszt's new music as the unhealthy creation of the godless.[17]

Weitzmann, on the other hand, became a loyal apologist for the music of Wagner and Liszt and accomplished that conversion—healthy or diseased—in a trilogy of treatises appearing in 1853 and 1854. The first of these is devoted to the augmented triad, the second to the history of the seventh chord, and the third, dedicated to Liszt, to the diminished-seventh chord.[18] What motivated Weitzmann's work was a deepening interest in enharmonic relationships and their unrealized potential for expanding the tonal system.

By virtue of their remarkable properties, the diminished-seventh chord and augmented triad stood out for Weitzmann as two dissonances worthy of special consideration. As the theorist recognized, the diminished-seventh chord had already been established in Western art music as an all too favored sonority. Carl Maria von Weber, for example, had treated the diminished seventh topically in *Der Freischütz,* premiered in 1821, where the chord appears, in first inversion and in a particularly dark scoring, to accompany references to Samiel. With its interlocking tritones, the chord is an appropriate symbol of that diabolical agent. After

Weber the diminished seventh enjoyed widespread acceptance; Liszt, too, employed the chord heavily in his music of the 1830s. Eventually, the sonority was so overused that it attained the dubious status of a cliché. In contrast, by 1853 the augmented triad had not yet won complete acceptance—certainly not by the theorists, who typically denied its existence or grudgingly viewed it as a fleeting passing chord [*"flüchtiger Durchgang"*]. The declared purpose of Weitzmann's treatise, *Der übermässige Dreiklang,* was to remedy this state of affairs: "It is my intention to illuminate by means of this treatise the darkness of the origin [of the augmented triad], to point out its extended family, to demonstrate its inseparable alliance with all the diminished-seventh chords which have long been indigenous here, and in general to present a detailed exposition of its mysterious and versatile character."[19]

After a short historical survey of earlier thought about the triad,[20] Weitzmann begins by establishing the augmented triad as one of four natural triads. Like the major, minor, and diminished triads, the augmented is built on thirds; taken together, the four triads exploit all combinations of major and minor thirds (i.e., major-minor, minor-major, minor-minor, and major-major). Next, Weitzmann shows how an augmented triad may be created by half-step motion from a major or minor triad. Twelve examples are offered for study. In six of them, major triads and their inversions serve as generating harmonies; in the other six, minor triads and their inversions produce the augmented triad (ex. 1a).

Example 1. Weitzmann, *Der übermässige Dreiklang.*

Stepwise motion is the rule throughout these examples; in addition, there is in each example at least one common tone between the generating triad and the resulting augmented triad.

Weitzman shows that, like the diminished triad, the augmented is a symmetrical sonority: specifically, it consists of two major thirds bounded by a minor sixth or its enharmonic equivalent. Unlike other triads, which produce combinations of fourths and thirds when inverted, the augmented triad maintains its succession of thirds under inversion—at least in sound, and in notation by means of enharmonic respelling (ex. 1b). From this symmetry emerges the principle that any augmented triad may be spelled in root position or in first or second inversion, without altering its sound (ex. 1c). Of course, the respellings carry different harmonic implications, and it is exactly this notational ambiguity, this "*Mehrdeutigkeit,*"[21] that composers are to exploit when using the augmented triad. For Weitzmann, the augmented triad thus becomes a highly versatile tool in modern music.

From another perspective, that of sound rather than of notation, Weitzmann observes that there are only four different augmented triads. As these four must serve twenty-four major and minor keys, their versatility is readily demonstrable. Indeed, in a chapter titled "Extended Family of the Augmented Triad [*Ausgebreitete Verwandtschaft des übermässigen Dreiklanges*]" Weitzmann is able to relate each augmented triad to no fewer than twelve keys.[22] Here we reach the heart of his theoretical system. In contrast to earlier theorists, who placed the augmented triad on the third degree of the minor scale, Weitzmann takes pains to establish a counterpart on the lowered sixth degree of the major scale. To accomplish this, he first inverts a C-major triad to produce an F-minor triad (ex. 2a). The augmented triad Ab–C–E, a by-product of this opera-

Example 2. Weitzmann, *Der übermässige Dreiklang.*

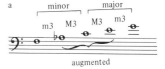

tion, is shared by the keys of C major and F minor, although in each case the triad relies on a "*Nebenton,*" that is, a pitch outside the particular scale. Thus Ab and E♮ serve as the supplementary tones in C major and F minor, respectively, the former as the lowered sixth and the latter as the raised leading tone. Harmonically the augmented triad resides on the third degree of F minor and on the lowered sixth degree of C major.[23]

Having established the concept of supplementary tones, Weitzmann illustrates how a single augmented triad may relate to a variety of keys, specifically, to twelve keys divided into two groups of six (see ex. 2b). First, the triad may progress to the major triads based on each of its three pitches. For example, the augmented triad Eb–G–B may be linked to the Eb-major, G-major, and B-major triads by lowering the appropri-

ate supplementary tone—the lowered sixth degree of each key—by half step (i.e., C♭ in E♭ major, E♭ in G major, and G♮ in B major). Second, the same augmented triad may be related to the relative minor keys of the three tonalities by raising the appropriate supplementary tone—the raised leading tone of the relative minor key—by half step (i.e., B♮ in C minor, D♯ in E minor, and F✳ in G♯ minor). Finally, Weitzmann derives the second group of related tonalities by reversing the major and minor modalities of the first group. In these examples one pitch acts as a common tone, while the other two descend or ascend by a half step. These six tonalities, E♭ minor, G minor, B minor, C major, E major, and A♭ major, are more distantly related to the augmented triad (see ex. 2b).

Part of Weitzmann's treatise concerns such practical matters as the doubling of triad members in four-part harmony (and the proscription against omitting one of its tones), the proper notation of the triad (that is, according to the harmony that follows it), and its possible resolutions. Weitzmann's enthusiasm for his fledgling harmony is perhaps most evident when he addresses the last issue: in a chapter titled "The Resolutions of the Augmented Triad [*Die Auflösungen des übermässigen Dreiklanges*]" he collects no fewer than thirty-two resolutions, each precisely analyzed.[24] The majority involve common tones, which ensure a smooth progression of the voices. For these cases Weitzmann summarizes four practical rules: (1) each pitch of the triad can descend by step while the other pitches remain stationary; (2) each pitch of the triad can ascend by step while the other pitches remain stationary; (3) each pitch of the triad can remain stationary while the other two pitches ascend by step; and (4) each pitch of the triad can remain stationary while the other two pitches descend by step.

These thirty-two progressions entail resolutions to major or minor triads. Not content with this number, however, Weitzmann also investigates what he calls "*Trugfortschreitungen*," or deceptive progressions. For instance, an augmented triad may "resolve" to a diminished-seventh chord; vice versa, a diminished-seventh chord may progress to an augmented triad. In these deceptive progressions Weitzmann uncovers a special relationship that links the four augmented triads with their counterparts, the three diminished-seventh chords. Each augmented triad may

progress by one common tone to each diminished-seventh chord; conversely, each diminished-seventh chord may be tied by one common tone
to each augmented triad (ex. 2c).[26]

Example 2—*Continued*

By thus relating the augmented triad to the diminished-seventh chord,
Weitzmann sought to strengthen its place in the family of dissonances
and to secure its position in the chromatically and enharmonically
charged music of his day. Four final examples afford a brief glimpse of
how Weitzmann proposed to exploit the newly uncovered resources of
the augmented triad. In one example a simple chain of fifths is harmonized by augmented triads (ex. 3a). A chain of fifths supports another

Example 3. Weitzmann's
augmented triad
progressions.

example, too, but here Weitzmann harmonizes the sequence with mix-
tures of seventh chords and augmented triads (ex. 3b), yielding a passage

almost entirely generated by ascending and descending chromatic lines.
In the severe chromaticism of this example Weitzmann reveals his most
daring musical thought, in which he approaches Liszt's later experiments
and looks forward to Hugo Wolf's mannered musical language.

Thus our "abandoned" triad found a secure place in Weitzmann's harmonic system, and its special properties were explicated in detail for the first time. Weitzmann's ideas, in turn, won recognition from Liszt, who greatly respected the theorist. It was Liszt who supported the publication of Weitzmann's progressively spirited prize essay "Clarifying Explanation and Musico-theoretical Justification of the Transformation and Development of Harmony Brought about by Artistic Creations [Erklärende Erläuterung und musikalisch theoretische Begründung der durch Kunstschöpfungen bewirkten Umgestaltung und Weiterbildung der Harmonik]" in the *Neue Zeitschrift für Musik* of 1860;[26] it was Liszt who paid tribute to the theorist by declaring "Weitzmanns are rare [*Die Weitzmanne sind selten*]";[27] finally, as we shall see, it was Liszt who accepted Weitzmann's challenge to composers to determine in their music the future destiny of the sonority.[28]

3

Reviewing a decade of Liszt's activities in Weimar as conductor and composer, Richard Pohl characterized the years 1852 to 1862 as a period of spiraling artistic revitalization, of accelerating, progressive change unmatched since the time of Beethoven, and before him, of Gluck. Pohl predicted a bright future for German music. There was good enough reason for his optimism: Liszt had begun to perform the works of Wagner, Berlioz, and other "forward-minded" composers and had begun to bring out his new series of symphonic poems. In several glowing articles Franz Brendel, editor of the *Neue Zeitschrift für Musik,* announced that Weimar was fast becoming a musical mecca, as it had been a literary one under Goethe.[29] Brendel might well have added his voice to Pohl's rallying cry, "We must go forward because we cannot go backward."[30]

For Liszt, this process of artistic quickening was hastened in no small way through his ongoing experiments with the augmented triad. In 1853, when Weitzmann's treatise appeared, Liszt brought out his *Pensée des morts* (S173/4), a thorough recasting of the considerably earlier *Harmonies poétiques et religieuses.* Among the many revisions in the later version is one stunning addition, a clamorous cadenza featuring augmented triads, first in a whole-tone progression and then in stark parallel motion over a rushing chromatic scale (ex. 4). Liszt thus accomplished in one bold stroke what A. B. Marx had not dared to attempt. This giddying cadenza is not for mere virtuoso display but derives its meaning from what follows: the mournful strains of a psalm intonation with its text, "De profundis clamavi," superimposed.

In much the same way, the revision of "Vallée d'Obermann" for the

Example 4. Liszt, *Pensée des morts* (S173/4).

Années de pèlerinage, published in 1855, shows Liszt's intensifying aware-ness of the augmented triad. The basic motive of this work describes a series of thirds descending from the third scale degree: in E minor a seventh chord (G–E–C–A), and in E major, the key of the conclusion, two major thirds (G♯–E–C), or an augmented triad (ex.5a).[31] In the re-vised version Liszt added the augmented triad to the final cadence, where it strengthens the motivic cohesiveness of the work (ex.5b).[32]

During Liszt's tenure in Weimar the augmented triad thus became a highly visible color in his harmonic palette: its frequency of use began to rival that of the diminished-seventh chord. This decisive turn was in-debted in no small way to Liszt's new concentration on programmatic music; as he fully realized, the triad is one effective agent of transmit-ting those extramusical, poetic ideas that inform his orchestral music of the Weimar period. One representative example occurs in the first sym-phonic poem, the so-called *Bergsymphonie* (1850), also known by Victor Hugo's poem that inspired it, "Ce qu'on entend sur la montagne."

Example 5. Liszt, "Vallée d'Obermann."

From the collection *Feuilles d'automne,* comprising forty poems of distinctly melancholic tone, "Ce qu'on entend" poetizes the opposing forces of nature and humanity as conflicting sounds heard atop a mountain summit. The human element, which drew from Hugo harshly dissonant language, received from Liszt a discordant musical counterpart in which the augmented triad figures prominently. Hugo's "exploding chords [*accords èclatants*]" and the "clangor of armor [*le choc d'armures*]" found their musical realization in the two passages shown in ex. 6a and 6b.

Example 6. Liszt, *Bergsymphonie* ("Ce qu'on entend sur la montagne").

Undoubtedly the major masterwork of the Weimar years was the "Faust" Symphony. Its long gestation began in the mid-1840s, when Liszt apparently sketched the famous opening theme, the center of my discussion. The work was not performed in its final version until 1857.[33] Critics recognized its significance early on: Pohl, for example, viewed it as the successor to Beethoven's Ninth Symphony on account of the culminating *chorus mysticus* that intones the closing lines of Goethe's drama. Pohl also praised Liszt's programmatic method in the symphony's three movements—conceived as character sketches of Faust, Gretchen, and Mephistopheles—as a particularly subtle yet forceful "psychological conditioning process [psychologischer Gestaltungs-Prozess]."[34] By this means Liszt attempted to portray musically the inner nature of the characters, and to give force to his programmatic ideas he required a special type of music.

To capture the essence of Faust, Liszt created the celebrated tonally unfocused opening of the symphony, in which he marshaled all twelve pitches of the chromatic scale. This extraordinary passage is often cited as a proto-twelve-tone row,[35] and recently Allen Forte has offered a pitch-class set analysis that attempts to reveal an organization based on chromatic tetrachords.[36] Historically more to the mark, however, and surely of more relevance to Liszt, is an interpretation that demonstrates the derivation of the theme from augmented triads. Already in the nineteenth century Pohl, for one, was impressed that "here for the first time in the entire literature of music a complete theme is constructed simply from the augmented triad—a startlingly new musical discovery, in the fullest sense of the word, that can ill be ignored by future harmony instructors and composers."[37]

Liszt hit on that bold invention as a means of characterizing Faust before his fateful encounter with Mephistopheles. The inspiration for this remarkable music is, most likely, Faust's opening monologue in his study, where Goethe reveals him as a man disenchanted with life and groping to extend the limits of his knowledge; hence the decidedly experimental nature of the opening theme, the meaning of which transcends the limits of a conventional tonal analysis.[38] To return to Pohl's interpretation: the opening theme begins "the first movement without any preparation in unending bitterness and inner desolation, as if uprooted by the most acrid doubts, and actually takes us at once into the middle of the situation, showing us Faust's portrait by means of a few strokes with the greatest mastery."[39] "Bitterkeit [bitterness]," "herbsten Zweifeln [acrid doubts]"—these words recall the extramusical references of the augmented triad mentioned earlier in this chapter. Liszt now boldly brought those associations to a new limit of expressiveness.

Example 7a. Liszt, "Faust"
Symphony, first movement.

The first twenty-two measures of the symphony, in fact, represent a self-contained passage almost entirely derived from the augmented triads of the opening theme (ex. 7a). This passage, severed from the main

body of the movement by a long pause, depicts Faust's self-imposed isolation. Muted strings attack *fortissimo* the first pitch, Ab, itself a strange
effect, before the four triads are outlined at a *piano* level. Next the winds,
marked *dolente,* perform a suspension figure harmonized by the last two
augmented triads of the sequence. This dolorous figure is repeated in the
lower register of the bassoons and clarinets. Finally the two triads are
combined in a descending, intercalated arpeggiation leading to a low E
and a pause in m. 11, the exact midpoint of the passage.

As the reduction in ex. 7b shows, in these eleven measures Liszt un-

Example 7b. Reduction,
"Faust" Symphony, first
movement.

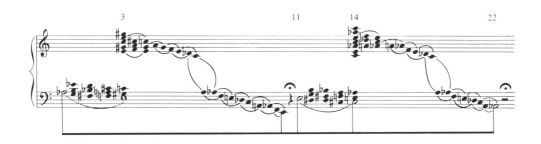

folds a descending chromatic scale in the bass from Ab to E and then
prolongs the E through a register transfer to the octave below. In the
second half of the passage he repeats the process, beginning on E and
descending chromatically to C. This time the arpeggiation is directed to
conclude on Ab, a critical revision that completes a larger-scale arpeggiation of the augmented triad Ab–E–C–Ab. The passage is, in short,
symmetrical and circular, commencing and ending on Ab and defining
no particular key. It is a fitting musical expression of Faust's frustration
that, ultimately, "wir nichts wissen können [we cannot know anything]."

Robert Morgan has offered a similar analytical reduction of the opening of the symphony,[40] and his reading of the first pitch provides a
convenient comparison with Allen Forte's pitch-class set analysis, which
seeks to link the opening to the "experimental mode" of Liszt's late
music. Morgan treats the entire passage as a dissonant prolongation of
the augmented triad Ab–C–E and therefore posits a parenthetical augmented triad above the initial Ab in the bass. Forte, on the other hand,
hears the Ab as the first member of the tetrachord formed by the first
four pitches (Ab–G–B–Eb) and then proceeds to read the following measures as a series of seven interlocking forms of that tetrachord (set 4–19
in Forte's system). Of course, each tetrachord contains as a subset an
augmented triad (set 3–12 in Forte's system); that is to say, set 3–12 is

included within set 4–19. Nonetheless, whether such tetrachords carried meaning for Liszt during the 1850s—indeed, the early sketches for the theme date back to the 1840s—is at the least questionable. On the other hand, it is plausible, as I argue later, that the freely atonal formations of Liszt's radical late music grew out of chromatic embellishments to the augmented triad, a view not at all incompatible with Forte's final assessment. And the critical work that prepared the way for those widely ranging experiments—for what Forte has termed "a process of accretion to the augmented triad"[41]—was unquestionably the "Faust" Symphony.

In Goethe's monologue Faust scorns philosophy and religion and turns instead to magic to satisfy his quest for knowledge. In a similar way Liszt shuns the trappings of traditional tonality and advances instead the mysterious qualities of the augmented triad, which is now boldly explored outside a tonal context. The entire passage is dimly lit by dark scorings and muffled strings, the musical equivalent of the reflected moonlight that envelops Faust in his study. Allying the augmented triad with magic or some kind of altered state thus acquires a topical significance in the "Faust" Symphony, as it does after Liszt in works such as Dukas's *L'Apprenti sorcier* (1897), the finale of Schoenberg's Second String Quartet ("Entrückung," 1908), or Busoni's *Doktor Faust* (1924). Actually, this device did not originate with Liszt. In *Roméo et Juliette* (1839) Berlioz relies on augmented triads in his delightful characterization of Queen Mab, the "fairies' midwife" who "gallops night by night through lovers' brains." In the admonition scene from act 3 of *Lohengrin* (1848) Wagner employs the harmony at the passage, "So ist der Zauber, der mich dir verbunden [Thus is the spell that has bound me to you]."[42] Finally, earlier composers had employed extraordinary effects—including augmented triads and whole-tone scales—to suggest magical properties.[43] None, however, had explored the triad to the extent that Liszt did in the opening of "Faust," and none had conceived a passage so extensively based on the sonority.

Recognizing the magical properties of Liszt's symphony, Pohl characterized the opening as "vielsagend (wie vieldeutig)"; he might as well have applied Weitzmann's word, *mehrdeutig,* to describe the ambiguous tonal implications of the augmented triad. Liszt's opening *is* atonal, at least on the surface; nevertheless, it bears on the fundamental tonal relationships of the entire symphony.[44] In particular, those mysterious augmented triads of the opening measures determined Liszt's tonal planning of the whole. The three pitches of the underlying arpeggiation, A♭, C, and E, are the three principal tonalities of the composition. The first movement is in C minor, but it has as an important subsidiary idea a grandiose theme in E major. The slow movement is in A♭ major, but it recalls the suspension figure of mm. 4 and 5 in C minor and also in E major. In addition, the final passage of the middle movement oscillates between A♭ and E. The diabolical third movement, a grotesque parody of the first, revives C and E as tonal centers. The concluding *chorus mysticus,* which exults in the *"Ewig-Weibliche,"* begins, appropriately enough, in A♭ major, Gretchen's key, before turning to the magnificent conclusion in C major. This overview does little justice to the manifold ways in which Liszt relates the augmented triad to the structure of his symphony, but at least one conclusion emerges from the analysis: the sonority now works on many intricate levels of Liszt's music, a common denominator in a highly sophisticated network of associations—thematic, motivic, harmonic, tonal, and programmatic. Liszt's psychological process penetrates to the core of Faust's character, and it does so by relying on the previously imponderable properties of the augmented triad.

4

In Liszt's music of the post-Weimar period are laid bare the ultimate consequences of his treatment of the augmented triad. The increasingly abstract nature of this austere music, its systematic reduction of the compositional means, and its eventual dissolution of tonal principles baffled many of Liszt's contemporaries and remain perplexing to this day. In the closing decades of his life Liszt became convinced that the traditional Western tonal order was more or less superannuated and that composers should seek a new means of tonal organization.[45] In place of diatonic scales he proposed whole-tone, gypsy, octatonic, and other chromatically altered scales—well in advance, it should be noted, of Busoni's extrapolation of "artificial" scales[46]—and instead of relying on a harmonic hierarchy based on major and minor triads, Liszt developed other alternatives, among them constellations of chromatic harmonies revolving around an augmented triad.

All these innovations brought Liszt irreversibly to the brink of atonality. As we have seen, the beginning of the "Faust" Symphony initiated this process, although that beginning did not preempt the fundamental tonal order of the symphony. Also, the symphony was conceived on too large a scale to permit the fateful final step into an atonal realm. To accomplish this step, Liszt found it convenient to work with music of smaller dimensions. In particular, he turned to piano music, devoting new attention to shorter works for that instrument.

"Aux cyprès de la Villa d'Este," from the third volume of the *Années de pèlerinage* (1869), is one of several threnodies from the late period; its extramusical associations alone mark it as a potential source of prominent augmented triads. One particular augmented triad, F♯–B♭–D, is especially active throughout the introduction of the composition (ex. 8a),

Example 8a. Liszt, "Aux cyprès de la Villa d'Este."

where it may be linked as an antecedent or consequent to several major and minor triads (ex. 8b). Each progression moves by stepwise motion with one or two common tones, recalling the progressions from Weitz-

Example 8b. Reduction,
"Aux cyprès de la Villa
d'Este."

mann's treatise cited in ex.2b. Liszt avoids defining G minor, the key suggested by the signature of two flats; instead, he implies that key by its dominant, which appears in both its major and minor forms. The solemn preface concludes with the opening augmented sonority, however, which claims harmonic priority for the passage.

Associating the augmented triad with nondiatonic scales was another means by which Liszt approached the final threshold. As early as 1850, in the Fantasy and Fugue for Organ on the pseudochorale "Ad nos, ad salutarem undam" from Meyerbeer's *Le Prophète,* Liszt had produced a large-scale work based on a tritonal axis, with whole-tone passages and supporting augmented triads (and diminished-seventh sonorities).[47] Even more remarkable in this direction was "Der traurige Mönch" (S348), a recitation for voice and piano written in 1860 but not published until 1872. Nearly the entire setting derives from whole-tone formations (an important by-product of which are augmented sonorities) and looks forward to a somewhat similar experiment, Debussy's "Voiles," based entirely on whole-tone and pentatonic formations. The poem "Der traurige Mönch," a ballade by Lenau, concerns a haunted tower inhabited by a spirit in the guise of a melancholic monk. With such a subject augmented triads were almost de rigueur for Liszt, who introduces this apparition with alternating minor and augmented triads (ex.9). Liszt referred to the

Example 9. Liszt, "Der
traurige Mönch."

work as "immeasurably desolate [*bodenlos wüst*]" and its mysterious harmonies as "monstrous [*ungeheuerlich*]."[48]

"Aux cyprès de la Villa d'Este" and "Der traurige Mönch" begin to exhibit the simplification of means that became increasingly common in Liszt's late music, in stark contrast to the effusiveness of his earlier music. In a series of piano pieces from the 1880s, nearly all of them conceived as dirges, Liszt carried the process to its natural conclusion, methodically stripping away ornamental detail and leaving in place unaccompanied melodic lines and disturbingly sparse textures—in short, music of the barest means. In these works, including the piano pieces "Nuages gris," "La lugubre gondola I and II," "R. W. Venezia," "Unstern," "Am Grabe Richard Wagners," and "Trauer-Vorspiel," as well as the sacred work *Via crucis,* the background structure is pushed toward the foreground, and the structural role of the augmented triad, which now operates on the most fundamental level, is highlighted.[49]

Example 10. Liszt, "Nuages gris."

The conclusion of "Nuages gris" (1881) illustrates the new compositional severity (ex. 10). In the treble Liszt writes an ascending chromatic

scale in octaves prolonging F♯, the leading tone of the "tonic" G minor. We hear in the bass an ostinato figure that alternates between B♭ and A and in the middle register a series of harmonies including a complete sequence of augmented triads. The goal of the passage is the remarkable open-ended cadence consisting of two chords. The first combines the bass and chord of m. 42 with the leading tone F♯. In the final sonority Liszt allows the F♯ to "resolve" to G but otherwise retains the preceding chord, including its embedded augmented triad. As others have noted, Liszt might easily have resolved the penultimate chord by step to G minor.[50] Instead this resolution is obviated, or distorted, by the augmented triad, literally upending the tonal center of the work, G, and denying its place as a tonal root. In this way Liszt effects a radical reordering of harmonic logic, subordinating conventional triads to more adventuresome, atonal complexes—in this case, one centered on the augmented triad.[51]

As a final example I consider briefly "La lugubre gondola I," written only six weeks before Wagner's death early in 1883. This funereal barcarolle unfolds as a slowly descending sequence of augmented triads. The opening melody itself suggests a chromatic embellishment of the augmented triad C–F♭–A♭; the accompanying ostinato figure presents a more direct statement of the same triad, respelled enharmonically and inverted as E–C–A♭ and embellished by the auxiliary tone D♭ (ex.11a).

Example 11a. Liszt, "La lugubre gondola I."

Despite the signature of four flats, suggesting the key of F minor, a conventional tonal analysis is vitiated by the lack of firm tonal cadences.

Rather, the piece's cohesion depends on its sequential underpinnings, as shown in the reduction in ex. 11b. The opening material returns trans-

Example 11b. Reduction, "La lugubre gondola I."

posed down a step in m. 39 and again, another step lower, in m. 77, where a blurring tremolando replaces the methodic ostinato in eighth notes. In the final portion of the piece Liszt effects two more transpositions of the augmented triad, completing the sequence. As a final masterstroke Liszt omits the C of the last triad, reducing the final augmented triad to the nebulous interval E–A♭.

5

Liszt's development and emancipation of the augmented triad are among his many innovative accomplishments that influenced generations of later composers. But recognition of his role in this development did not go unchallenged. Schoenberg, for example, attempted to make a case for Wagner's use of the sonority, citing the famous motive from the "Ride of the Valkyries" in the third act of *Die Walküre* as a departure point ("Ausgangspunkt") for further experimentation.[52] (Surely a more momentous example from Wagner is act 1, scene 3, of *Siegfried,* in which Mime attempts to teach the young hero the meaning of fear in a scene suffused with augmented triads.) Schoenberg to the contrary, the case for Liszt's influence seems clear: his music represents the crucial nineteenth-century link in the evolution of the augmented triad. Works such as Wolf's songs "Das verlassene Mägdlein" or "Bei einer Trauung" from the *Mörike Lieder,* in which sequences of augmented triads underscore bitterly ironic texts; the second movement of Mahler's Fourth Symphony, in which an augmented triad introduces the eerie, altered sound of a *scordatura* solo violin; Schoenberg's op. 11, no. 1, in which augmented triads are discernible in the welter of atonal sound; the second movement of Bartók's Suite op. 14, constructed on an interlocking series of augmented triads; or "Vom Tode Mariä I" from Hindemith's *Das Marienleben,* which uses augmented triads to symbolize the death of Mary—are all indebted, directly or indirectly, to Liszt's pioneering treatment of the sonority. The examples could be extended to include Debussy, Ravel, Scriabin, Busoni, Berg, and many other composers of the first rank who followed Liszt.[53] It is only fitting, then, that as the twentieth century draws to a close, we acknowledge Liszt for raising the augmented triad from neglect and for developing to the fullest its special properties—in short, for joining Weitzmann in regaling the sinister guest.

NOTES

1. Ferruccio Busoni, *The Essence of Music and Other Papers,* trans. Rosamond Ley (New York: Dover, 1965), 138.

2. See my "The 'Unwelcome Guest' Regaled: Franz Liszt and the Augmented Triad," *19th-Century Music* 12, no.2 (fall 1988): 93–115, on which parts of this chapter are based.

3. August Göllerich, *Franz Liszt* (Leipzig: Reclam, 1908), 21.

4. A brief historical overview, including a valuable summary of Liszt's use of the augmented triad, is offered in Serge Gut, *Franz Liszt: Les Éléments du langage musical* (Paris: Klincksieck, 1975), 290–94. In seeking to establish Liszt as the liberator of the augmented triad (a view to which I subscribe), Gut perhaps takes unnecessary pains to dismiss its earlier history; he views examples cited from Monteverdi, Schütz, Purcell, Lalande, Bach, Rameau, Haydn, and Mozart as rare and isolated. Examples of the triad in the eighteenth and early nineteenth centuries are, however, not all that uncommon; more to the point is that composers before Liszt used the triad in a severely limited number of ways.

5. Jean-Philippe Rameau, *Traité de l'harmonie* (Treatise on harmony) (Paris, 1722; facs. New York: Broude, 1965), 273.

6. Johann David Heinichen, *Der General-Bass in der Komposition* (Thoroughbass in composition) (Dresden, 1728; facs. Hildesheim: Georg Olms, 1969), 100.

7. Johann Phillip Kirnberger, *Die Kunst des reinen Satzes* (The art of strict composition) (Berlin, 1776; facs. Hildesheim: Georg Olms, 1968), 1:39.

8. Georg Andreas Sorge, *Vorgemach der musikalischen Composition* (Anteroom to musical composition) (Lobenstein, 1745–47), 1:19–20; 2:75, 118–20.

9. Daniel Gottlob Türk, *Anweisung zum Generalbassspielen* (Instruction in thoroughbass playing) (Vienna, 1824), 182–85.

10. Gottfried Weber, *Versuch einer geordneten Theorie der Tonsetzkunst* (Attempt at an ordered theory of composition) (Mainz: B. Schotts Söhne, 1830), 111.

11. Adolf Bernhard Marx, *Die Lehre von der musikalischen Komposition* (Precepts of musical composition) (Leipzig: Breitkopf & Härtel, 1847), 271.

12. "Gehen wir aber auf den grossen Dreiklang zurück, und erhöhen die Quinte, so schreit uns der übermässige Dreiklang schrillend an: eine Folge solcher Akkorde ist aber (bis jetzt wenigstens) noch gar nicht gewagt worden,—und wüssten auch wir nicht zu motiviren.—Sie könnte sich nur etwa in dieser bitterbösen Weise [example] darstellen" (Adolf Bernhard Marx, *Allgemeine Musiklehre: Ein Hülfsbuch,* 4th ed. [Leipzig: Breitkopf & Härtel, 1850], 322).

13. Ebenezer Prout, *Harmony: Its Theory and Practice* (London: Augener, 1903), 85.

14. Arnold Schoenberg, *Harmonielehre* (Vienna, 1911; 7th ed., 1966), 467–68, published in English as *Theory of Harmony,* trans. Roy E. Carter (Berkeley: University of California Press, 1978), 390.

15. Some biographical details are provided in the *Allgemeine deutsche Biographie*

41 (Leipzig, 1896), 635, and in Paul Bekker, "Zum Gedächtnis Karl Friedrich Weitz-manns" (In memory of Carl Friedrich Weitzmann), *Allgemeine Musik-Zeitung* 35, nos. 32–33 (Aug. 1908): 577–78.

16. Letter of 15 March 1857 to Franz Hauser in *The Letters of a Leipzig Cantor,* ed. A. Schöne and F. Hiller, trans. A. D. Coleridge (London, 1892; rpt. New York: Vienna House, 1972), 2: 100.

17. Ibid., 2: 134–35 (letter of 3 January 1860 to Hauser).

18. Carl Friedrich Weitzmann, *Der übermässige Dreiklang* (Berlin, 1853); *Geschichte des Septimen-Akkordes* (Berlin, 1854); and *Der verminderte Septimen-Akkord* (Berlin, 1854).

19. "Es ist nun meine Absicht, durch diese Schrift das Dunkel seiner Abkunft zu lichten, seine ausgebreiteten Verwandtschaften nachzuweisen, sein unzertrennliches Bündniss mit allen bei uns längst heimischen verminderten Septakkorden darzuthun, und überhaupt eine ausführliche Darstellung seines geheimnissvollen und vielseitigen Charakters zu geben" (Weitzmann, *Der übermässige Dreiklang,* 1).

20. With citations from Rameau, Tartini, C. P. E. Bach, Rousseau, Kirnberger, Antonio Eximeno, Albrechtsberger, Gottfried Weber, Dehn, and A. B. Marx. Weitz-mann's verdict about their work is less than enthusiastic: "The result of all research about our chord that has been presented thus far is, then, the following: it is posi-tioned on the third degree of the minor scale, it arises through the raising of the fifth of the major triad, and it is only able to move in two to three strictly circumscribed ways [Das Resultat aller bis dahin mitgetheilten Forschungen über unsern Akkord ist also das folgende: er hat seinen Sitz auf der dritten Stufe der Molltonleiter, er entsteht durch die Erhöhung der Quinte des harten Dreiklanges und ist nur fähig, zwei bis drei abgemessene Schritte zu thun]" (*Der übermässige Dreiklang,* 4).

21. Ibid., 13–15.

22. Ibid., 17–19.

23. Ibid., 16–17.

24. Ibid., 24–29.

25. Ibid., 29–30, 22–23.

26. *Neue Zeitschrift für Musik* 52 (1860), passim.

27. See Lina Ramann, *Lisztiana: Erinnerungen an Franz Liszt in Tagebuchblättern, Briefen und Dokumenten aus den Jahren 1873–1886/88* (Lisztiana: Reminiscences of Franz Liszt in Diary Excerpts, Letters and Documents from the Years 1873–1886/88), ed. Arthur Seidl and Friedrich Schnapp (Mainz: Schott, 1983), 277.

28. Weitzmann, *Der übermässige Dreiklang,* 32.

29. Franz Brendel, "Ein Ausflug nach Weimar" ("An excursion to Weimar"), *Neue Zeitschrift für Musik* 36 (1852): 37–40, 120–21; 37 (1852): 225–27, 237–40, 251–54.

30. "Wir müssen vorwärts, weil wir nicht rückwärts gehen können" (Richard Pohl, "Liszt's Faust-Symphonie (1862)," *Gesammelte Schriften über Musik und Musiker,* 3 vols. [Leipzig: Bernhard Schlicke, 1884], 2: 248).

31. The E-major version of the motive describes part of the whole-tone scale (G♯–F♯–E–D–C), which, as Liszt discovered, is compatible with the augmented triad. He exploited this association more extensively in *Der traurige Mönch,* discussed later.

32. For further evidence of Liszt's heightened use of the augmented triad in the re-vised version of "Vallée d'Obermann," see Allen Forte, "Liszt's Experimental Idiom and Music of the Early Twentieth Century," *19th-Century Music* 10, no. 3 (spring 1987): 212–13. Forte applies a hybrid analytical approach drawing on Schenkerian reduction methods and pitch-class set analysis.

33. For a review of the convoluted chronology of the work, see László Somfai, "Die Gestaltwandlungen der *Faust-Symphonie* von Liszt," in *Franz Liszt: Beiträge von unga-rischen Autoren,* ed. K. Hamburger (Budapest, 1978), 292–96.

34. Pohl, *Gesammelte Schriften,* 2:270.

35. See, for example, Constantin Floros, "Die Faust-Symphonie von Franz Liszt: Eine semantische Analyse," *Musik Konzepte 12: Franz Liszt,* ed. Heinz Karl Metzger and Rainer Riehn, 42–87 (Munich: edition text + kritik, 1980), 52; László Somfai, "Die Metamorphose der 'Faust-Symphonie' von Liszt," *Studia musicologica* 5 (1961): 286; F. Ritzel, "Materialdenken bei Liszt: Eine Untersuchung des 'Zwölftonthemas' der Faust-Symphonie," *Die Musikforschung* 20 (1967): 289–94; K. W. Niemöller, "Zur nicht-tonalen Thema-Struktur von Liszts *Faust-Symphonie,*" *Die Musikforschung* 22 (1969): 69–72; and N. Nagler, "Die verspätete Zukunftsmusik," *Musik-Konzepte 12: Franz Liszt,* 24–25.

36. Forte, "Liszt's Experimental Idiom," 217–18.

37. "[H]ier zum erstenmal in der gesamten musikalischen Litteratur ein ganzes Thema lediglich auf den übermässigen Dreiklang baut ist—eine überraschend neue musikalische Erfindung, im vollsten Sinne des Worts, welche von künftigen Harmonielehren, sowenig wie von nachfolgenden Komponisten ignoriert werden darf." Pohl, *Gesammelte Schriften,* 2:284. For other readings of the opening as a sequence of augmented triads, see Diether de la Motte, *Harmonielehre,* 2d ed. (Kassel: Bärenreiter Verlag, 1978), 238, and Robert Morgan, "Dissonant Prolongations: Theoretical and Compositional Precedents," *Journal of Music Theory* 20 (spring 1976): 60–62.

38. Constantin Floros, who has attempted a semantic analysis of the symphony, suggests that the theme relates "to the erudition of Faust, to his tendency toward reflection and speculation, to his craving for enlightenment, to the brooding aspect of his personality [auf die Gelehrsamkeit Fausts, auf seine Neigung zur Reflexion und zur Spekulation, auf seinen Drang nach Erkenntnis, auf die grüblerische Seite seiner Persönlichkeit]." He concludes that the augmented triad is an emblem for Faust ("Die Faust-Symphonie," 64).

39. "[I]n seiner unendlichen Bitterkeit und innerlichen Verödung, wie von herbsten Zweifeln durchwühlt, ohne alle Vorbereitung den ersten Satz, und führt uns sofort recht eigentlich mitten in die Situation, zeichnet uns Fausts Bild in wenigen Strichen mit grösster Meisterschaft." Pohl, *Gesammelte Schriften,* 2:284.

40. Morgan, "Dissonant Prolongations," 61.

41. Forte, "Liszt's Experimental Idiom," 227.

42. Transcribed by Liszt for piano solo (S 446, 1854).

43. E.g., Glinka's whole-tone passages for the magician Chernomor in *Ruslan and Lyudmila* (1842). Regarding the interest of later Russian composers in the augmented triad, see Richard Taruskin, "Chernomor to Kashchei: Harmonic Sorcery; or, Stravinsky's 'Angle,'" *Journal of the American Musicological Society* 38, no.1 (spring 1985): 72–142.

44. See also Floros, "Die Faust-Symphonie," 60–62, and Morgan, "Dissonant Prolongations," 62.

45. Cf. Ramann, *Lisztiana,* 276–77.

46. Ferruccio Busoni, *Sketch of a New Esthetic of Music,* trans. T. Baker (New York, 1911; reprinted New York: Dover, 1962), 90ff.

47. See R. Larry Todd, "Liszt, Fantasy and Fugue for Organ on 'Ad nos, ad salutarem undam,'" *19th-Century Music* 4, no.3 (spring 1981): 250–61.

48. In a letter of 10 October 1860, cited in *Franz Liszts Musikalische Werke* (Leipzig: Breitkopf & Hartel, 1922), 7/3:xii.

49. Several are analyzed by means of pitch-class sets by Forte, including two stations from *Via crucis,* "Trauer-Vorspiel," "Unstern," and "Nuages gris" ("Liszt's Experimental Idiom," 217–28). Forte shows that the augmented triad and tetrachord 4–19, encountered earlier in the "Faust" Symphony, figure prominently in these works. In more traditional terms, set 4–19 may be described as an augmented triad with an added chromatic auxiliary note (e.g., C–C♯–E–G♯).

50. See, for example, Bernard C. Lemoine, "Tonal Organization in Selected Late Piano Works of Franz Liszt," *Liszt-Studien 2,* ed. Serge Gut, 123–31 (Munich: Emil Katzbichler, 1981), 123–24.

51. Other analysts have taken a somewhat different approach to the conclusion of "Nuages gris." Jim Samson, although recognizing the augmented triad as the "central harmonic unit," views the final chord as a whole-tone chord; see his *Music in Transition: A Study of Tonal Expansion and Atonality, 1900–1920* (London: Dent, 1977), 18. Lawrence Kramer adopts a similar view in "The Mirror of Tonality: Transitional Features of Nineteenth-Century Harmony," *19th-Century Music* 4, no.3 (spring 1981): 205. Allen Forte focuses his attention on the penultimate chord where he finds a pentachord that contains as subsets both the augmented and diminished triads ("Liszt's Experimental Idiom," 226).

52. Schoenberg, *Harmonielehre,* 468.

53. Some additional examples are tangentially discussed in Simon Harris, "Chord-Forms Based on the Whole-Tone Scale in Early Twentieth-Century Music," *Music Review* 41 (1980): 36–51; see also James M. Baker, *The Music of Alexander Scriabin* (New Haven, Conn.: Yale University Press, 1986), passim.

Dramatic Recapitulation and Tonal Pairing in Wagner's *Tristan und Isolde* and *Parsifal*

WILLIAM KINDERMAN

The subject of Wagner's large-scale formal and tonal procedures in his later works has long remained a controversial issue for critics and analysts. In a series of volumes published more than a half-century ago, Alfred Lorenz sought to defend Wagner from charges of formlessness by dividing up the continuous flow of the music into a succession of closed schematic forms.[1] The artificiality of Lorenz's method is by now generally recognized, and the forms he perceived often turned out, under scrutiny, to be a product of his own "diligent obsessions," in the words of Anthony Newcomb.[2] Perhaps in part because of the declining prestige of Lorenz's analytical enterprise in recent decades, the large-scale formal and tonal context of the works from *Tristan* to *Parsifal* has become a topic conspicuously avoided in much scholarship and, in at least one recent study, even an object for disdain.

Carl Dahlhaus has argued that in these works "form as 'architecture' was replaced by form as 'web,'" but his conclusion, that "Wagner renounced an architectonic foundation for musical forms," seems too sweeping, for it does not take into account the formal context of the music on the largest scale.[3] The context of Dahlhaus's observation concerns Wagner's abandonment of the foursquare phrase construction and regularity of metric pulse common in earlier music. A broad, unbroken musical continuity is indeed a quintessentially Wagnerian feature, but this does not preclude hierarchical formal structures in the work as a whole, as Dahlhaus implies it does when he writes of "the establishment of a thematic network or web as the basis for musical form in place of the architectural principle of the balance between related parts, in detail as well as a whole."[4]

More recently, in an article on *Tristan,* Carolyn Abbate takes a position far more extreme than Dahlhaus's, bluntly characterizing studies addressing larger formal relations in Wagner as "reductive analyses" that "emphasise Wagner's commonality with lesser works or ordinary values." According to Abbate, "the 'insights' generated by such analysis . . . indeed shrink Wagner into the negligible."[5] Nevertheless, Abbate does not examine in detail any of the analyses that she describes as reductive. Her own discussion of the *Tagesgespräch* from act 2 of *Tristan* builds on an analysis by Dahlhaus concerning the relation and occasional divergence of music and text and does not address issues of large-scale form. I return later to her contention that to perceive larger formal or structural relations in Wagner's works is to "shrink him into the negligible."

In this chapter I attempt to show that Wagner did indeed employ an architectural principle in the music of his later works, one based on the recapitulation or transformation of extended musical passages, often in conjunction with a pairing of keys. The development of this procedure was undoubtedly connected to Wagner's elimination of set-numbers and his creation of a continuity of music and drama from the beginning to the end of an act in the works beginning with *Das Rheingold*. As Donald Francis Tovey once wrote, "the revolution effected by Wagner . . . concerns the time-scale of music. . . . Wagner's achievement consisted in refashioning the whole texture and form of music until it covered the drama on a time-scale measured by hours instead of minutes."[6] On such a massive time scale the recall of motives and themes and the interaction or divergence of words and music—however important—would not suffice to articulate the major events of the drama. Wagner's later music, although more autonomous and less dependent on the text in specific details, often assumes an even greater and more generalized dramatic function. Not surprisingly, Wagner's use of extended, varied musical recapitulation and tonal pairing assumes special prominence in connection with some of the most complex and central dramatic ideas of his dramas, such as the ascent of the lovers into "Night" in *Tristan und Isolde* or the threat to the Grail in *Parsifal*.

The rest of this chapter is divided in three parts. The two main sections present analyses of *Tristan* and *Parsifal,* tracing the unfolding and dramatic development of the music heard from the very outset of each work.[7] More than *Die Meistersinger* or the *Ring* cycle do, *Tristan* and *Parsifal* invite close comparison in their dramatic and musical structures, and they offer two of Wagner's most impressive examples of tonal pairing. Although not exhaustive, the analyses not only address large-scale relations but also constitute an attempt at a detailed critical reassessment of some important musical gestures (e.g., the complex, evocative dissonances of the "Tristan" chord and the C-minor inflection within the opening Communion theme in *Parsifal*), a reassessment made possible precisely on account of the relation of these gestures to the context of the whole. The third section returns to the broader aesthetic issues raised by Wagner's formal procedures in his later works.

TRISTAN UND ISOLDE

I

The largest single formal gesture in the music of *Tristan* occurs at the very end, in Isolde's so-called "Liebestod." This passage represents not only part of a recapitulatory synthesis but also the completion and resolution of a modulatory framework that embraces the entire work. The "Liebestod" is related to the climax of the love duet in act 2 as a recapitulation of its last eighty-odd bars, written in a slightly different notation with a new vocal counterpoint for Isolde, but it is also intimately linked with the prelude to the first act. The first seventeen bars of the prelude and an even longer passage at the climax of the "Liebestod" are based on the same underlying progression, which is reinterpreted in the "Liebestod" so that it appears in B major instead of its original tonality of A minor. This change in tonality, together with accompanying changes in the thematic material and orchestration, is perfectly adapted to convey the dramatic point of the work: the unceasing, unfulfilled yearning of the lovers at last finds its resolution and triumphant conclusion in Isolde's "Liebestod."

The opening musical progression of the prelude clearly bears a symbolic relationship to the drama. It consists of a chromatic ascent in the upper line, divided in successive phrases between the oboe, clarinet, flute, and strings. The first phrase ascends from G♯ to B, harmonized as a dominant-seventh chord of the implied tonic, A minor (see ex. 1). The second and third phrases rise from B to D and D to F♯, harmonized by the dominant sevenths of C and E, respectively. The last of these phrases is then repeated an octave higher and fragmented as the E♯–F♯ semitone is detached from it. This semitone to the sixth degree of the scale is repeated five times, which lends a sense of urgency to the melodic ascent when it finally continues. In m. 16 the chromatic line rises to G and G♯, harmonized once again as the dominant seventh of A minor. The first sixteen bars thus comprise a chromatic ascent through an entire octave from G♯, the leading tone of the implied tonic, and the tonal implication of the passage is confirmed through use of the dominant sevenths of the triadic degrees of A minor. In the seventeenth bar and elsewhere throughout the work, however, when this passage is recapitulated, it

Example 1. *Tristan und Isolde,* beginning of prelude, act 1.

leads to a deceptive cadence. The tonic triad of A minor is avoided. The upward chromatic progression rising to a deceptive cadence symbolizes the theme of longing for the unattainable so central to the drama.

The importance of this progression is reflected not only by the frequent recurrence of its opening measures throughout the work but also by its recapitulation in full toward the end of each of the three acts. In act 1 it is recapitulated at the drinking of the love potion, beginning at Isolde's words "Ich trink' sie dir! [I drink it for you]," which are set to the first notes of the opening cello motif from the prelude.[8] In this passage the recapitulation is actually expanded by the interpolation of material in the pauses between the opening phrases; twenty-six bars are directly recalled in a passage of forty-five bars. The second recapitulation of the prelude occurs at the end of act 2, where Tristan confronts Marke after the king's lament. The final recapitulation takes place at the last encounter of Tristan and Isolde in act 3, immediately before Tristan's death. In each of these passages the prelude is recalled in its original tonality of A minor, and conspicuous features of the orchestration are retained.[9]

The opening progression from the prelude is thus treated as a structural musical element on the level of the whole drama.

The dramatic relation between this progression from the prelude and the music of the "Liebestod" is illustrated most vividly in the last section of the opera, beginning at the lovers' final encounter. Tristan's physical collapse as he falls into Isolde's arms is marked by the beginning of the recapitulation from the prelude, and the breaking off of the passage symbolizes Tristan's death. Isolde's ensuing extended monologue serves as a transition to the "Liebestod." Gradually, Isolde's words reveal her to be removed from the level of the visible action, and the process of immersion in an inner, or ideal, world is mirrored by the appearance of music recalled from the love duet in the second act. After her words "The wound? Where? Let me heal it!" Wagner first recalls the music from that part of the love duet that will begin the "Liebestod," and at the end of Isolde's monologue this material foreshadowing the "Liebestod" reappears (see ex. 2). This music is first heard in the second-act love duet

Example 2. *Tristan und Isolde,* act 3, recall of material from second-act love duet.

to Isolde's words "So stürben wir, um ungetrennt, ewig einig, ohne End [So would we die, to be eternally one, indivisible, without end]." Its motivic configuration of a rising fourth and appoggiatura, which tends to be treated in rising sequences of great breadth, is related to the initial descending fourth and appoggiatura of the rising sequential progression at the climax of the "Liebestod," which I discuss in detail later.

Isolde's last words in this passage contradict the whole basis for the visible dramatic action. Moments earlier Tristan dies from his self-inflicted wound, but Isolde's words address Tristan as if he still lives or has returned to life:

Nicht meine Klagen darf ich dir sagen?	*Are you deaf to my words?*
Nur einmal—ach! nur einmal noch!	*Only once—oh! Only once more!*
Tristan! Ha! Horch! Er wacht!	*Tristan! Ha! Hark! He wakes!*
Geliebter!	*Beloved!*

This "awakening" of Tristan coincides, moreover, with the recall of the material from the love duet foreshadowing the "Liebestod." At this crucial point in the drama, the two levels of action—inner and outer, invisible and visible, Night and Day—become dissociated and no longer bear any direct relation to one another. The music from the love duet is abruptly interrupted in the ensuing fight scene between Kurwenal and Melot, during which Isolde falls and remains unconscious, oblivious of the outward action. The fight scene and the allied passages for Brangäne and Marke are merely a parenthesis in the main action, which resumes in Isolde's "Liebestod."

At the beginning of the "Liebestod" the music from Isolde's earlier passage is resumed at her words beginning "mild und leise [gently and quietly]"; as I have shown, both of these passages recall an important section of the love duet preceding the climactic passage that will be recapitulated in full. The effect of recapitulation from the love duet is thus much broader and deeper than the restatement of a single earlier passage and represents an extended recapitulatory synthesis. In its musical and dramatic construction this recapitulatory synthesis bears a striking resemblance to analogous passages in the final act of *Götterdämmerung,* composed more than a decade later. In *Götterdämmerung* Siegfried's recollection of Brünnhilde immediately before his death is so intense that he believes he is once again united with her on her rocky height. Like Isolde in *Tristan,* Siegfried addresses Brünnhilde directly, in the present tense. In both works a dichotomy is formed between the outward dramatic action and an inner, spiritual plane of action embodied through recapitulation. Thus Isolde's "Liebestod" corresponds to the music from Brünnhilde's awakening recapitulated in *Götterdämmerung,* the composition of which was doubtless influenced by *Tristan.* In *Tristan,* however, unlike *Götterdämmerung,* the completion of the recapitulation acts as the culmination and resolution for a whole complex of chromatic music heard since the beginning of the work, four hours earlier. The recapitulatory synthesis in *Tristan und Isolde* is shown in table 1.

2

Wagner himself never used the term *Liebestod,* or "love-death," to refer to Isolde's final passage. The name "Liebestod" was first applied to the

Table 1. *Tristan und Isolde,* Act 3 Conclusion

		Musical Material	Action	Schirmer Vocal Score, Page Numbers
Internal Action		Recall of progression from prelude, act 1	Tristan's death	276/5–277/4
		Death motive; recall of music from "So stürben wir . . ." in act 2 foreshadowing Isolde's transfiguration	Isolde's monologue	277/4–282
External Action		Interruption in the recapitulatory synthesis; unrelated material	Fight scene	283–88
Internal Action		Death motive; recall of music from "So stürben wir . . ." in act 2	Marke's lament	288/4–293
		Large-scale varied recapitulation from the climax of the love duet, act 2, with cadence	Isolde's transfiguration ("Liebestod")	293–301

conclusion of *Tristan* by Liszt in his piano reduction of the passage, and the term has since become universally associated with it.[10] Wagner did employ the term *Liebestod,* but with reference to the first-act prelude, whereas he called Isolde's final passage a "Verklärung," or transfiguration. The word *Verklärung* also appears in Wagner's stage directions for the last moments of *Tristan,* when Isolde is to appear as transfigured. The intriguing aspect of this description, however, is its implication for the music. *Verklärung* implies a glorification, or elevation, but also a transformation, a change in appearance. Taken literally Wagner's description might seem to suggest the existence of a specific musical relationship between Isolde's final passage and the rest of the opera.

A link between Isolde's "Liebestod" and the prelude to the first act is also suggested by Wagner's concert arrangement of the prelude. Since the end of the prelude modulates from the tonic A minor to C minor in preparation for the Sailor's Song, Wagner revised the end of the piece for concert performance by adding twenty-four bars in A major drawn from the very end of Isolde's "Liebestod." The last bars of the concert ending, in fact, consist of a nearly exact transposition of the end of the "Liebestod" from B major into A major.

Example 3. Excerpt from Wagner's concert ending of the *Tristan* prelude.

The transitional bars in Wagner's keyboard score of the concert ending, dated "Paris, 15 December, 1859," are shown in ex.3.[11] Particularly

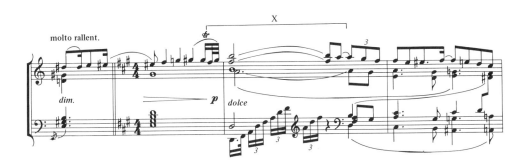

interesting here is the point at which Wagner joins the two pieces structurally, grafting the end of the "Liebestod" onto the end of the prelude. The moment of joining is actually the cadence to the long chromatically ascending progression first heard at the beginning of the prelude (compare ex.1). This cadence, and the entire ascending passage that precedes it, has an exact counterpart at the climax of the "Liebestod," where the progression is transformed in accordance with the demands of the drama.

The climax of the "Liebestod" bears a relationship with the beginning of the prelude that is much more intimate than has hitherto been realized. Some analyses of *Tristan* have isolated aspects of this progression, but the full scope of the relation seems to have been overlooked, since it must be analyzed not in terms of leitmotivs but with a view to Wagner's use of larger dimensions of tonality. Kurth, for instance, singles out the melodic cambiata figure that emphasizes the cadential arrival in each passage—the point where the prelude and "Liebestod" dovetail in Wagner's concert ending of the prelude (see ex.3, where the motif is designated as *X*).[12] Instead of relating this melodic figure to its broader context, however, as part of a cadential articulation, Kurth was content to identify it as an important but neglected leitmotif and assigned it a name, the "fate motif [*Verhängnismotiv*]." In the musical context of the prelude, however, this motif is inseparably bound up with the long chromatically ascending passage that precedes it; it is not, strictly speaking, an independent thematic unit but part of a cadence that gathers up what has preceded it and brings the music to a point of harmonic and rhythmic articulation. The relationship between the prelude and "Liebestod" is based not on motivic recall but rather on the reinterpretation and transformation of an extended passage, culminating in the cadence.

It is important in this connection to reassess the tonal structure of the music associated with the lovers' sphere, particularly the progression from the A minor of the prelude to the B major of the "Liebestod." Lorenz was baffled by this aspect of *Tristan,* which unlike *Parsifal* or *Die Meistersinger* does not end in the key in which it began.[13] Seen in relationship to the drama, however, the progression seems fitting and inevitable: the unsettled A minor and stable, unequivocal B major reflect the dramatic progression from the agony of yearning to its mystic transfiguration at the end of the opera. To accomplish this dramatic end, in fact, Wagner embodied in *Tristan* a logical extension of the historical development of tonality and musical structure reaching back to Beethoven.

Charles Rosen, among others, has drawn attention to the fact that romantic compositions from the 1830s frequently begin from a point of tonal instability, which undermines the classical canon of a closed framework.[14] Rosen cites in particular Schumann's Fantasy in C, op.17, the first movement of which delays appearance of the C-major triad in root position until its closing measures; this is but one example among many. From Chopin to Mahler there is a marked tendency for composers to avoid clear tonic articulation at the beginning of a work and postpone resolution of the unstable opening material to a later point. Nor is this practice unknown before the 1830s; it is foreshadowed in works by Haydn and Beethoven. In some of Beethoven's later compositions, such as the Piano Sonata in A, op.101, and the String Quartet in C♯ Minor, op.131, the first strong tonic downbeat is delayed until the beginning of the last movement, creating a structural tension spanning the whole work. This dimension of Beethoven's late style is especially noteworthy here in view of Wagner's deep interest in these pieces (particularly op.131) during the 1850s, immediately preceding the composition of *Tristan.*[15] A remarkable aspect of the C♯-Minor Quartet that must have appealed to Wagner is its formal continuity, for it embraces seven highly dissimilar movements within a single coherent tonal plan. As exemplified in Beethoven's op.131, the principle of delayed resolution represented not an attack on formal coherence but rather a crucial means for imposing formal coherence on a temporal scale larger than had hitherto been contemplated.

By the 1830s Chopin extended this tendency to postpone strong tonic articulation into the practice of starting outside the tonic key altogether, in a secondary tonality that can still be treated in such a way as to imply the eventual tonic. Chopin's second scherzo thus begins in B♭ minor, but the overall tonic of the piece is actually D♭, and the opening material in B♭ is resolved to the tonic, in somewhat varied form, in the coda.[16] This practice of directional tonality is a fundamental aspect of the musical language of Wagner's later works. It is especially in *Tristan,* however, that directional tonality, in combination with thematic transformation and extended musical recapitulation, assumes outstanding dramatic importance.

By withholding strong tonic articulation of B major until the climax of Isolde's "Liebestod," Wagner established a powerful formal relation spanning the entire course of the drama. The most obvious dimension of this relation is the completion in the "Liebestod" of the progression from the love duet, where the emphatic cadence to B major is cut off by the arrival of Marke and Melot and the dawning of Day. The overpowering affirmation of this cadence in the "Liebestod" owes not a little of its effectiveness to the fact that it supplies the structural goal implied by the long sequential ascent heard in the love duet.[17] In a deeper sense, however, both passages represent a transformation of the crucial progression first heard at the beginning of the prelude to the first act. In the love duet and "Liebestod" the underlying progression from the prelude is reinterpreted so that it achieves stability and clarity of definition. This progress toward tonal stability in particular is thus identified with the progress of Tristan and Isolde into the realm of Night.

Like the beginning of the prelude, the climax of the "Liebestod" consists of a long chromatic ascent from G♯ through an entire octave leading to a cadence (see ex. 4). Here, however, the progression undergoes a process of thematic transformation to reflect the character of ecstatic abandonment demanded by the dramatic context. Unlike the prelude, it contains no pauses between segments of the chromatic ascent, and its orchestration is filled out so that the chromatically ascending line, which is divided between the woodwinds and strings in the prelude, is now doubled in the winds and strings simultaneously. Despite these changes and the difference in tonality, the underlying progression is the same as that in the prelude. In both passages Wagner emphasizes the last stage in the chromatic ascent by reiterating the semitone to the sixth degree of the scale below the anticipated tonic note: the five repetitions of the semitone G–G♯ or F⁎–G♯ in mm. 14–17 of the example thus correspond to the five repetitions of the semitone E♯–F♯ in ex. 1. The tension generated by these repetitions finds resolution in the cadential arrival in m. 18,

Example 4. *Tristan und Isolde,* act 3, showing the chromatic ascent in Isolde's transfiguration. Piano reduction.

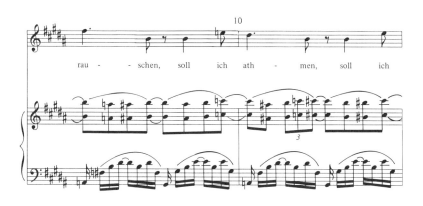

Süss   in Düf-ten mich ver-hau - chen?   In dem

wo - - gen-den   Schwall,   in dem tö - - nen-den

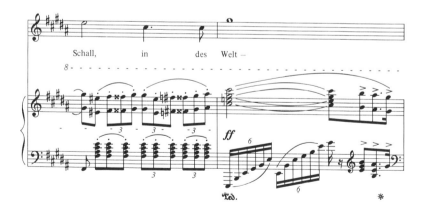

Schall,   in   des   Welt —

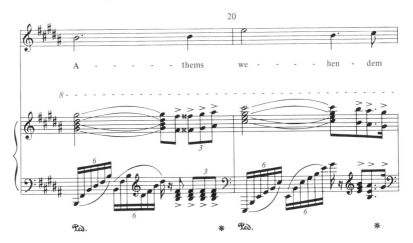

which corresponds unmistakably to the deceptive cadence in m. 17 of the prelude. The relationship between these passages becomes fully apparent at the moment of cadence to B major.

A remarkable example of thematic development in this passage consists in Wagner's treatment of the expressive appoggiatura figure derived from the deceptive cadence in the prelude. In the "Liebestod" this appears not only at the climax but also at the beginning of the chromatic ascent. In both instances Wagner resolves the appoggiatura on C♯ not to the B-major tonic triad but to the fifth of the subdominant triad and connects the resolution through a linear descending fourth to a second appoggiatura to the tonic triad. It is this structural moment that serves as the point of connection between the prelude and "Liebestod" in Wagner's concert ending of the prelude (compare ex. 3). The thematic substance from the prelude is developed here as one aspect of the transformation of the cadence, which is the central structural and dramatic idea of the passage.

More lies behind this relation than the device of the interrupted cadence, however, for the sonority of the progression from the prelude is also transformed. This brings us to the matter of the first vertical sonority of the prelude, the so-called Tristan chord, the chord that has provoked countless attempts at analysis from theorists.[18]

Analysts have often attempted to identify this chord in terms of traditional functional harmony, but the sonority has steadfastly resisted such classification. It consists of a minor triad with added sixth, a genuinely ambiguous harmonic sonority. In a sense, of course, the dissonance and harmonic ambiguity of the chord embody the dramatic point of the progression: the retention of dissonance and absence of resolution lend to the passage a mysterious aura; its tonal instability is inseparable from its expressive content. In the context of the whole work, furthermore, this sound is treated not as an abstract chord but as a referential sonority often associated with its original orchestration and pitch level from the beginning of the prelude, with G♯ in the uppermost voice and F in the lowest. This spacing and pitch level are retained, for instance, at those important dramatic moments when the prelude is recapitulated at length, as occurs toward the end of each act. The significance of the Tristan chord consists not in its abstract configuration but in the sound itself and its evocative relationship to the drama.

It is within this context that we may most profitably view the passage described by Wagner himself as a *Verklärung,* or transfiguration. In the prelude each of the opening phrases employs the Tristan chord, which gives rise to the chromatically ascending line in the uppermost voice. At the corresponding moment at the beginning of the "Liebestod," on the other hand, we hear a B-major chord preceded by its subdominant, a harmonic pattern foreshadowing the concluding plagal cadence in the last measures of the work. The G♯ that initiates the chromatic ascent in the "Liebestod" is thus not a chord tone but an upper appoggiatura to a B-major triad, whereas the analogous G♯ in the prelude sounds like a lower appoggiatura to A.[19] This difference in the resolution of the G♯ is the result of a subtle change in the crucial sonority of the Tristan chord when the entire progression is transformed in the "Liebestod."

The harmonic basis for the transfiguration in the "Liebestod" is the replacement of the Tristan chord by a closely related sonority, an appoggiatura chord to B major. This sonority shares all the tones of the Tristan chord with one striking exception: F♮, the lowest tone of the Tristan chord, is altered to F♯ (see fig.1). The difference of this semitone deci-

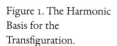

Figure 1. The Harmonic Basis for the Transfiguration.

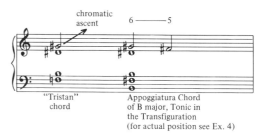

sively changes the character of the chord, and even the tonality of the entire passage. The disappearance of the F purges the harmonic complexity of the Tristan chord, which is thereby replaced by the more straightforward appoggiatura chord of B major.

This B-major chord is now treated as the tonic, but its first appearance in root position is postponed until the powerful cadence that caps the chromatic ascent through the octave. At this point the pattern of subdominant resolutions to B major is repeated in rhythmic augmentation. With the arrival of the resolution to B major, the final cadence is imminent, but five measures before the end Wagner recalls the crucial sonority of the Tristan chord as a final reminiscence, clarifying the harmonic basis for the transfiguration (see ex. 5). In this final reminiscence the B-major

Example 5. *Tristan und Isolde,* act 3, conclusion.

tonic triad is connected directly with the Tristan chord, recalled in its original spacing and distinctive orchestration. This time, however, the tonic note B sounds softly in the bass through the reminiscence, and the Tristan chord passes not to the dominant seventh of A minor, as in the prelude, but to an E-minor triad, the penultimate subdominant chord of the final cadence. The Tristan chord, symbol of the unfulfilled yearning of the lovers throughout the drama, is superseded by the stable, unequivocal triad of B major.

3

A "secret of form" in Wagner's *Tristan,* in the sense of a hidden transition within the overall formal progression, is lodged in the relationship between the prelude and "Liebestod" conveying the dramatic theme of transfiguration.[20] It has two distinct aspects. Rhythmically, the arrival associated with the implied cadence of the opening progression is avoided during the course of the entire work. Only at the climax of the "Liebestod" is the cadence provided, with a powerful structural downbeat marking the moment of arrival. The strength of this articulation rivals anything in the classical symphonic repertory. Harmonically, on the other hand, the ambiguous Tristan chord is superseded by the tonic triad of B major. Both events converge in the great cadence to B major just analyzed, which embodies the dramatic transfiguration of Isolde.

As has often been observed, there is a conspicuous absence of stage action in *Tristan*. The most important elements in the action are internal and psychological, and their expression is therefore heavily dependent on the music. Because of its independence from spatial localization, music is ideally suited to embody this inner sphere of action, dissociated from the outward events of the drama. In the philosophical tradition that influenced Wagner through Schopenhauer, in fact, music is extolled precisely on account of its independence from the phenomenological world, the external world of appearances.

In *Tristan*, furthermore, the development of the famous chromatic idiom associated with the lovers is explicitly identified with the realm of Night, in the ideology of Night and Day derived from the literature of early romanticism.[21] The realm of Night is ultimately incompatible with Day, or external reality: the inward mystery of Night vanishes under its illumination. The resolution of this dichotomy is possible, therefore, only through the transcendence of Day. The end of *Tristan* assumes an otherworldly or religious dimension as a consequence of the triumphant affirmation of Night in Isolde's "Liebestod."[22]

Since it symbolizes nothing less than the transcendence of the external world, there is the risk of an evacuation of definite, objective content from the text of the "Liebestod." Indeed the words do not relate to any aspect of the visible action, although they refer precisely to the music. Isolde asks repeatedly whether those around her share her vision, and her words identify this vision explicitly with the orchestral music of the passage. The broad crescendo that extends over the entire passage is literally described in the text. Beginning "gently and quietly [mild und leise]," by the appearance of the chromatically ascending progression it is "resounding more brightly [Heller schallend]," and it reaches its climax in the "ringing sound [tönenden Schall]" of the great cadence to B major. Isolde's final text is like a commentary on the effect of the music in the nineteenth-century tradition of poetic interpretation to which Wagner himself contributed in his prose writings. Metaphysics aside, the conclusion of *Tristan* is a hymn to music, and specifically to the formal resources of music on which the strength of articulation in the "Liebestod" depends.

To articulate the *Verklärung,* or transfiguration, at the end of *Tristan* Wagner employs a combination of recapitulation, thematic transformation, and directional tonality to cap a formal structure that operates on the level of the entire work. The fundamental aspect of this structure is a reinterpretation of the progression from the beginning of the prelude such that it receives its definitive expression in the "Liebestod." The formal gesture at the end of *Tristan* is consistently foreshadowed from the very beginning of the drama, in the progression leading to the deceptive cadence and in the sound of the Tristan chord, which is supplanted in the "Liebestod" by the appoggiatura chord to B major and turned into the tonic sonority. The overall progression from A minor to B major acts, therefore, much like a gigantic transition, or a tonal pairing, on the level of the whole work. At the same time, the tonal pairing of A and C from the first act (see the introduction to this volume) is shifted downward to A♭/C♭[B], first in the progression from "O sink hernieder, Nacht der Liebe [Descend, night of love]" (and even more tangibly from "So stürben wir, um ungetrennt") to the end of the love duet in act 2 and then in Isolde's closing "transfiguration," from "mild und leise" to the final B-major chords.

PARSIFAL

I

In a fundamental sense *Parsifal* inverts the message of *Tristan*. Parsifal's denial of the temptation of the senses is connected to his capacity for compassion: agapē overcomes eros. Musically, there can be no resolution of chromaticism into diatonicism here, as in *Tristan;* instead, there is a purification from dissonance and chromaticism of the diatonic Grail themes and motives, which are integrated and combined for the first time in the closing recapitulatory synthesis at the end of act 3, after Parsifal appears as redeemer and reveals the Grail. By contrast, the prelude to act 1 presents the themes associated with the Grail successively, while investing the first of them—the so-called Last Supper or Communion theme—with a dissonant tension of dramatic import.

Wagner composed the music of *Parsifal* mainly during 1877–78, precisely twenty years after the composition of *Tristan*. His sketches and drafts show in detail how he first devised music for the ritual Grail scene before composing the prelude to act 1, which foreshadows the scene in the temple.[23] A tonal pairing of A♭ and C is worked out elaborately in the prelude and in many related passages, becoming in effect a symbolic tonal representation of the changing state of the Grail. The central dramatic tension consists in the threat to the Order of the Grail posed by the plight of Amfortas, whose festering wound opens afresh when he reveals the Grail at the communion service. This threat to the Grail is removed only in act 3, when Parsifal appears as redeemer, bringing the Holy Spear gained during his victorious encounter with Kundry and Klingsor in act 2. To embody this dramatic tension in the music, Wagner juxtaposes the sonorities of A♭ major and C minor already in the opening Communion theme, which comprises several motives capable of independent development (see ex. 6).

Example 6. *Parsifal,* act 1, beginning of prelude.

Wagner himself once described this theme as symbolic of the theological virtue of love, although he also indicated on another occasion that "the pain of Amfortas is contained in it."[24] Both elements seem to be reflected in its motivic structure. The first two bars of this unaccompanied theme rise in a suspended, syncopated rhythm through the A♭-major triad and stepwise through the octave; stress on the strong beats of the meter occurs only in m. 3, where the descending semitone A♭–G brings the change in harmony to C minor. This downward shift of a semitone is emphasized not only by the rhythm of the passage but also by the crescendo to *forte* in m. 3; a decrescendo to *piano* marks the return to A♭ and to the initial syncopated melodic idiom in the last bars of the theme. The harmonic tension created by this striking inflection casts a shadow of ambiguity over the tonic key of A♭ major, which sounds, momentarily, like the flat sixth of C minor. As is later made clear, this tension introduced by the motive in m. 3 after the stable beginning in A♭ embodies in germinal form the dramatic relationship between the anguished, sinful condition of Amfortas and the purity of the Grail.[25]

A♭ major and C minor are used in the tonal structure of the prelude's opening as keys for the larger thematic statements, each of which is twenty bars long. In turn, this key relation parallels the tonal framework of the entire act, which closes in the major mode of C. The anticipation of the act's polar tonalities represents one aspect of a general musical foreshadowing in the prelude of the Grail scene at the end of the act.

All the music of the prelude is associated with the Grail and serves to anticipate the scene in the temple. Thus, the prelude's opening statements of the Communion theme in the keys of A♭ major and C minor are recapitulated in these same keys in the Grail scene, where they are sung to the Communion text. Two other motives from the prelude—motives that Wagner associated with the theological virtue of faith—are also prominent in the Temple scene (the initial appearance of these motives is shown in ex. 7, where they are designated as the Grail motive and Faith

Example 7. *Parsifal*, act 1, prelude.

motive).[26] The most telling and dramatically significant anticipation of the Grail scene, however, is contained in the last section of the prelude. This passage foreshadows the music of Amfortas's great lament, as well as a number of other passages associated with Amfortas, and it also prepares the transition from the Transformation music into the Grail scene.

This final section of the prelude represents a development of the opening Communion theme, which is greatly expanded from within. Its first three bars are treated sequentially, with the motive from the third bar serving as a pivot for modulations to keys rising in thirds. This tonal

(Der Vorhang öffnet sich vor der Bühne)

Example 8. *Parsifal,* act 1, conclusion of prelude.

framework thereby parallels on a larger structural level the intervallic pattern of rising thirds in the theme itself. Subsequently, the increasingly chromatic texture of the passage culminates in the isolation and development of the descending semitone figure at its original pitch level, A♭–G (see ex. 8). Here the semitone is reinterpreted as an ascending appoggiatura and repeated threefold. Syncopations and diminished and minor harmonies contribute to the passage's expressive intensity. At the end of Amfortas's tortured narrative in the Grail scene, this poignant appoggiatura is set to the two syllables of "*Wunde* [wound]."

The chromatic intensity of this passage abates as the music approaches the cadence in A♭, corresponding to m. 6 of the original theme, in the closing bars of the prelude. Here again, the thematic model of the Communion theme is greatly expanded: the cadential dominant chord is protracted for eight bars, while the serene, rising triadic figure penetrates the highest register in the violins. Nevertheless, the expected cadence in A♭ is not granted: as the curtain opens, trombones behind the stage sound the head of the Communion theme on the pitch level of F♭, with the effect of a deceptive cadence. The diatonic rise through the octave drops from F♭ to E♭ through the same crucial descending semitone figure that will remain attached to this theme until Parsifal's return of the Holy Spear in act 3.

In *Parsifal,* as in *Tristan,* the denial and postponement of cadence provide a means of sustaining musical tension on the largest scale, thereby reflecting the progress of the drama. As I have discussed, the definitive cadence in *Tristan* is postponed until Isolde's transfiguration in the closing moments of the drama; only here is the inherent ambiguity and instability of the music associated with the lovers and the realm of Night fully resolved. In *Parsifal,* by contrast, it is the music associated with the

Example 9. *Parsifal,* act 1,
conclusion of the
Transformation music.

Grail that undergoes an analogous process of resolution in the key of
A♭ when its elements of intrinsic ambiguity and instability are eventually removed. In the first Grail scene this is not yet the case. Accordingly,
the music of the processional entrance into the Temple of the Grail is
marked by a striking modulation to C, which then becomes primary in
the tonal pairing.

The transition is accomplished through two modified appearances of
the deceptive cadence from the end of the prelude (see ex. 9). In the third
measure of the example, the circle-of-fifths progression, having reached
the dominant of A♭, resolves deceptively to F♭ as the trombones behind
stage play the beginning of the Communion theme, ending in the semitone descent to E♭ in the fifth bar. Moments later, the sequential restatement of this motive a minor third lower in the trombones outlines the
semitone D♭–C, opening the gateway to C major, which is articulated
by the fixed pitches of the temple bells. The remainder of the scene is
framed by the processional motive heard in the bells in their associated
tonality of C major.

Dramatically, the center of gravity of this first Grail scene is less in the
ritualistic passages than in Amfortas's lament immediately preceding
the communion service. Amfortas at first refuses to perform his duty.
The core of his narrative is a description of his experience at a previous
service when the Grail was revealed. In the music of this passage, the so-
called Grail motive appears in C major, followed by the head of the Communion theme treated developmentally, beginning in C minor. This de-
velopmental passage is foreshadowed in the final section of the prelude;
both passages give striking emphasis to the semitone motive in the third
bar of the Communion theme, which is exploited to reflect the inevitable
opening of the wound when Amfortas is confronted by the purity of the
Grail. Amfortas's hopeless predicament can be remedied only through
the intervention of a witness to the scene, "the pure fool," Parsifal.

2

In a letter to Mathilde Wesendonk written on 30 May 1859, during the
composition of *Tristan,* Wagner describes the figure of Amfortas as "my
Tristan of the third act with an inconceivable intensification."[27] Later in
the same letter he writes: "And yet there is still another difficulty with
the character of Parzival: he is absolutely indispensable as the chosen redeemer of Amfortas: but should Amfortas be shown in a true, revealing
light, he will be of such enormous tragic interest, that it will be more
than difficult to create another main interest against him, and yet this
principal interest must be centered in Parzival, if he is not to appear

at the end as a cold Deus ex machina."[28] Nearly two decades after he wrote this letter, Wagner faced the challenge of transferring the principal dramatic interest from Amfortas to Parsifal in musical terms. A crucial aspect of this dramatic progression would be to treat Parsifal's response to Kundry's seduction attempt in act 2 such that it projects not utter passivity on the part of Parsifal but self-possession, shown through his identification with and compassion for Amfortas and his conscious realization of the nature of his mission. This action is internal and psychological and therefore heavily dependent on the music for its expression.

This moment in the drama parallels and combines aspects of two climactic passages in the *Ring* cycle: Brünnhilde's awakening in *Siegfried* and Siegfried's later recollection of her awakening just before his death in *Götterdämmerung*. Like the young Siegfried's encounter with Brünnhilde, Parsifal's encounter with Kundry is deeply psychological in a manner anticipating Freud; Kundry's kiss is "the last mother's greeting" as well as the "first kiss of love." At the same time, Parsifal's recollection of and identification with Amfortas parallels Siegfried's identification with Brünnhilde immediately before his death. Both become oblivious of their surroundings and wholly absorbed in their vision as something more real than external reality.

Parsifal might be regarded as the last of a long line of Wagnerian characters—reaching back to Senta in *The Flying Dutchman*—who undergo a symbolic transfiguration in the course of the drama. The transfiguration of Parsifal from the naïve youth of act 1 into redeemer, however, goes further in this respect than anything in Wagner's earlier works. In *Tristan* and in the *Ring* Wagner allies the transfigurations of Isolde and Siegfried, respectively, with the dramatic theme of the promise of salvation through love while giving striking emphasis to this aspect of the drama through his musical setting. The massive musical recapitulations of *Tristan* and *Götterdämmerung* serve precisely this end. *Parsifal,* by contrast, progresses beyond the dramatic framework of these earlier works; the Amfortas of act 1 corresponds already to the Tristan of act 3, and the transfiguration of Parsifal's character occurs already in act 2, not as a final concluding gesture, as in Isolde's transfiguration or Siegfried's vision of Brünnhilde before his death. The transfigurations of Siegfried or Isolde represent an end point in the dramatic progression or even a disappearance of the character from the level of the visible action, as implied in Isolde's symbolic death. The corresponding moment of the *Parsifal* drama, on the other hand, is not an end point but a new beginning: Parsifal's discovery of the nature of his mission as redeemer.

How, then, does Wagner embody in his music this shift of the principal dramatic interest from Amfortas to Parsifal? The device of recapitulation plays a crucial role. The last fifty bars of Parsifal's passage in response to Kundry's kiss are to a considerable extent a varied recapitulation of several passages from Amfortas's lament in act 1. In particular, the Communion theme is transferred to Parsifal, in C minor and A♭ minor, to reflect his identification with Amfortas and his memory of the Savior's cry that led him to the realm of the Grail. The use here of recapitulation is dramatically apt, since it expresses Parsifal's capacity for compassion as his means of insight into the plight of Amfortas while transferring the musical material associated with the Grail to the future leader of the Order of the Grail. Amfortas, it will be recalled, is incapable of serving his office after the scene witnessed by Parsifal in act 1.

In a sense Kundry's delivery of the kiss is also a recapitulation, although its musical setting is heard for the first time in act 2. Before the beginning of the drama, she had delivered the kiss to Amfortas, tempting him into sin and allowing Klingsor to inflict the wound. It is significant in this regard that the descending semitone so frequently heard in association with Amfortas's wound is derived from the chromatic motive of Kundry's seduction (see ex. 10). Kundry's motive circles around the dissonant interval of the tritone; its circular motion evokes the image of the

Example 10. *Parsifal*, act 2, setting of Kundry's kiss.

biblical serpent ready to strike.[29] As Kundry embraces Parsifal, the ascending chromatics from her motive reach the semitone E♯–F♯, which is repeated three times during the kiss. On the third repetition, this F♯ becomes G♭, as the direction of the semitone is inverted. As Parsifal grips his heart in anguish, we hear the motive from the third bar of the Communion theme associated with the wound of Amfortas.

The full symbolic significance of this musical setting of Kundry's kiss seems to have been overlooked in the literature on *Parsifal,* although the motivic relations themselves have been carefully examined.[30] This motivic derivation of the descending semitone of the Communion theme from Kundry's chromatic music points to the prehistory of the drama—Kundry's earlier seduction of Amfortas—as the dramatic source of these same musical tensions from the beginning of the work. In this sense, the time scale of the music extends beyond the beginning of the drama. Kundry's kiss serves then as the point of connection between the sublime, diatonic realm of the Grail and the diabolical, chromatic realm of Klingsor; from her kiss comes the "pollution of the sanctuary" reflected in the chromatic contamination in the third bar of the Communion theme. Thus the drama's crucial turning point comes in this replay of the earlier seduction scene, with Parsifal taking the place of Amfortas.

After receiving Kundry's kiss, Parsifal reacts by identifying Amfortas's wound with his own experience of the temptation of sin. The wound can then be seen as a symbol, as the outward, visible embodiment of the inner, spiritual condition of sin. This relation is expressed musically through the initial derivation of the descending semitone from Kundry and its use moments later at Parsifal's exclamation "Amfortas!" Its clearest expression, however, is at the end of Parsifal's passage, where the musical setting of his question "How do I atone for my guilt?" corresponds to the setting of Amfortas's words "close the wound" at the end of his lament in act 1. Both passages in turn arise as a development of the semitone motive first heard at the end of the prelude, which in its turn is derived from the dissonant inflection within the Communion theme and, ultimately, from Kundry's poisoned kiss.

The musical significance of this relation extends even beyond these examples in a complex network of passages spanning the entire work. The setting of Kundry's kiss is already foreshadowed at the same pitch level, for instance, in the music of Gurnemanz's narrative in act 1, when he describes Kundry's seduction of Amfortas. It is surely not coincidental, furthermore, that the motivic fifth F–B♭ highlighted in the setting of Kundry's kiss recurs so prominently in act 3 in music connected with the death and funeral procession of Titurel, which is associated tonally with B♭ minor. No less significant is the reappearance of the descending semitone G♭–F at Kundry's baptism by Parsifal, where the crucial pitch G♭ is reinterpreted enharmonically as F♯ and subsequently resolved into B major in the music of the Good Friday spell. The most central relation, however, is that connecting Parsifal's response to Kundry's kiss with the Grail scene in act 1. Here the tonal pairing of A♭ and C again assumes an important role.

Parsifal's rejection of the temptation of sin, embodied in the kiss, is paralleled by his identification with the Grail, embodied in the two appearances of the Communion theme in the keys of C minor and A♭ minor. The first appearance of the theme corresponds exactly, in key and orchestration, to Amfortas's description of the communion service in act 1; according to Wagner's performance directions, as transmitted by Felix Mottl, Parsifal is at this point "totally in the state of being in which he has seen Amfortas."[31] Moments later Parsifal's trancelike vision culminates in his quotation of the Savior's cry that led him to the Grail: "Deliver, rescue me from hands sullied by guilt [Erlöse, rette mich aus schuldbefleckten Händen]!" (see ex.11). According to Mottl, this line is

Example 11. *Parsifal*, act 2, Parsifal's quotation of the Savior's cry.

to be sung with "terrifying expression."[32] The unusual use here of the minor mode of A♭ contributes to the intensity of expression, as does the fact that the dissonant turn to the C-minor harmony of the theme is sung by Parsifal himself. Once again, the words here refer to the sin of Amfortas and not merely to its external manifestation in the wound. Only when this sin is overcome can the diatonic purity of the Communion theme be affirmed.

3

One decisive moment remains in the development of the music associated with the Grail: Parsifal's return with the Holy Spear and his assumption of the role of leader of the Order of the Grail. Here, finally, the threat to the Grail is removed; also removed is the dissonant or chromatic contamination of the Communion theme. The tonal pairing is eliminated in favor of a symphonic synthesis and resolution of the motives of the Grail in A♭ major.

Lorenz and other analysts have pointed out the motivic change in the Communion theme in act 3: the downward semitone of its third bar is replaced by a rising whole tone.[33] This new form of the Communion theme appears first when Parsifal presents the spear to Gurnemanz and subsequently throughout the closing Grail scene. The first appearance of this new version of the theme is shown in ex.12. Lorenz regarded this change as the product of a new motivic combination in which the series of rising tones to the new resolution outlining a fourth comprises a rhythmically varied form of the Spear motive from m.4 of the original Communion theme (cf. ex.6, where the Spear motive consists of a rising fourth, A♭–D♭).[34] This interpretation, however persuasive, leaves out of account the broader structural and dramatic implications of the change, which consists not of an assimilation of the Spear motive per se but of an alteration in one note, a purging of the crucial descending semitone that represents a primary source of musical tension throughout the drama. Once again, an analogy might be drawn with *Tristan,* in which the change of a semitone in the harmony of the crucial Tristan chord provides the new sonority to be treated as tonic when the ascending chromatic progression from the first-act prelude is transformed and resolved in Isolde's transfiguration. In both cases Wagner presents a theme at the outset of the work containing elements of musical tension and complexity that are identified throughout with aspects of the drama and resolved only at its conclusion. This is an essential aspect of Wagner's "Copernican revolution," in Tovey's words, with its immense expansion of the time scale of musical form.[35] In this equation of music and drama

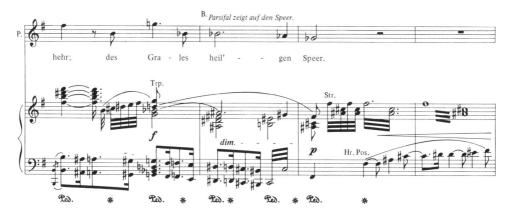

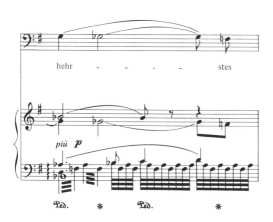

Example 12. *Parsifal*, act 3,
setting of Parsifal's
revelation of the Spear to
Gurnemanz.

the formal consolidation of the primary musical complex occurs only at the end of the entire work, where it is dramatically motivated.

In *Parsifal* the primary musical complex associated with the Grail undergoes a formal synthesis and resolution when the shrine is opened in act 3. Essential to this resolution is the new version of the Communion theme, cleansed of its descending semitone. Since this new version comprises only the first two bars of the original Communion theme with a new resolution, I refer to it as the Communion motive. The Communion motive parallels the Spear motive and the so-called Grail motive, both of which contain a rising fourth, as well as the remaining motive associated with the Grail, the so-called Faith motive, whose descending fourths are frequently inverted to rising fourths in the contrapuntal texture. In the closing music it becomes evident, for the first time, that all the motives associated with the Grail are closely related thematically.

At the same time, these related motives are joined into larger formal units. The Grail, Communion, and Faith motives are combined in direct rhythmic succession, forming an eight-bar thematic statement that is treated in sequence, leading to the imitative entries of the Communion theme in the chorus, to the text "Erlösung dem Erlöser [Redeemed the Redeemer]!" The formal and thematic integration of this passage symbolizes the spiritual wholeness of the redemption. Never before in the work is such integration evident in the music associated with the Grail. In the first-act prelude, by contrast, these motives are merely juxtaposed, without being directly connected to one another.

At the moment of Kundry's death Wagner recalls for the last time the chromatic semitone relation that plays such an important role throughout the drama. As Kundry sinks lifeless to earth, the music shifts upward melodically from A♭ to A♮, heard as part of an A-minor triad that is emphasized by the dynamics and orchestration. This is a rhythmically augmented form of a progression previously heard in association with the semitone in the third bar of the Communion theme. At its final appearance at the end of *Parsifal,* this semitone shift is absorbed into a larger cadential progression in A♭ major. When this cadence is reached, the visual dramatic action is at an end, and the stage curtains are slowly drawn closed. Fifteen bars of music remain, however, leading to the final cadence of the work.

In the closing bars of *Parsifal* the Grail and Communion motives are overlapped and combined to form the final cadence (see fig. 2 and ex. 13). In the first two measures of the example the first half of the Grail motive appears in its rhythmically augmented form in the highest register. This expanded form of the motive, in a similar register and orchestration, is

Figure 2. Overlap of
Motives at Conclusion of
Parsifal.

Example 13. *Parsifal*, act 3,
conclusion.

heard several times in the first Grail scene of act 1 and again in the closing
moments of act 2, where Parsifal makes the sign of the cross, banishing
Klingsor's evil magic. Whereas the tonality of these earlier appearances
of the augmented motive is C major, however, it is now heard in A♭
major, further resolving the tension of the tonal pairing.

The rest of the Grail motive is omitted in the final cadence, since its
pitches are duplicated when the Communion motive, heard on the subdominant, rises stepwise from B♭ to E♭, the fifth of the tonic triad reached
in the third-to-last bar. In its pitch level on D♭ and orchestration of trom-

bones and trumpets, this final appearance of the Communion motive exactly corresponds to its earlier appearance at the moment of entrance into the Temple of the Grail in act 1 (see ex. 9). There, as we have seen, it resolves downward by semitone to C, as C major becomes primary in the tonal pairing. Here, by contrast, the Communion motive resolves upward to E♭ in the final sonority of the work. The arrival of this final tonic chord of A♭ major thus provides the simultaneous resolution of the Grail and Communion motives, standing in place of the dissonance that has represented a primary source of musical tension from the beginning of the work, four hours earlier. In these closing bars both motives are subsumed into the final subdominant cadence, completing and perfecting the musical form as an audible symbol for the utopia of redemption. Moreover, the dramatic resolution of tensions not only takes place on a motivic and harmonic level but unfolds on the expanded time scale of Wagner's mature tonal practice. The full significance of these closing passages of resolution in *Parsifal* becomes evident only in relation to the tonal pairing of A♭ and C heard from the opening of the first-act prelude.

How can we reconcile the presence of such large-scale relations in Wagner's music and drama with Dahlhaus's claim that "Wagner renounced an architectonic foundation for music forms" or Anthony Newcomb's claim that "the essence of Wagnerian form lies in its ambiguity and incompleteness"?[36] Ambiguity and incompleteness do indeed characterize the form of limited sections or dramatic scenes in the music dramas; in these works a dramatic scene rarely provides a discrete unit of organization for the musical setting. In fact, Wagner's renunciation of an architectonic foundation for musical forms (in the plural) may be regarded as a direct corollary to his explicit identification of the musical form (in the singular) with the entire drama, as Wagner himself pointed out in his essay "On the Application of Music to the Drama" (1879): "The new type of dramatic music, in order to comprise an artwork as music, must nevertheless attain the unity of a symphonic movement. This will be achieved when it spreads itself by means of the deepest internal relations over the entire drama, not just over small, isolated, arbitrarily separated parts of the whole."[37]

This procedure is demonstrated in works such as *Tristan* and *Parsifal,* where a primary musical complex associated with central aspects of the drama undergoes a formal evolution prolonged over the entire duration of the work. Not all the music is organized in relation to this primary musical complex; episodic portions of the drama, such as the Flower Maidens' scene in *Parsifal,* for instance, are given an appropriately episodic treatment in the music. Passages constituting the primary musical complex can be heard in relation to one another, even over vast stretches of musical time, because parallels in the dramatic situation are reflected by the recall or reinterpretation of the same thematic material, reinforced by control of the tonality and orchestration. A special burden carried by this musical complex is to convey in sound the resolution of dramatic tensions at the conclusion of the work. Here it is the resolution of ambiguities and strength of formal articulation in the music that play an indispensable dramatic role.

But can it be correct that "the 'insights' generated by such [large-scale structuralist and reductive] analysis do indeed shrink Wagner into the negligible, by the very discourse of the interpretation"?[38] The error behind such attitudes is that the aesthetic ramifications of Wagner's central innovation—his equating of the music's development with the development of the entire drama—are thereby ignored and even denied. To perceive relations between parts of a Wagnerian work does not entail that we "reduce" it to only these aspects; on the contrary, any such inquiry should enable us to move out in any direction to address other features. And any suggestion that our aesthetic experience of these music dramas may be tainted by an awareness of their inner workings can be safely dismissed. Indeed, it is perhaps above all through a renewed appreciation of Wagner's dramas as "deeds of music become visible"[39] that justice can be done to the most valuable legacy of this controversial artist.

NOTES

1. The analyses of Lorenz were published as *Das Geheimnis der Form bei Richard Wagner,* 4 vols. (Berlin, 1924–33; rpt. Tutzing, H. Schneider, 1966).

2. See Anthony Newcomb, "The Birth of Music out of the Spirit of Drama," *19th-Century Music* 5, no.1 (summer 1981): 39–40 and 46 n.16.

3. Carl Dahlhaus and John Deathridge, *The New Grove Wagner* (London: Macmillan, 1984), 126. This material was first published in the *New Grove Dictionary of Music and Musicians,* ed. Stanley Sadie (London: Macmillan, 1980).

4. Dahlhaus and Deathridge, *The New Grove Wagner,* 127.

5. Carolyn Abbate, "Wagner, 'On Modulation,' and *Tristan," Cambridge Opera Journal* 1 (1989): 37.

6. Donald Francis Tovey, "The Main Stream of Music," published in *The Main Stream of Music and Other Essays,* 330–52 (London: H. Milford, 1949), 350–51.

7. The discussion of *Tristan* incorporates material that appeared in different form and in German translation in "Das 'Geheimnis der Form' in Wagners *Tristan und Isolde," Archiv für Musikwissenschaft* 40, no.3 (1983): 174–88; the *Parsifal* analysis includes material published in different form in "Wagner's *Parsifal:* Musical Form and the Drama of Redemption," *Journal of Musicology* 4, no.4 (fall 1985–86): 431–46, and 5, no.2 (spring 1987): 315–16.

8. In this instance the first note of the cello motive is not A but A♭, which is the usual form of the motive in the work as a whole.

9. In act 2, for instance, where some aspects of the orchestration are changed substantially, the prominent role of the oboe is retained. In act 1 the orchestration is retained in all essentials, as is necessary to ensure the recognition of the entire passage when it is expanded by the interpolation of new material.

10. See Robert Bailey, "The Genesis of 'Tristan und Isolde' and a Study of Wagner's Sketches and Drafts for the First Act," (Ph.D. diss., Princeton University, 1968), 88; see also Paul Bekker, *Richard Wagner: His Life in His Work,* trans. M. M. Bozman (London: Dent, 1931), 303–5.

11. Wagner sent this keyboard score with an accompanying letter to Mathilde Wesendonk on 19 December 1859. See *Letters of Richard Wagner,* ed. Wilhelm Altmann, trans. M. M. Bozman, 2 vols. (London: Dent, 1927), vol. 2, no. 451. The score was published as an insert after p. 272 in *Richard Wagner, Wesendonk Briefe* ed. Julius Kapp (Leipzig: Hesse & Becker Verlag, 1915). The full orchestral ending incorporated into the prelude was published by Breitkopf und Härtel as *Vorspiel zu Tristan und Isolde* (Leipzig). A recent discussion of the concert ending is offered by Robert Bailey in *Prelude and Transfiguration from Tristan and Isolde* (New York: Norton, 1985), 26–27.

12. See Ernst Kurth, *Romantische Harmonik und ihre Krise in Wagners "Tristan und Isolde"* (Berlin: Hesse Verlag, 1923; rpt. Hildesheim: G. Olms Verlag, 1968), 501–5.

13. Lorenz, *Geheimnis der Form,* 2:173–80. To explain the tonal plan of *Tristan,* Lorenz devised elaborate arguments purporting to show that the actual "tonic" of the whole work is E major. Yet E major appears very infrequently in *Tristan,* and the work does not sound as if it ends in the dominant. The artificiality of this scheme is only too apparent.

14. Rosen, *The Classical Style: Haydn, Mozart, Beethoven* (New York: Viking, 1971), 451–53.

15. Wagner's interest in the music of Beethoven's last creative period, and in the C♯-Minor Quartet in particular, has been discussed in an article by Amanda Glauert, "The Double Perspective in Beethoven's Opus 131," *19th-Century Music* 4, no. 2 (fall 1980): 113–20.

16. For a discussion of these tonal procedures in Chopin, see William Kinderman, "Directional Tonality in Chopin," in *Chopin Studies,* ed. Jim Samson, 59–75 (Cambridge: Cambridge University Press, 1988).

17. The dramatic significance of this formal relationship in the music has been pointed out by Joseph Kerman in his book *Opera as Drama* (New York: Knopf, 1956), 212.

18. A critical discussion of the older analytical literature is found in Lorenz, *Geheimnis der Form,* 2:194–96. For a more recent discussion, see Heinrich Poos, "Zur Tristanharmonik," in *Festschrift Ernst Pepping,* ed. Poos, 269–97 (Berlin: Verlag Merseburger, 1971), 269–73.

19. In the literature on the prelude it is a matter of some controversy whether the G♯ functions as an appoggiatura in the strict sense of the word. See William J. Mitchell, "The Tristan Prelude: Techniques and Structure," *Music Forum* 1 (1967): 174–76.

20. In his letter to Mathilde Wesendonk dated 29 October 1859, Wagner identifies the secret of his musical form as "the art of transition," citing an example from the love duet in the second act of *Tristan.* Wagner's original text is as follows: "Meine feinste und tiefste Kunst möchte ich jetzt die Kunst des Überganges nennen. . . . Das ist denn nun auch das Geheimnis meiner musikalischen Form, von der ich kühn behaupte, daß sie in solcher Übereinstimmung und jedes Detail umfassenden klaren Ausdehnung noch nie auch nur geahnt worden ist [I now wish to call my finest and deepest art the art of transition. . . . That is also the secret of my musical form, of

which I boldly claim that in its unity and clear comprehensive span embracing every detail it has never before even been envisioned]" (*Richard Wagner, Wesendonk Briefe* 262). An English translation is found in *Letters of Richard Wagner,* vol. 2, no. 442.

21. A seminal work in this tradition is "Hymns to the Night by Novalis" (Friedrich von Hardenberg), from 1800.

22. Joseph Kerman has interpreted *Tristan* as a religious drama in *Opera as Drama,* 192–216.

23. For a relevant discussion of Wagner's compositional process, see my study "Die Entstehung der 'Parsifal'-Musik" (The genesis of the music to *Parsifal*), *Archiv für Musikwissenschaft* 52, no. 1 (1995): 66–97; esp. 88–91.

24. For the reference to "Liebe [love]" in association with the Communion theme, see the programmatic commentary on the prelude sent by Wagner to Ludwig II in connection with a private performance on 12 November 1880 at Munich, reproduced in *Dokumente zur Entstehung und ersten Aufführung des Bühnenweihfestspiels Parsifal,* ed. Martin Ceck and Egon Voss, vol. 30 of *Richard Wagner Sämtliche Werke,* 31 vols. (Mainz: B. Schott's Söhne, 1970), 45. With reference to the later appearance of the Communion theme in the first Grail scene, Cosima Wagner wrote in her diary on 10 August 1877 the following: " 'Die Schmerzen Amfortas' sind darin enthalten' sagt mir R." (*Dokumente,* 24).

25. A chromatic intensification of this descending semitone is already evident in the statement of the Communion theme in C minor, where the semitone C–B is stressed twice, in different registers, and fully exploited in the expanded version of the theme at the end of the prelude, foreshadowing the lament of Amfortas.

26. See Wagner's previously cited programmatic commentary on the prelude, *Dokumente zur Entstehung,* 45.

27. "Mein Tristan des dritten Aktes mit einer undenklichen Steigerung" (*Wagner, Wesendonk Briefe,* 207).

28. "Und noch dazu hat's mit dem Parzival eine Schwierigkeit mehr. Er ist unerlässlich nötig als der ersehnte Erlöser des Amfortas: soll Amfortas aber in das wahre, ihm gebührende Licht gestellt werden, so wird er von so ungeheuer tragischem Interesse, dass es mehr als schwer wird, ein zweites Hauptinteresse gegen ihm aufkommen zu lassen, und doch musste dieses Hauptinteresse sich dem Parzival zu wenden, wenn er nicht als kalt lassender Deus ex machina eben nur schliesslich hinzutreten sollte" (ibid., 210).

29. It is interesting in this connection that an entry in Cosima's diary dated 3 June 1878 describes Kundry's motive as a "winding" or "serpentine motive of love's desire" (" 'ein Augenblick dämonischen Versenkens,' wie R. die Takte bezeichnet, welche den Kuss Kundrys begleiten, und worin das tragische, wie Gift sich schlängelnde Motiv der Liebessehnsucht vernichtend wirkt"). This passage is cited in *Richard Wagner Sämtliche Werke,* 30: 33.

30. A thorough discussion of the motivic relationships in *Parsifal* is contained in Hans-Joachim Bauer, *Wagners Parsifal: Kriterien der Kompositionstechnik* (Munich, 1977). For a recent discussion of harmonic relations in this setting of Kundry's kiss, see David Lewin, "Amfortas's Prayer to Titurel and the Role of D in *Parsifal*: The Tonal Spaces of the Drama and the Enharmonic Cb/B," *19th-Century Music* 7, no. 3 (April 1984), 348–49.

31. "Ganz in dem Zustand, in dem er Amfortas gesehen hat." (See the vocal score of *Parsifal* edited and annotated by Mottl [Frankfurt: C.F Peters, 1914, 1942], 187).

32. "Mit furchtbarem Ausdruck!" (ibid., 187).

33. See Lorenz, *Geheimnis der Form,* 4:14.

34. See ibid., 13–14. The head of the Communion theme with this new upward resolution has often been described in the literature as the Redemption motive.

35. See Tovey, "The Main Stream of Music," 350–51, where he writes that "the revolution effected by Wagner is not less important—or, as Kant would say, not less Copernican—than any previous event in musical history."

36. Newcomb, "The Birth of Music," 64.

37. "Dennoch muss die neue Form der dramatischen Musik, um wiederum als Musik ein Kunstwerk zu bilden, die Einheit des Symphoniesatzes aufweisen, und diess erreicht sie, wenn sie, im innigsten Zusammenhange mit demselben, über das ganze Drama sich erstreckt, nicht nur über einzelne kleinere, willkürlich herausgehobene Theile desselben" (*Richard Wagner, Gesammelte Schriften,* 10 vols. [Berlin: Deutsches Verlaghaus Bong, 1907], 10:185).

38. Abbate, "Wagner, 'On Modulation,' and *Tristan,*" 37.

39. Wagner's formulation, "ersichtlich gewordene Taten der Musik," appears in his 1872 essay "Über die Benennung 'Musikdrama'" (On the term "music drama"), in *Gesammelte Schriften,* 9:306.

JOHN WILLIAMSON

I t has become something of a ritual to preface scholarly work on Hugo
Wolf with a complaint as to the "conspicuous lack of analytical investigation" accorded to so major a figure.[1] Deborah Stein's recent book robs
such a complaint of some of its force, but a single study cannot dissipate
the standard picture of Wolf, which takes as its starting point the not-
insignificant relationship of music to poem that Wolf's songs raise in a
particularly intense form. Stein discusses this issue only in a brief section
at the start of her monograph, more as genuflection than debate, since it
is marginal to her essentially theoretical perspective.[2]

Wolf has been consistently judged according to a yardstick that takes
the notion of fidelity to the text as central to his creative intention—a
valid point, and one to which Wolf himself gave considerable credence.
Whether it is central to his aesthetic success is more debatable. A representative example of such an approach to Wolf is the following remark
by Jack Stein: "If one thinks of a song as an extension into musical terms
of the essence of the poem, and this is precisely how Wolf conceived
them, there are plenty of misses in his 53 Mörike songs."[3] Such a conclusion rests on rather shaky foundations. That the essence of a poem is
open to interpretation, often of a radical kind, is something that literary criticism has shown clearly (as Stein virtually concedes later when he
notes that "the most important feature of almost any lyric poem is not
likely to be its literal meaning, but rather its connotations, its ambiguities, its 'paradoxes'").[4] Even allowing that such an essence is deducible
from poetic content, it does not answer the questions begged by the
relationship between the evaluation of the text and the composition of
specifically musical inspirations: motives, extended melodies, and forms.
These may be prompted by some feature of the text, but there remains
the problem of how the musical extension of poetic content takes place.

Usually analysis reveals a relatively limited number of musical rhetorical devices that have no "absolute" equivalents in literary terms. It is on these musical devices, the imaginative use of musical parameters, that convincing extensions are usually based. The stimulus may be poetic, but the execution is for much of the time as subject to musical laws and structures as any piece of instrumental music. In a sense this casts doubt on the view that the presence of a text may affect the structural assessment of such matters as monotonality.[5] The point of the query is not to deny such an idea, however, but merely to draw a line between precompositional stimuli insofar as they bear on the overall shape or character of a song and musical events that comprise tonal structures. Musical factors in Wolf are ultimately relatable to musical logic, however much they may lean on types that are principally suitable to vocal music. There is no denying that text and music in many cases work together to guarantee aesthetic success; such cooperation is in no sense an extension of some absolute essence, however, and the choice of a feature of the poem to yield a unifying motive is in almost every case an act of interpretation defying a simple definition of "miss" in literary terms.

That such a statement of first principles should still be necessary in Wolf's case is indicative of the extent to which Wolf has been the prisoner of the literati. Even a casual inspection of the musical content of his mature songs, however, should have revealed not a composer dependent on the text for his historical stature but perhaps the most compelling harmonist of his time and place, possessed of a structural grasp of harmony adequate to dealing with the post-Wagnerian world that did not yet shade off into the more radical and (at least in part) uncontrolled experiments of his contemporaries, Mahler and Strauss. Citing an important exchange from 1890 between Emil Kauffmann and Wolf, Decsey shows that Wolf was aware of this aspect of his music. Kauffman, in an otherwise favorable piece on Wolf, had drawn attention to Wolf's perhaps most radical feature:

Harmonic asperities and liberties are used to express the highest suffering, sudden dissonances persist in unresolved tension, which must offend the hardened ears of even the most full-blooded Wagnerian, and which make an appearance where Wolf is influenced by Wagner not always in his own interest as in the "Peregrina" songs and in the darker songs, "Das verlassene Mägdlein," "Seufzer"—these are the solitary stains, which in no way detract from the overall effect, on the otherwise pure, richly shining tone pictures.

To this Wolf responded by claiming that "each of my dissonances, however sharp, is justified according to the strictest rule of harmony."[6] To provide an illustration of this, Decsey simply reproduced without com-

Example 1a. "Seufzer,"
mm. 1–2 in E minor.

ment the opening bars of "Seufzer" (ex. 1a) (although he then noted at least one other witness for the prosecution who found this opening "wahnsinnig [insane]").

One hopes that Wolf's confidence would not have been shaken by what theory has made of these admittedly daring opening bars. Theory in this context means principally Ernst Kurth. It is an indication of his fascination with "Seufzer" that he returned to it three times in his *Romantische Harmonik* (Romantic Harmony). On two of these occasions he was content to cite the song in support of his interest both in tonalities with roots a third apart and in the third of the chord as potential leading note.[7] On earlier pages, however, he devoted a much more extensive commentary to the opening bars (which he reproduced a minor third higher, as in ex. 1b, in accordance with the higher of the two printed editions).

Example 1b. "Seufzer,"
mm. 1–2 in G minor as in
Kurth.

The harmony is passing: F♯–A♭–C–E♭, an alteration of the diminished seventh of G minor; the long-held G in the upper voice is a chromatic passing note of tension before the A♭ in spite of the fact that this is itself an alteration in the chord. Initially it is still worthy of note as an expression of the aspirations of the motion, as the bass part is notated G♭ instead of F♯ in the descent. But the first bar in addition hints at another type of interpretation; in the first place, it seems as if VII of G minor would move further with the second chord to IV of G minor, whereby the bass note A♭ would be a note of tension to G. This faltering in the inner dynamics at the alteration is characteristic of high Romanticism; fundamentally it is only an intensification of the inner transformations of tension which underlie each simple enharmony; the second interpretation however is only in appearance, to such an extent does that vague hinting at another type of interpretation *belong to the nature of the phenomenon; for already by means of the external dynamics, the swelling to forte at the second chord and the diminuendo towards the end of the motive, Wolf hints that he experiences the second melody note, the G, as note of tension, which strives towards the Ab, pressed on still more intensively to the progression towards the peak by the bass note Gb (F♯) of the second bar. . . . In Wolf's song these opening bars immediately experience a repetition, the final chord thus retains its original interpretation, then after the second time it experiences a reinterpretation to D-flat minor.*[8]

In accordance with his fundamentally harmonic approach to theory, Kurth was intent on assessing the degree to which these bars are based on altered chords, with a particular eye on the phenomenon of the altered note dependent on or subordinate to another altered note. This led him to make some statements that are fairly inconsequential from a theoretical viewpoint; it is hardly necessary to view the harmony F♯–Ab–C–Eb as an altered diminished seventh. One could also quibble with his description of this sonority in the first bar as passing, since there is nothing from which it might pass. Most unconvincing of all is his interpretation of the subsequent bars as being in Db minor. One goes to Kurth not necessarily for correct specific observations, however, but rather for certain general insights peculiar to his unique theoretical orientation; he was certainly right to insist on the unity of the harmony defined by that opening bar, in spite of the motivically important interval of a fifth between Eb and Ab. He also seizes unerringly on the crucial distinction between his theoretical F♯ and the notated Gb in ex.1b, noting the "intensification of the inner transformations of tension which underlie each simple enharmony." These transformations of tension in "Seufzer" are tantamount to a structural basis for much of a song that resists simple analysis according to standard models for tonality. Before addressing the problem typified by "Seufzer," however, it is well to define what in effect is a gap in theory where Wolf is concerned.

"Seufzer" represents a small category of songs that has not been systematically treated in the Wolf literature. Since Deborah Stein's monograph is the principal theoretic treatment of Wolf, her terms help to define the gap. The phenomenon exemplified by "Seufzer" resists simple incorporation into Schenkerian monotonality in a manner similar to certain earlier phenomena noted by Harald Krebs. His objection to analysis by means of the *Ursatz* in cases where the defining tonality arrives at a late stage, and where the head note of the fundamental line is similarly delayed, also works against "Seufzer."[9] Stein's alternative, directional tonality, is a much more convenient tool in the abstract. Her examples, however, tend to dwell within a type of song where an initial tonality is supplanted by a second; both tonalities in such a scheme should and can be defined fairly closely by traditional procedures such as tonicization (even if it may be veiled). "Seufzer" defies such a categorization by moving from an area of doubtful tonality to a final resolution into E minor. It does not suffice to categorize such doubtful tonality simply as suspended tonality, although it meets the requirements of Schoenberg's general definition of the term by its heavy dependence on "vagrant chords," and Schoenberg himself noted in passing that the music of Wolf provides examples of the phenomenon.[10] The gap in theory can be defined as the absence of explanation for that species of directional tonality whereby suspended tonality clarifies itself toward a final resolution. The first condition to be observed is the lack at the outset of a tonic defined by tonicization of a scale degree, or even the lack over long stretches of a root-position triad that might be tonicized. The second is that a final tonicizing cadence does ultimately arrive, bringing with it such vestiges of an *Ursatz* as the song can muster. The fundamental structure in such cases is tantamount to a final cadence of remarkable complexity in which the traditional *Bassbrechung* is often reduced to V–I. In such cases the limitations of Schenker's picture of monotonality are obvious and rich in historical implications that Schenker himself would have been the first to realize and possibly deplore.

The basis of the suspended area is often bound up closely with the tensions noted by Kurth in enharmony, but it also involves the prolongation of a dominant area. In particular, the progression V/V–V–I is often used at a deep level to supplant the *Bassbrechung* (with the subdominant area discussed by Deborah Stein relegated to the epilogue following the vestigial *Ursatz*). Three songs in Wolf's output fall unequivocally into this theoretical gap: "Seufzer" from the Mörike book, "Herr, was trägt der Boden hier?" from the *Spanisches Liederbuch,* and the late and relatively unappreciated "Sonne der Schlummerlosen," written to one of Byron's *Hebrew Melodies* in translation. This is not to deny that other songs exhibit related characteristics. A song like "Alles endet, was entstehet," however, which might seem a worthy climax to the procedures observed in the other three, lacks concision in following the two conditions outlined previously. The last of the religious songs in the *Spanisches Liederbuch,* "Wunden trägst du, mein Geliebter," also seems to be related to the others in its dense chromaticism; on close inspection, however, it too is less concise in its channeling of its chromatic and enharmonic energies, exhibiting phenomena that expand on rather than reproduce certain areas in the three songs selected for discussion. The latter stand

out for the ruthless economy with which they follow their often tortu-
ous path to the final elucidation of their tonality. Their unity of approach
seems, at least in two cases, also to reflect religious poetry (to which the
more general affinity of "Alles endet" and "Wunden trägst du" seems
to add some corroboration). Such literary unity is a fairly vague matter,
however, as brief examination of the texts makes clear.

It is a minor curiosity that none of the poems concerned was written
in German. The poem of "Seufzer [Sighs]" is a translation of a pas-
sion hymn by Venantius Fortunatus that Mörike included in the original
Latin in his novel *Maler Nolten,* giving his translation in a footnote.[11]
Its imagery is far from rich, leading to the suspicion that the density of
Wolf's setting is in large measure an attempt to give the austere text a
significance beyond the merely verbal.

Seufzer

Dein Liebesfeuer,	*The fire of your love,*
Ach Herr! wie teuer	*oh Lord, how dearly*
Wollt' ich es hegen,	*would I tend it,*
Wollt' ich es pflegen!	*and nurse it!*
Hab's nicht geheget	*I have not tended it*
Und nicht gepfleget,	*nor nursed it,*
Bin tot im Herzen,	*I am dead at heart,*
O Höllenschmerzen!	*oh pains of hell!*

By contrast, the Spanish poem contains ample imagery, albeit of a conventional kind.

Herr, was trägt der Boden hier?

Herr, was trägt der Boden hier,	*Lord, what does the soil bear here*
Den du tränkst so bitterlich?	*which you water so bitterly?*
"Dornen, liebes Herz, für mich,	*"Thorns, dear heart, for me,*
Und für dich der Blumen Zier."	*but for you a garland of flowers."*
Ach, wo solche Bäche rinnen,	*Lord, where such streams run,*
Wird ein Garten da gedeih'n?	*will a garden grow there?*
"Ja, und wisse! Kränzelein,	*"Yes, and know this: garlands*
Gar verschiedne, flicht man drinnen."	*of many kinds are woven in it."*
O mein Herr, zu wessen Zier	*Lord, for whose ornament*
Windet man die Kränze? sprich!	*do they coil the garlands? Tell me!*
"Die von Dornen sind für mich,	*"Those of thorn are for me,*
Die von Blumen reich' ich dir."	*those of flowers I offer you."*

Neither song uses a motive that is suggested by a specific feature of the text; motives are suggested by sentiments of a more general kind. For the Mörike setting, it has been plausibly suggested that the falling fifths noticeable from the first bar onward "express the constantly renewed spiritual burden of the penitent, while the small chromatic steps in the right hand reproduce his heavy sighs." [12] Equally plausibly, the dragging rhythm that in various forms dominates the Spanish song might have been suggested by "trägt [bears]" in the first line, with its suggestion of a burden to be borne (quite apart from the other meaning of *bear* directly relevant to the first line). Such suggestions penetrate to no deep level of meaning, however, and are less interesting than the proliferation of the motives in a musical sense. The analogies between the poems and Wolf's settings are matters of structure rather than of imagery.

The Byron setting, on the other hand, has a more convincing analogy between image and motive.

> *Sonne der Schlummerlosen*
>
> *Sonne der Schlummerlosen, bleicher Stern!*
> *Wie Tränen zittern schimmerst du von Fern;*
> *Du zeigst die Nacht, doch scheuchst sie nicht zurück,*
> *Wie ähnlich bist du dem entschwundnen Glück,*
> *Dem Licht vergang'ner Tage, das fortan*
> *Nur leuchten, aber nimmer wärmen kann!*
> *Die Trauer wacht wie es durch's Dunkel wallt,*
> *Deutlich, doch fern, hell, aber o wie kalt!*

The translation by Otto Gildemeister is a somewhat free rendering of Byron's poem; Wolf adjusted it only by substituting "nur" for Gilde-meister's "noch" at the start of line 6. [13]

> *Sun of the Sleepless*
>
> *Sun of the sleepless! melancholy star!*
> *Whose tearful beam glows tremulously far,*
> *That show'st the darkness thou canst not dispel,*
> *How like art thou to joy remembered well!*
>
> *So gleams the past, the light of other days,*
> *Which shines, but warms not with its powerless rays;*
> *A night-beam Sorrow watcheth to behold,*
> *Distinct, but distant—clear—but, oh how cold!*

The syncopations, and more particularly the combination of duplet and triplet in the piano, seem to spring from "zittern [tremble]" and "schimmerst [shimmer]" in the first line; these features were the first to be discussed by Georg Bieri in his brief account of a "moon-song" that he regarded with considerable justice as unique in its genre, certainly in comparison with "moon-songs" by Schubert, Schumann, and Wolf himself.[14] But again there is an equally convincing structural analogy. It is once more symptomatic of the prevailing literary approach to Wolf that Sams should find the structural analogy yet long for something more, perhaps beyond what should be expected of the songwriter. Sams asserts that "Sonne der Schlummerlosen" and its companion piece, "Keine gleicht von allen Schönen," contain "moments of rare beauty, coinciding with the key phrases of each poem, 'ach wie kalt' [sic] at the end of the first . . . but on the whole they lack depth and penetration. They give the impression of two adjacent pictures in a gallery; a winter moonscape, and a summer seascape, of flawless academic perfection, but somehow lacking in that rich inner life which Wolf at his most characteristic never fails to convey."[15] That moment of rare beauty is in musical terms something rather more, and to appreciate its relationship to what precedes it is to grasp the musical inner life that has all too often been ignored in favor of anecdotal appreciation of the tangible moment.

In describing "Seufzer" Sams refers to its "iron musical framework for a central poetic idea," which he saw in the phrase "the pangs of hell" and noted that such a procedure anticipated the religious songs of the Spanish book particularly closely.[16] If the framework is considered from a motivic aspect, the strictest of the three is unquestionably "Herr, was trägt der Boden hier?" Perhaps that is why this song has come to seem to be the group's representative, both in the attention paid it by Stravinsky (who arranged it and "Wunden trägst du, mein Geliebter" for instrumental ensemble in 1968) and in Eric Werba's claim that "it truly aimed at a new harmonic world."[17] Its opening motive dominates the song rhythmically. Its basic form is the only figure employed in the questioning opening to the dialogue of each stanza (ex. 2a). In the responses it is modified and is used either in overlap between voice and piano (ex. 2b) or in overlapping adjacency in the piano part (ex. 2c). The motive thus never

Example 2a. "Herr, was trägt der Boden hier," m. 1.

Example 2b. "Herr, was
trägt der Boden hier,"
mm. 7–8.

Example 2c. "Herr, was
trägt der Boden hier,"
mm. 23–24.

really relaxes its grip. A strong rhythmic profile is also present in "Sonne der Schlummerlosen," although more in the duplets and triplets of the piano, primarily in the left hand and less consistently in the right. As a result, the right is free in one section to develop a characteristically floating line (one of the memories of violin lines from the mature Wagner that one regularly finds in Wolf). The harmonic implications of this line are essentially static, as C♯6 moves to B♯5 for the foreground arpeggiation of a diminished seventh (mm. 13–15), B♯5–D♯6–F♯6–A6 (with the latter resolving at the last to G♯5). The character of this passage is rather unlike anything in "Herr, was trägt der Boden hier?" and serves to disguise one feature common to all three songs, namely, linear movement in sixths.

This is most obvious in "Herr was trägt der Boden hier" as a reflection of the consistency with which the questions pursue the motive of ex. 2a. The whole of the music for the first question in the poem can be regarded as a composing-out of a seventh chord on F♯ by a linear progression through the augmented fourth A♯5–E5, a movement into an inner part. The progression is almost entirely in conventional $^6_3$ chords decorated by suspensions and neighbor notes (ex. 3). That the motion is a mixture of semitones and tones rather than simply diatonic or chromatic explains the seventh that intrudes in the second bar. This linear progression establishes the prominence of A♯, whose enharmonic equivalent B♭ figures in the crucial progression of the close. The F♯-major resource of which it is part is the goal, as triad rather than seventh, of the first stanza, with a rare tonicizing progression at the words "Blumen Zier."

If such a progression seems to counter the previously elucidated first

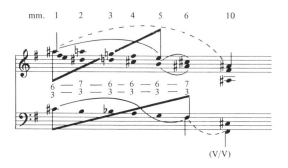

Example 3. "Herr, was trägt der Boden hier," reduction of mm. 1–10.

condition, it may still be conceded that Wolf goes out of his way to weaken the finality of the F♯-major triad as potential tonic. That the progression of mm. 1–6 prolongs a seventh chord rather than a triad is one countering force. Another is the D-minor triad at the start of the response, "Dornen, liebes Herz," especially since A4 is placed prominently at the top of the texture in both voice and piano. A tension is thus established between A and A♯; in Kurth's terms, because the A♯ is a major third over F♯ and thus possesses potential leading-note energy, it is liable to be unstable. This turns out to be the case. The A♯ remains prominent in the linear motion of the second question as the goal of the prolongation in the bass (ex. 4). The goal of the response is A4, however, this time as

Example 4. "Herr, was trägt der Boden hier," reduction of mm. 11–14.

seventh over B. Each response thus far replaces the ruthlessly channeled linear progressions with more striking ambiguities and juxtapositions.

Underlying the second response is a linear motion in the bass, D♯–E–F♯ (ex. 5); this is carefully disguised to underline the seemingly enigmatic sentiments expressed in the response. The prolongation of the E is particularly striking, with the augmented triad (over G) a notable fingerprint of Wolf's style. The goal, however, although approached hesitantly, remains consistent. The A♯ turns down to A♮, and F♯ major, once again with a seventh, yields to a seventh over B major. The A stands again at the top of the texture on the tellingly late turn to the seventh on "drin-

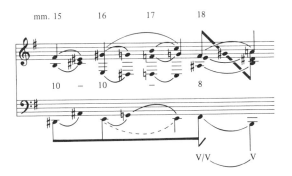

Example 5. "Herr, was trägt der Boden hier," reduction of mm. 15–18.

nen." Each of the first two stanzas thus ends with the goals previously noted as characteristic of Wolf's organizational substitute for the traditional bass arpeggiation, V/V and V in relation to E, the key of the close.

Having organized the first two questions on the basis of a chromatic linear progression, Wolf reduces the final question to a much more narcissistic hovering between first-inversion triads a third apart (ex. 6); A

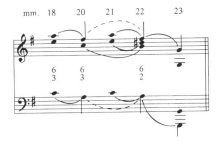

Example 6. "Herr, was trägt der Boden hier," reduction of mm. 18–23.

thus stands prominently either at the top or the bottom of the texture, and its importance is guaranteed by the manner of its resolution at the start of the final response. If the fundamental line about to be unrolled has a head note, it must be the G ($\hat{3}$) on which all parts converge in m. 23 (ex. 7). Spread across four octaves, without harmonic support, this is almost Wolf's last gesture at obfuscation in the response sections.

There remains the question of the A♯, however, which is raised bluntly by the contrary motion away from G, generating the unsupported tritone E–A♯ (which recalls the space defined in the topmost voice of the first question). By reading the A♯ as B♭, the all-important enharmony, the unsupported drift away from G is halted on the neighbor note, A4. Treated at first as part of a Neapolitan sixth, A4 is then brought back within the framework of E as the dominant seventh. This curious, tenta-

Example 7. "Herr, was trägt der Boden hier," reduction of mm. 23–27.

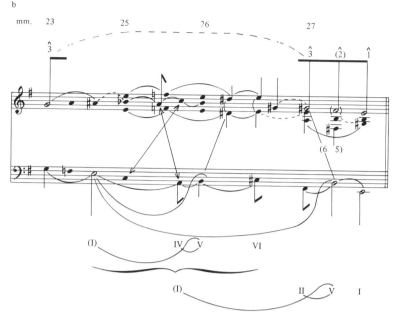

tive prolongation of a head note in itself tentative is deflected by a deceptive shift before the fundamental line is completed. Having achieved his head note, Wolf seems to lose interest in the F♯, which has been of such importance to this point as a structural focus; it is substituted in the completion of the fundamental line. The fundamental structure is thus subjected to particularly intense strain by the head note's lack of a clear statement of I in the bass arpeggiation, by the foreground A♯, and by the substitution of $\hat{2}$. To express the foreground tensions of the harmony, a Kurthian approach would latently convey, perhaps, the overriding tension between A and A♯, and the resolving enharmony of A♯ and B♭, more keenly than any notion of a governing head note.

This is not to abrogate monotonality, however, but merely to note the increasing strain of maintaining it in the era of chromatic harmony dominated by Wagner and Liszt. The motivic concentration of "Herr, was trägt der Boden hier?" becomes the opportunity for channeling the harmonic energies of chromaticism and enharmony toward a coherent structural entity. As previous comments on the central foreground arpeggiation suggest, "Sonne der Schlummerlosen" does not concentrate so intensively on a single motive, with the result that its handling of chromatic detail is looser but also richer and more allusive. It is less easy to locate an obvious chromatic tension like that of A and A♯ in the previous example. Perhaps G and G♯, B and B♯, and D and D♯ have something of the same force; ultimately, the undermining of the dominant of C♯

minor plays an important part in the final cadence. Nor does enharmony figure so prominently. Wolf instead resorts to a technique of harmonic deflection that only gradually crystallizes into the *Ursatz*. A facet of this deflection is that the initial I of the bass arpeggiation is even more strikingly absent than it is in "Herr, was trägt der Boden hier?"

"Sonne der Schlummerlosen" comprises three sections (in sharp contrast to the poem's two stanzas), each of which proceeds from the initial $\frac{6}{4}$ sonority over A in parallel to another $\frac{6}{3}$ over G. Already the parallel motion is more complex in structure (as well as being of more restricted compass) than the linear movements of the first two questions in the Spanish song. The third over the bass in both chords falls to a second on the first occasion (ex. 8a), although this fall is rendered obscure by regis-

Example 8. "Sonne der Schlummerlosen," reduction of mm. 1–16.

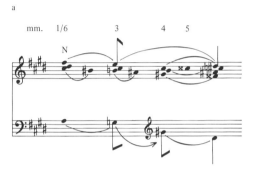

tral dislocation; in the right hand it is actually a rise of a seventh C♯5–B♯5, and in the left it is a fall of a ninth, C♯5–B♯3, although the latter is renotated as C4 to preserve the motivic character of the third, a local appearance that occurs with each return to the first $\frac{6}{3}$ in the initial position. The focus of the first progression is ultimately D♯ major, effectively V/V⁷ in relation to the final C♯ minor. The whole progression supports the first two lines. When it is repeated, "doch scheuchst sie nicht zurück" becomes the excuse for breaking the repetition (as in ex. 8b) to lead to a G-major triad. What G major stands for is of necessity obscure, given the

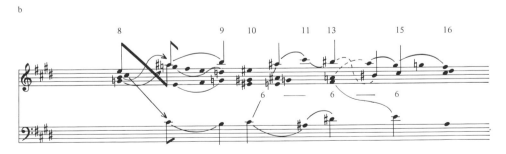

complete lack of a firm triad or tonicizing progression to this point. It feels like a substitute, in context probably for G♯ minor in first inversion. The subsequent movement of sixths that underlies the foreground arpeggiation of mm. 10–15 is directed toward a first-inversion C♯-minor triad, although this is characteristically delayed until the very end of the last bar of the progression (m. 15). That the dense chromatic foreground might be composed out of a background cycle of fifths (D♯–G♯–C♯) is plausible enough in theory, although it depends on taking a rather more meaningful view of chord inversions (a reflection perhaps of a historical reality) than Schenkerian theory traditionally permits. Such a viewpoint does not invalidate the fact that Wolf is again relying on successions of sixths, however overladen with other elements (which are necessary to realize the usual Schoenbergian vagrant chords) and that a chromatic alteration (G major for G♯ minor) is central to his deliberately ambiguous structure.

The third section proceeding from the $^6_3$ (beginning in m. 16) reproduces the start of the second as far as the G-major intrusion. From here (ex. 9), in conjunction with the text "deutlich, doch fern," everything

Example 9. "Sonne der Schlummerlosen," reduction of mm. 18–21.

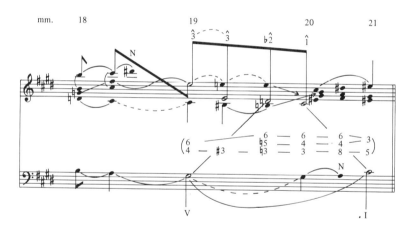

points toward the significance of "hell" as the head note of the fundamental line, which here lacks its supporting I. The $\hat{3}$ enters as E5, in the voice alone, supported by V in the piano and separated from its continuation, "aber o wie kalt," by the interval of a tenth. The G-major $^6_3$ is thus a neighbor note that moves back to the song's starting point, a $^6_3$ over A. Now A is treated as a neighbor note to the G♯, which forms V in the bass arpeggiation. Although this restatement of the initial sonority is no longer a $^6_4$ chord, the fourth above the bass, D♯6, is restored as a linear event. The lower octave doubling of this neighboring D♯6 and the multitude of covering tones are not graphed in ex.9 in order to clarify the underlying voice leading.

The unfolding of the truncated *Ursatz* is as involved as the halting motion of the song to this point seems to demand. Characteristically for his mature style, Wolf allows the sixth and fourth above V to resolve at different rates, then overshoots the tonic to land in one of his plagally biased epilogues. The agents of such an overshooting are $\hat{2}$ and $\hat{7}$, chromatically lowered from B♯ and D♯. As a result, the tonality of C♯ minor, so dimly observable through the seemingly drifting chromaticism, is postponed until the last two bars, where the *tierce de picardie* brings the final paradox: this song "in" C♯ minor contains not one single root position of the tonic triad. The final gleam of the major owes its "coldness" further to the high register in which the third of the triad stands against the long-delayed tonic in the bass.

Both "Herr, was trägt der Boden hier?" and "Sonne der Schlummerlosen" work out ideas that stem ultimately from the earlier "Seufzer." The merit of treating them before "Seufzer" is that they represent in some measure a clarification of ideas that the Mörike setting presents in a manner closer to the limit of what can be done with the traditional monotonal framework. The use of progressions in sixths, enharmony, cadences obscured by neighbor notes in both upper parts and bass, and a postlude fashioned from the prolongation of a deceptive cadence are all present with added intensity in "Seufzer." Ironically, the first two bars, those singled out by Decsey and Kurth, present a problem less in their content than in their long-term implications. They are in effect a voice exchange of a familiar kind, as illustrated in ex.10. An A would com-

Example 10. "Seufzer," voice exchange, mm.1–2.

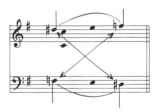

plete a German sixth of A minor, and the A is eventually supplied by the voice in the repetition of mm.1–4 at m.13. The enharmony E♭ for D♯ is what gives the song its substance, however, acting as the launching pad for the linear progression of mm.5–8, which is later expanded as mm.17–22; the song's structure is essentially two unequal musical strophes, featuring prolongation of the augmented sixth by voice exchange, linear progression, and cadence (with the voice entering only on the cadence of the first strophe). Wolf's goal is best illustrated from the second strophe. From the reading of D♯ as E♭ arises the $^6_4$ chord over A♭ from which the linear progression of $^6_4$ chords begins in each strophe. The central role of the interplay in the song between the F of the augmented sixth and the F♯ of E minor ($\hat{2}$) is illustrated by the start and conclusion of the linear progression (ex. 11). The conclusion of the progression also

Example 11. "Seufzer," reduction of mm. 17–23.

places F♯ against the D♯ associated by voice exchange with the original F. The final $^6_4$ (actually by now $^6_3$) at "(Her-)zen" in m. 22 is the neighboring chord that leads to the establishment of $\hat{3}$ (G) and I (E). The tension between F and F♯ thus acts as a structural framework in a manner familiar from "Herr, was trägt der Boden hier." The principal problem for the analyst is deducing how far this model can be applied to the first strophe.

In that strophe, the linear progression is rather differently structured and is furthermore two bars shorter than that of the second strophe. In addition, the first strophe ends with a half cadence, aiming for B major (as V). The starting point of the progression is again the $^6_4$ over A♭, but the conclusion plays tantalizingly with a variety of possibilities. Kurth would probably have seen this variety as the product of alterations that are themselves dependent on alterations. The chord highlighted in m. 8 (ex. 12a) would lead naturally to a $^6_4$ over B2 if B♭4 and D♭3 were read as A♯4 and C♯3, which is what Wolf does imply in the long run (it should be pointed out that he notated them as A♯ and C♯ in his slightly later orchestration). But D♭3 does not go to B2; it moves to C3, which supports B4 in the top part. This in turn pushes up to C5, a "resolution" that occurs as C3 in the bass falls to F♯2. The coherence of the passage at least in part depends on the fact that B♭/A♯ could equally well be supported by D♭/C♯ or C; with the latter as bass, the resource of m. 8 would be the

Italian sixth of E minor (C–E–A♯). It is tempting to see the whole of mm. 9–10 as a projection of V/V–V, with two possible alterations in the form of registrally displaced chromatic passing notes. This at least would conform with the venerable if theoretically debatable view that all augmented sixth chords are (like diminished and half-diminished sevenths in some cases) altered versions of V/V⁷ without the root in all cases save the French sixth. The progression of mm. 8–10 thus becomes a contrapuntal spinning-out of a single progression, while the individual lines generate clashes of remarkable richness and diversity at the first entry of the voice on a B that is notably awkward to pitch even by Wolf's notoriously demanding standards. The voice itself has a further layer to add to the dense foreground. Its stepwise descent from B4 to F♯4 bears a resemblance to an interrupted motion from $\hat{5}$ to $\hat{2}$ over V (ex. 12b), a suggestion of Schenkerian orthodoxy that belongs only to the foreground, however, given the weak support of G4 ($\hat{3}$) and initially of B4; the relationship of ex. 12b to 12a is of surface allusion, not genuine analytical reduction. Furthermore, the variation in the voice part in mm. 11–12 shows the real

Example 12. "Seufzer," reduction of mm. 5–12.

significance in musical terms of this highly charged entry, the restatement of D♯5 as at the opening in time for the second strophe (ex. 12c).

The interpretation that sees in mm. 8–10 an elaboration of V/V–V
finds some support in a close reading of the ascent of mm. 5–8. Although
this has been hitherto taken at face value as a linear progression of $^6_4$s, it
might equally be taken as a decorated progression of $^6_3$s. The reason is
obvious: the linear motion, in particular the independent movement of
the inner part, creates a pattern of 4–3 in each measure (ex. 13). It is the at-

Example 13. "Seufzer,"
mm. 5–6.

traction of this completely semitonal ascent that insufficient information
is presented to define exactly which notes stand in a subordinate relation.
The reading presented in ex. 14a is thus at the very least an urgent possibility, turning the whole ascent enharmonically into the prolongation of
V/V shown in ex. 14b. By analogy with this, the progression of the linear movement in the second strophe becomes V/V–V, albeit with both

Example 14. "Seufzer,"
reduction of mm. 6–9.

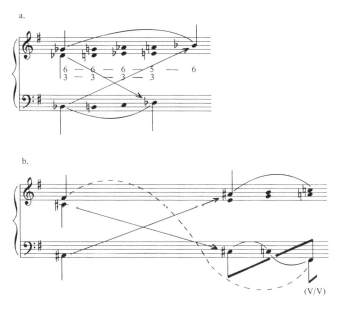

chords in inversion (again suggesting a historical reality that Schenker resolutely ignored). If the opening bars are further to be considered as an outgrowth of the dominant area of E minor, then the whole of the first twenty-two bars should be considered a fluctuation between V and V/V of greater complexity than anything in "Herr, was trägt der Boden hier?" and "Sonne der Schlummerlosen."

Example 15. "Seufzer," reduction of mm. 22–31.

This interpretation is reinforced by the intensity of the final cadence (ex. 15). Here Wolf does support $\hat{3}$ (G4) with I (E), but in a supremely

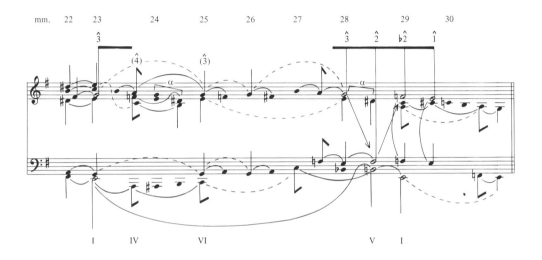

climactic moment he replaces B by the neighboring C in the piano, while introducing B4 in the voice part as neighbor note to A as the *Ursatz* moves upward to its own neighbor note. The original F is retained as part of the Neapolitan sixth used to support the neighboring $\hat{4}$. Once this expressive neighbor is left, the head note is restored over VI, while the foreground draws attention to the time-honored bearer of expressive anguish, the leading note approached from $\hat{3}$ by diminished fourth (α). The cadence is prolonged by the neighboring chord VI (whereas "Sonne der Schlummerlosen" uses a form of deceptive cadence), and $\hat{3}$–$\hat{2}$ is dwellt on in expressive suspensions, such as the diminished fourth, ancient signifiers, whose effectiveness here stems as much from the remarkable structural control displayed as from their well-known affective properties. The tension between F and F♯ persists to the end. A notable instance is the manner in which the presence of F once more threatens to move off at a tangent by means of B♭ in m. 28. The B♭, however, is interpreted as if it were A♯, the same relationship as in "Herr, was trägt der Boden hier?" although with a different context. In the completion of the *Ursatz* in the final bars, F as $\flat\hat{2}$ again supplants F♯ in the topmost part by way of the leading note (α), and the final movement in the bass is the Phrygian second adding its archaic touch to a song that uses strikingly radical means to conjure what Frank Walker called a "medieval atmosphere."[18] One can well appreciate Walker's comment that the archaic harmonies of the subsequent "Auf ein altes Bild" grew out of the closing bars of "Seufzer," although there is a profound difference between the chromatic dissonance of the latter and the diatonic dissonance of the former.

In analyzing "Seufzer," it is hard not to be impressed by the degree to which Schenker's particular picture of monotonality retains relevance. Without it, analysts would lack the pegs on which to hang such fundamental tools for their investigations as V/V and V. It might be possible to construct a picture of the areas of suspended tonality at the outset of "Seufzer" and "Sonne der Schlummerlosen" with the aid of another analytical tool, and doubtless the increasing use of Fortean methods is something that must be expected in the repertory of late-nineteenth-century chromaticism. It must be a set theory comprised with some directional principle, however, and that directional principle will presumably be latently tonal. The presence in all three songs of the vestiges of a fundamental structure in Schenkerian terms (even if for "Sonne der Schlummerlosen" only in the form that Schenker regarded as appropriate to "a true prelude"),[19] in which $\hat{2}$ is always either substituted or chromatically altered to the Phrygian second, precludes talk here of an alternative to monotonality. Rather, Wolf stands on ground that has been regarded as ripe for the abandonment of tonality itself but refuses, like most of his contemporaries, to make that step, a refusal that he shared with younger Viennese contemporaries for whom atonality and twelve-note serialism became tangible realities. Moreover, it is arguable that from a theoretical point of view, construction by third and stress on the subdominant area are potentially more destructive of monotonality than anything in the three songs considered; they undermine tonality in episodes rather than monotonality in the whole.

What Wolf offered in "Seufzer" was a method of retaining the closed world of monotonality with all its dense connections while absorbing the chromatic implications of Wagner, Liszt, and also Bruckner, yet he achieved it without any of the structural expansion that is so noticeable a feature of at least two of those three composers. The consequentiality of Wolf's harmony depends perhaps less on those famous but overemphasized texts than on the scale that they dictated, a scale within which potentially disruptive forces could be controlled and in which the capacity of Wagnerian chromaticism for modulation, highlighted by Kurth as the leading-note potential of the third, could be curbed. Within these limits, it is time to proclaim Wolf as perhaps the most complete master of harmonic tension in the abstract of his age and place, the creator of the most convincing synthesis after Wagner of chromaticism, enharmony, and where it suited him, monotonality.

NOTES

1. For example, Tim Howell, review of *Hugo Wolf's "Lieder" and Extensions of Tonality,* by Deborah J. Stein, *Music Analysis* 7, no.1 (1988): 93; some reasons for this omission were given in an unpublished paper by Amanda Glauert, "Hugo Wolf: Poet or Musician?" presented at the Conference of Nineteenth-Century Music, University of Birmingham, July 1986.

2. Deborah J. Stein, *Hugo Wolf's "Lieder" and Extensions of Tonality* (Ann Arbor: UMI, 1985), 4–5.

3. Jack Stein, "Poem and Music in Hugo Wolf's Mörike Songs," *Musical Quarterly* 53, no.1 (Jan. 1967): 22.

4. Ibid., 23.

5. See, for instance, Harald Krebs, "Alternatives to Monotonality in Early Nineteenth-Century Music," *Journal of Music Theory* 25, no.1 (spring 1981): 14. Since writing this brief theoretical discussion, I have drawn comfort from Kofi Agawu's claim that "carefully construing the purposes of a song analysis may further reveal the wisdom in the claim that there is no necessary relationship between the words and music of a song" ("Theory and Practice in the Analysis of the Nineteenth-Century *Lied,*" *Music Analysis* 11, no.1 [Mar. 1992]: 23).

6. Ernst Decsey, *Hugo Wolfs Schaffen, 1888–1891* vol.2 of *Hugo Wolf,* 3 vols. (Leipzig: Schuster and Loeffler, 1903–04), 114–15; *Briefe an Emil Kauffmann,* ed. Edmund Hellmer (Leipzig: Breitkopf und Härtel, 1903), 8; further reference to Wolf's reply can be found in Eric Sams, *The Songs of Hugo Wolf* (London: Methuen, 1961), 4–5. A recent discussion of the Wagnerian influence on Wolf's "Das verlassene Mägdlein" is offered by William Kinderman in "Zwischen Schumann und Hugo Wolf. *Das verlassene Mägdlein* von Felix Draeseke" (Between Schumann and Wolf: *The Forsaken Maiden* by Felix Draeseke), in *Draeseke und Liszt: Draesekes Liedschaffen* (Draeseke and Liszt: Draeseke's Songs), ed. Helga Lühning and Helmut Loos, 205–17, Veröffentlichungen der Internationalen Draeseke-Gesellschaft, vol.2 (Bad Honnef: Gudrun Schröder Verlag, 1988), 208–9.

7. Ernst Kurth, *Romantische Harmonik und ihre Krise in Wagners "Tristan,"* 3d ed. (Berlin: Max Hesses Verlag, 1923), 226–67 and 520.

8. Ibid., 197–99.

9. Krebs, "Alternatives to Monotonality," 9.

10. Arnold Schoenberg, *Theory of Harmony,* trans. Roy E. Carter (London: Faber, 1978), 384.

11. Eduard Mörike, *Maler Nolten: Bearbeitung,* ed. Herbert Meyer, vol.4 of *Werke und Briefe,* ed. Hans-Henrik Krummach, Herbert Meyer, and Bernhard Zeller, 13 vols. (Stuttgart: Ernst Klett Verlag, 1966–68), 369. Mörike left his translation of "Seufzer" in at least two versions; it is arguable that the principal variant, which substitutes "War Eis im Herzen [there was ice in the heart]" for "Bin tot im Herzen [I'm dead at heart]," makes a more striking effect by balancing the images of fire and ice (Mörike, *Werke und Briefe,* 3:400–401, 5:236–38).

12. Anton Tausche, *Hugo Wolfs Mörikelieder in Dichtung, Musik und Vortrag* (Vienna: Amandus-Edition, 1947), 93.

13. Byron, *Lord Byrons Werke,* 6 vols., trans. Otto Gildemeister, 4th ed. (Berlin: Georg Reimer, 1888), 3:145.

14. Georg Bieri, "Hugo Wolfs Lieder nach verschiedenen Dichtern," *Schweizerische Musikzeitung* 75, no.11 (1 June 1935): 402–3.

15. Sams, *The Songs of Hugo Wolf,* 258.

16. Ibid., 63.

17. Erik Werba, "Hugo Wolfs Liedschaffen aus der Sicht von Heute," *Österreichische Musikzeitschrift* 33, no.2 (Feb. 1978): 62.

18. Frank Walker, *Hugo Wolf: A Biography,* rev. ed. (London: Dent, 1968), 233; I want to thank Christopher Lewis for a very pertinent question that led me to rethink my reading of this final cadence.

19. Heinrich Schenker, *Free Composition,* trans. and ed. Ernst Oster (New York: Longman, 1979), 89; Schenker is here discussing Chopin's Prelude op.28, no.2, as an example of an incomplete fundamental structure (V–I). This passage is one obvious starting point for Robert P. Morgan's article "Dissonant Prolongations: Theoretical and Compositional Precedents" (*Journal of Music Theory* 20, no.1 [spring 1976]: 49–91). Although none of Morgan's examples is especially similar to the tonal strategies of the three Wolf songs considered here, I must acknowledge the general relevance of his arguments to my approach. In particular his concern with the manner of the prolongation seemed important enough to justify copying his title.

Tonal Dualism in Bruckner's Eighth Symphony

WILLIAM E. BENJAMIN

Whatever the tonal complexities of Anton Bruckner's Eighth Symphony, it is not beyond question that these pose genuine alternatives to monotonality. One can of course describe the first themes of both the first and last movements as tonally deviating,[1] but neither movement puts into doubt the status of C as initial tonic, except by way of beginning with an upbeat segment (very short in the first, long in the last, and striking in both) of secondary function that resolves to C; in addition, neither departs from a modulational path that is more or less conventional in its broad outlines, even if filled with ingenious elaborations, and that strongly implies C as terminal tonic.

On the face of it, then, this might seem to be an instance of anacrusic secondary tonalities, like the B♭ minor of Chopin's second scherzo or, perhaps more relevant to Bruckner, the implied A at the start of Beethoven's Ninth Symphony. Impressive and historically important as these instances undoubtedly are, they are in a way theoretically unproblematic, even if analytically engaging; that is, they suggest not radical revision in explanatory approach but only special attention to the way in which the unusual openings condition the harmonic and rhythmic-gestural plans of the main bodies of these movements.[2]

It is also open to question whether directional tonality[3] itself poses a significant challenge to monotonality, since in most works where it is manifestly pertinent—acts in Wagner's mature operas, movements of Mahler's symphonies, and so on—directional tonality may have more to do with the music's total semiotic context, and specifically with its symbolic functions, than with its status as formal object engendering experiences of tonal coherence. Indeed, one can argue convincingly that, with the great expansion in the scale of ambitious musical discourse over the course of the nineteenth century, global harmony loses its identity as primary structure in many larger movements, including many that are overtly monotonal. In other words, without saying that thematic transformation replaces harmonic structure as the primary agent of co-herence, one might speak of the thematicization of harmony, that is, of harmony becoming part of the color of a theme and of harmonic relations being brought into play to reinforce networks of themes in their transformational interrelations. The thematicization of harmony in turn implies that the field of large-scale structure is partially vacated, left open to new shaping forces, and helps to explain the progressive shift in the second half of the century from a preoccupation with structures defined in terms of a conventional syntax (of harmony, meter, and phrase structure) to one with structures whose dimensions are natural, continuous, and scaled by intensity (dynamics, density, and aspects of timbre).[4]

As a consequence of this shift, the listener can intellectually construct the apparent monotonality of many late-romantic works but perhaps not experience it as such. In more specific terms, the fact of beginning and ending in the same key may lead to an experience only of *return to,* and not of the *motion within* or *prolongation of* that, properly speaking, constitutes monotonality. What this means, in effect, is that for a large corpus of works by Wagner, Mahler, Strauss, and others, beginning and ending in different places may be aurally equivalent to beginning and ending in the same place. If so, the two would be variants of one type, consisting in a modulational-thematic trajectory with plotlike connotations. They would differ in semantic value, that is, in terms of the specific stories for which they might be used, but not as structural types, since in each case unity would be experienced in terms of shapes of varying intensity and not in terms of key or chord.

Even allowing for some overstatement of them, these considerations encourage the previously made supposition, that large-scale late-romantic directional tonality is more a problem in the endlessly fascinating topic of late-nineteenth-century musical semantics than an issue for music theory in its traditional role of exploring and anchoring the experience of tonal coherence. If valid, such a view would reorient the search for alternatives to monotonality toward other expressions of tonal dualism in the music of the period as bearing perhaps more crucially on both listening and compositional technique.

I explore three categories of tonal dualism in this chapter. All have been subject to prior investigation, although not, as far as I know, with regard to their interaction and cogenerative role within a single context. The first is the concept of mixture, extended beyond the standard major/minor type to include a variety of interweavings of pairs of modes with a single tonic, as treated in a well-known study by John Vincent.[5] Examples of this first category are the mixture of major and Phrygian—each being the other's intervallic inversion—and of Phrygian with a "synthetic" scale, as in the pairing at the start of Liszt's B-Minor Sonata. The second category consists in an opposition of harmonic systems around a single tonic, for example, the opposition of harmony controlled by the V to that controlled by the IV, as discussed by Deborah Stein in her work on Hugo Wolf.[6]

Both of these categories depart from what might be called standard tonality, and not insignificantly, but they do not necessarily challenge the principle of tonal monopoly, whereby at every level of the music's hierarchical structure, each point in the music's time affiliates to one and only one harmony, and each harmony to only one tonic.[7] This is not the case with the third category, however, which covers what might be viewed as expressions of dual or multiple prolongation within sections of a work. These involve the occupation of a time span (at some level) by two or more underlying harmonies, affiliated to different tonics by virtue of distinct webs of voice leading through which they are expressed.[8]

Bruckner's Eighth Symphony, composed between 1884 and 1890, is deeply rooted in exactly these three dualisms, the interrelated use of which generates its very tight repertoire of motives, linear patterns, and chord progressions and contributes powerfully to the determination of its special range of moods and meanings, which have been the subject of much previous commentary. All three are well illustrated in the opening theme from the Finale, surely one of the most terrifying visions ever depicted in the realm of tones. Ernst Kurth, whose voluminous monograph remains an unsurpassed monument of insightful criticism of the composer, notes the affective dualism of this music, the way it begins in Bruckner's most turbulent and frightening vein, only to etherealize into an atmosphere of "religious solemnity."[9] Nevertheless, Kurth's analysis of the harmony, which is fragmentary here, does not show how it constitutes an extremely clear expression of this affective progression.

The music is presented in ex. 1, a piano reduction overlaid with analytical commentary. It begins with two upbeat measures that introduce the wild accompaniment figure of repeated quarter notes with grace notes. There follows a phrase of five double measures, extended to seven through the lengthening of the fanfare in the fifth double measure (mm. 11 and 12 of the score). The harmony of this passage consists of a progression from an F♯, presumably the root of an F♯-major triad, to a D♭ triad, that is, a root motion equivalent to a perfect fifth up or perfect fourth down. But which is it? Are we dealing here with a progression

Example 1. Sketch of final
movement, opening theme.

C minor: (III)   IV   ♭II   V♮   I

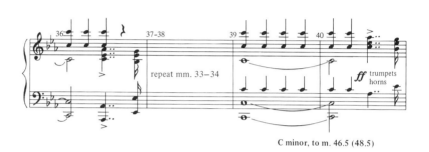

C minor, to m. 46.5 (48.5)

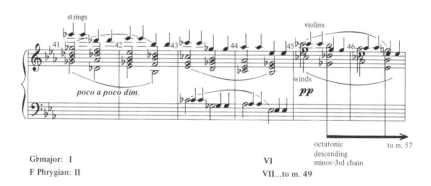

G♭ major: I   VI
F Phrygian: II   VII...to m. 49

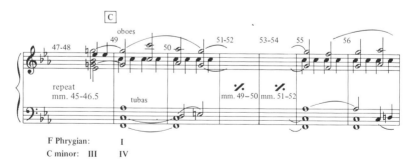

F Phrygian: I
C minor: III   IV

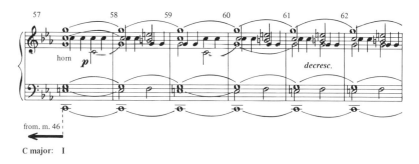

toward a dominant, hence of the I–V type, or one *from* a subdominant, and therefore of the IV–I type?

A number of factors support provisional adoption of the I–V hypothesis. The phrase is patently one of intensification, reaching a climax on the D♭ chord (m. 11), and may thus be heard to interpret the abstract intensification represented by the syntactic shift away from a tonic. Less tenuous, for those who reject the tension metaphor for harmonic progression, are considerations of rhythm and voice leading: the return of the opening F♯ as the root of a G♭ chord in m. 9 implies a prolongation of that tone that more easily fits the status of I than that of IV, and the rising stepwise motions in all upper voices between the chord at m. 9 and that at m. 11 are more readily heard as realizing an opening gambit from I to V than they are as executing some sort of plagal cadence.

These points are contradicted by one that is theoretically deeper and that takes us beyond the confines of the first phrase. If we believe the phrase to embody a I–V motion, we are thinking of the D♭ chord that begins in mm. 9–10 as hierarchically inferior to the F♯/G♭ chord that initiates the phrase; if we take it as a IV–I motion, the D♭ chord becomes hierarchically superior (as a tonic chord). Therefore, the two chords will yield opposite results if we make a reduction of the phrase to only one harmony. We will choose the tonic chord in either case, that is, the F♯/G♭ chord if we think I–V and the D♭ chord if we think IV–I.

As I observed, looking to the passage as a whole and considering what happens when we regard the first phrase as I–V, we are left with an F♯ chord in the first phrase and an A♭ chord in the second phrase (at rehearsal letter A), this being an exact transposition of the first up a tone. In the third phrase (at B), which is harmonically conventional and begins and ends with its tonic chord, we are obviously left with a C-minor triad. Putting the three together, we get the succession F♯ major–A♭ major–C minor, in which the chords sit side by side, as it were, without achieving a tonal accommodation or implying a continuation that would establish their tonal meaning. If we neglect primary evidence and choose the IV–I interpretation, however, we get the succession D♭ major–E♭ major–C minor, a strong pattern in which the final chord acts as a modal tonic by melodically assimilating the first, which in turn governs the second as model. In other words, we are able to sense an underlying ♭II–I motion, elaborated by sequence to include a medial III.

The meaning of this pattern is further clarified through consideration of the fourth phrase, which begins at m. 41. This concludes the theme and is the longest of all so far, encompassing fourteen double measures. The first part of this phrase is a little obscure, although it can be seen that its first measure (m. 41) presents in microcosm the progression underlying the whole first phrase (G♭ to D♭, and its fourth measure (m. 44) relates in the same way to the second phrase. The second part of the phrase (at letter C), however, is transparently a plagal cadence to a C-major chord. If we now omit the third phrase with its conventional cadence, we see an overall pattern of plagal motions that moves convincingly to the global tonic: F♯/G♭ to D♭, A♭ to E♭, F to C. The principal voice emerging from this takes the main elements in the first two phrases, the D♭ and E♭, and joins them to the complete plagal cadence of the last phrase, thus: D♭, E♭, F, C. In effect, phrase four retraces the quasi-Phrygian close adumbrated in phrase three, but it does so more elaborately and in a manner more consistent with the plagal progressions of the first two phrases (see ex. 2).

I have implicitly been discussing two types of dualism: the question of coexisting tonal fields and that of competing harmonic systems. Of

Example 2. Large-scale harmonic structure in the opening theme of the final movement.

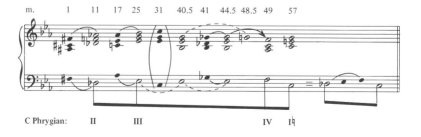

course, these are intimately connected, since the question as to whether the progressions of the first two phrases are plagal or half cadential is really a decision as to local key. If the first phrase is plagal, it sounds as if it is in D♭; if half cadential, as if it is in G♭. In my view, to listen sensitively to this passage is to keep these possibilities in the balance until the fourth phrase, where the plagal interpretation is confirmed, and this means experimenting within phrase one (and two) with various rhythms of shift between projected tonics and thereby coming to hear some variable time span within this phrase as a zone of hierarchical indeterminacy or prolongational overlap.

I have also touched on the third dualism, that of mixture. What is the passage as a whole, if not a gigantic Phrygian cadence that starts on D♭, the leading tone and hence the point of maximal melodic tension; prolongs it through the upward melodic third, F, reached through the passing tone E♭; and relaxes into the cadential C? Now we see where Kurth's metaphor of wildness evaporating into limpid spirituality takes root. In addition, the purpose of the conventional chordal syntax of phrase three becomes clear: to change the passage's environment at the phrase level from one of tonal indeterminacy to one of sharp tonal focus, all within a larger determined structure that is modal and plagal. This change is appreciable when the previously described triad succession underlying phrase two is compared with its diminutions scattered throughout phrases three and four (in mm. 32, 36, 40, 46, and 48): the latter are univalently perceived as plagal progressions to the III of C minor and thus in contrast to their preceding middleground model. Unusually, then, mixture operates in this passage not between passages at the same level but across the levels, with a large-scale Phrygian pattern governing a progression in which two chromatic and tonally indeterminate phrases are succeeded by two diatonic phrases in minor (or minor-major mixture, if the chord at mm. 57–65 is taken into account).

Finally, the idea of Phrygian/minor mixture provides an opening into the first part of phrase four. On the face of it this is in G♭ major, harmonizing that scale with a series of plagal progressions. However, the G♭ triad, although locally the tonic here, is never cadentially stabilized. Instead, the segment may be heard as progressing from the G♭ chord at m. 41 to the E♭-minor chord at m. 44.5, the latter an alternative harmonizer of the prolonged melodic G♭. This progression is a Phrygian way of approaching F as a tonic, and the F-minor chord at m. 49 may be heard as such. This chord's link back to mm. 41–44 is supported by the way in which the progressions in mm. 32 and 36, both of which lead directly to F-minor chords, are recalled by the similar progression in mm. 44, which thereby seems to call forth an F-minor chord in turn, the difference being that the use of an E♭-*minor* triad in m. 44 gives the F-minor triad in m. 49 a Phrygian tonic cast.

It may be objected that the G♭ in m. 44 is "rectified" in mm. 46 and 48 by the restoration of a G♮, which is then extended through mm. 49–55 as a suspension. As I hear them, however, mm. 45–48 do not destroy the strong Phrygian effect produced by connecting the content of mm. 41–44 to that of mm. 49–67. Instead, I hear the content on the more local F (Phrygian) level as cutting across that on a more global C (minor) level, the span of which is the whole of phrases three and four. In this way, both G♭ and G♮ are heard as ways of getting to F, the former having to do with the immediate context, which is interrupted by a shift to the larger context, to which the latter is relevant. In effect, the novelty in the composition of structures is a rhythmic one, because local structures are allowed to cut across global ones. I return later to this aspect of rhythmic originality in Bruckner.

A possibly more serious objection to the notion of F as a Phrygian tonic at m. 49 rests on the nonequivalence of the G♭-major collection in mm. 41–44 with a Phrygian collection on F, with the former including C♭, and the latter, C. To counter this it need only be pointed out that the previously outlined Phrygian conception rests on a reduction of the content of mm. 41–45 to its first and last chords, neither of which contains C or C♭. Therefore, mm. 41–45 are Phrygian (in F) at one level and major (in G♭) at a more immediate level, in just the way that mm. 1–30 initiate a Phrygian progression (in C) at the level of the passage as a whole while expressing indeterminacy with respect to the circle of fifths when considered on their own.

I have written at such length on this theme because it is so magnificent an example of Bruckner's art and because it instantiates, in complex interaction, all the issues I wish to discuss. The remainder of this chapter divides into three parts: first, a careful look at the opening measures of the first movement; second, an overview of key structure in the first movement as a whole; and finally, some critical remarks of a general nature about the composer. I do not touch on the middle movements, except to say that the Scherzo is totally based on plagal and, to a lesser extent, Phrygian relations and evinces the same manner of dualism of (local) key center that I have been discussing, and that the Adagio, wonderful as it is, is on the whole more conventional in terms of the concepts advanced here.

MOVEMENT 1: THE OPENING MEASURES

I turn now to the first movement, with its mysterious, recondite, even risky opening, clearly influenced by the start of Beethoven's Ninth.[10]

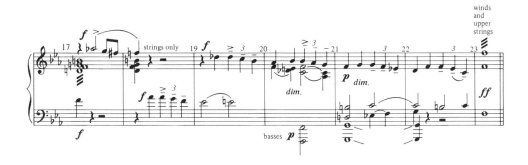

Example 3. Piano reduction of the first movement, opening theme, antecedent.

This is reproduced in piano reduction as ex. 3. Several English-speaking commentators read mm. 1–4, rather superficially, as being in B♭ minor and have the music switching inexplicably to C minor in m. 5.[11] Some German-language sources, however, present a more coherent picture. Kurth places mm. 1–4 in C, but on the subdominant, and has mm. 5–6 resolving this subdominant to a fleeting tonic and passing on to a weakly asserted dominant expressed in the clarinet motive that prefigures, in rhythm, the chromatic motives of mm. 9–10, 13–14, and 17–18. He understands the A♭-minor triad in m. 9 as reverting suddenly, after the clarifying tonic in mm. 7–8, to a dark subdominant region. Although Kurth does not offer a complete monotonal analysis of mm. 1–22, he makes it clear that he hears the chords of mm. 9–16 as determined by the chromatic rise from the G4 at m. 8 to the B4 at m. 17 and as leading to the dominant seventh that harmonizes that B4, with mm. 19–22 providing the half cadence of an antecedent phrase.[12]

Such analysis in terms of the opposing regions of a single tonic has some merit, but it makes the music sound unproblematic by glossing over and suppressing contradictory evidence. Haas, for example, agrees with Kurth that the opening harmony of the movement is a IV, but he reveals his dilemma by saying that this anomaly is rectified at the start of the recapitulation, where he hears the theme in the oboe (at mm. 282–85) as representing I.[13] Unfortunately, the oboe statement is a tone higher than that in the low strings in mm. 2–5 and therefore ought to represent V. Alternatively, if the theme in the recapitulation represents I, the theme at the start must also represent I, but now in B♭ minor, and this puts us back to that other, less coherent reading of the opening. In effect, the problem with maintaining that the music opens with a subdominant is that the first figure sounds so much more like a dominant.

The first step toward a more adequate reading lies in trying to fill out the harmonic texture implied in attributions of harmonic function to various spans of music. In other words, if there really are subdominants and dominants in this music, it should be possible to add missing chord members to the skeletal outline provided by the composer. I have attempted to do just this in ex. 4. The harmonic analysis underneath the example may appear traditional, but a close look at the "pivotal" harmonic areas, enclosed in boxes, will indicate otherwise: in the case of both modulations, from F to C and from C to G, a progression involving the I and V of an initial key is reinterpreted as one involving the I and IV of a succeeding key.[14] Instead of preparing for and introducing a modulating dominant, the pivotal segments avoid such a dominant entirely. Also nontraditional is the use, in each successive key, of a modal (Phrygian) ♭II. The parallels with the opening of the last movement are clear and striking.

A description in terms of a series of rapid modulations, however unconventional in structure, only serves to demonstrate how much this theme sounds like material from a development section—a quality it shares with the themes of many late-nineteenth-century composers but that still fails to capture the theme in its particularity. To grasp the latter is to question whether there is a higher-level prolongational structure by means of which mm. 1–22 can be reduced to a simple progression in C. By reverting to a traditional cadence preparation in mm. 19–22, the music signals the primacy of C, but it does not follow that this reversion establishes hierarchical determinacy in the preceding music. Of course, it is possible to claim that mm. 1–8 prolong I and mm. 9–18 do the same

Example 4. First movement, opening measures, with inner voices added to clarify harmonic implications.

for V, as the previous analysis implies, but little in the music substantiates this. One must reckon with the fact that C harmonies are presented only in mm. 5 and 7, whereas an F harmony occupies mm. 1–4. Initial placement, length, and the ambiguity of the C major's point of initiation (whether in m. 5 or m. 7) seem to favor F as the basic harmony of these measures. But now a strange circumstance rears its head: a convincing result is obtained if F is literally prolonged as a pedal in mm. 1–8, but this result has the paradoxical consequence of making the F harmony resume the role of V and points to B♭ as tonic. This suggests a different kind of synthesis of the passage, as a IV–V progression in C, with the IV expanded as the V of B♭. Here, however, we are in the grip of a rhythmic indeterminacy, since it is impossible to say at what point in the music the IV progresses to the V: the F pedal can be sustained convincingly through mm. 5–14, whereas the prolongation of a G harmony may be located as early as m. 5. The chord at m. 9 emerges uncannily as a reproduction of the Tristan chord if one respells it as B–D♯–G♯ and imagines F sustained below it. This can be heard as an altered V in C or as a chromatic variant of V in B♭ (or IV in C).[15] Example 5 is an attempt to capture this striking complexity. Note in particular the way that slurs in this example overlap, showing spans in which two harmonies are

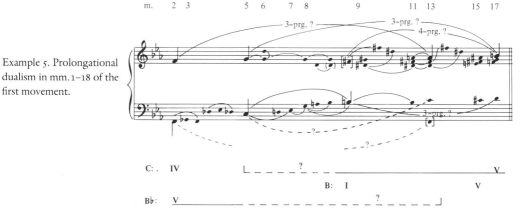

Example 5. Prolongational dualism in mm. 1–18 of the first movement.

simultaneously prolonged and violating the conditions for a strict prolongational hierarchy. In effect, we have in this passage an example of music in which there is a lengthy span—mm. 5–14, the region of overlapping slurs—that cannot be reduced to a single harmony, or said to affiliate to a single tonic at every level, without falsifying its meaning.

TONAL ORGANIZATION IN MOVEMENT 1

An important aspect of Bruckner's style is its discontinuous, or nonlinear, presentation of secondary tonalities.[16] In more conventional styles a secondary tonality will occupy a continuous span, large or small, typically coinciding with a thematic segment or, more locally, with a subthematic extension or interpolation. In Bruckner, however, it is also common for secondary keys to be presented in discontinuous fragments, interrupting an equally discontinuous represention of the primary tonality asserted as primary largely by way of somewhat greater overall length, stability of expression, motivic density, and the like. An example is provided by the antecedent phrase complex of the second theme in the first movement, mm. 51–72. The primary key is clearly G major, evident in the opening four measures and in the terminal half cadence. G♭ major, C major, and A$_{\text{minor}}^{\text{major}}$ function as secondary keys, but instead of occupying continuous segments within the complex, they are applied to noncontiguous and motivically divergent blocks, giving the music a nonlinear, modular aspect. So, for example, G♭ major is applied to mm. 55–58 and 63–64, whereas mm. 59–60 and 67–68 are in C and mm. 61–62 and 65–66 are in A.

It can be objected, of course, that recurring key networks are accidental in tonal music, in the sense that they are by-products of prolongation. Indeed, a smoothly prolongational analysis can always be constructed that will make these networks disappear, or at least greatly lessen their apparent significance. One analytical strategy might be to refer this G-major theme, and many others like it, to the model of classical development sections: key would be displaced by chord as the starting point of structure, and the theme would no longer be seen as being in a certain key but as prolonging some chord of the key of the whole movement. In my view, however, precisely the opposite view is warranted: the theme does sit in a key but does not have the sound of prolonging any chord in a continuous way. What this implies, then, is a theory of *tonal space in terms of keys* that will generate descriptions of underlying keys emerging, in particular contexts, from discontinuous networks of surface keys. Such a theory would correspond to the sense of large-scale tonal structure articulated, at the start of this chapter, as being appropriate to many longer works of the late romantic period, in the sense that it could account for monotonal and "tonally deviating" movements in the same terms, namely, as differing productions resulting from differing orders of and balances among foreground keys. A theory based on chord prolongation, on the other hand, has to view the two categories as essentially distinct.

I am not ready to present a theory of this kind, but ex. 6 attempts a description of how the first movement as a whole may be heard to trace a succession of keys in which discontinuous relationships are significant and some keys emerge as more important than others. This sketch is not a finished product but merely an attempt to capture aspects of a certain kind of synthesis without imposing on the music a degree or type of (prolongational) unity that it does not easily support. It is important to understand that the sketch is not a reduction of the music's bass line; it is, rather, a representation of the tonics that emerge as the music is heard in time. Some of these tonics are only implied and do not appear as chord roots in any voice. Three types of notes are used—filled but stemless, filled with stems, and open with stems—to indicate in the usual way degrees of stability or importance. Two types of slurs appear: dotted slurs connect two representations of the same key separated by music in other keys, that is, where there is no continuous sense of a single key; solid slurs indicate the prolongation of a particular key (*not* of a chord) through other, more foreground keys. Solid slurs and dotted slurs overlap in many configurations, and as was implied in earlier comments on the opening measures, solid slurs may overlap as well. Occasionally a solid slur emanates from a note without connecting to another, indicating a prolonged key that does not return at the foreground.

Three further symbols used in the sketch require explanation. An aster-

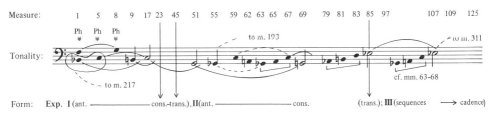

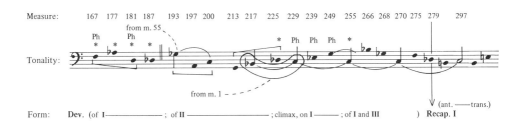

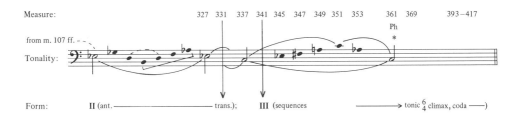

Example 6. A tonality sketch of the first movement.

isk over a note indicates a key that is established without stating its dominant chord, normally through a plagal approach to the tonic chord. In some of these cases the dominant chord does appear, but only after the key is established. The symbol "Ph" over a note indicates a pronounced Phrygian coloring to the key. Finally, the single vertical double slash (preceding m. 193) indicates a textural/rhythmic caesura in the music.

I now review the sketch by means of a verbal summary. As it touches on the first theme, this commentary largely encapsulates the detailed remarks already made.

The first theme contains an antecedent and a consequent. The antecedent begins with keys rising by fifths: F, C, G, all of Phrygian cast and all established without dominant preparation. These keys overlap in time. The key of C returns in m. 17 and may be regarded as prolonged throughout mm. 1–17. An implication of B♭ also underlies mm. 1–11, if the opening F is mentally retained during these measures as a bass pedal. This key may be heard as picked up again in m. 217, in the middle of the development, where there is an imposing pedal on F as a dominant. Beginning in m. 9 there is a strong current of B major, which overlaps slightly with the reassertion of C, at m. 17, by means of the latter's dominant chord (see ex. 5 and note 16). This B major provides the first instance of an important relationship, that between keys a half step apart, with one arising in the elaboration of the other.

Although the consequent of the first theme begins similarly to the antecedent, small changes, together with the strong C ending of the antecedent, work to place it in an unambiguous C tonality. The consequent cadences at a point of key elision, a half-cadential V doubling as the initial I in G major.

The second theme, in G, is organized in turn as an antecedent followed by a consequent. The antecedent introduces local (discontinuous) key networking, with Gb represented in mm. 55–58 and 63–64, and C in mm. 59–60 and 67–68. The half-step relationship between the underlying G and the more local Gb is motivic, reflecting the C/B duality in mm. 9–18, for example. Also pervasive is the chaining of keys by minor thirds (Gb, A, C in the antecedent). The consequent introduces a different chain of keys related by minor thirds (Ab, B, D).

The third theme, the tonal preparation for which begins at m. 85, is in Eb, prolonged through m. 166 by means of a greatly extended cadence. At mm. 101–7 there is yet another chain of minor-third-related keys, repeating the pattern at mm. 63–69.

The development section begins at m. 167 with a most interesting series of progressions that tonicizes, in order, F, Ab, D, and Db. Note that the first three of these lie in a minor-third chain and the last two are related through a half step; the series as a whole thus conforms to established patterns. Interestingly, none of these tonics is prepared by a dominant, and the first and third are strongly Phrygian. The caesura preceding m. 193 prevents one from hearing the Db tonic as the dominant of the succeeding Gb tonic. The latter is more convincingly networked to Gb at m. 55, with which it has the strongest motivic (second-theme) affinities.

The development of second-theme materials pursues the minor-third-related-keys motive, progressing from Gb to C through A. What amounts to a false retransition begins at the arrival in C, on the V pedal in m. 200. This has the most interesting shape, since the key of C is virtually swallowed up by that of Bb, also represented by a V pedal, at m. 217. This Bb is followed by a Phrygian C at m. 229, coinciding with the augmentation of the movement's principal motive in the bass at m. 225, where the development climaxes.[17] The pairing of these two keys relates back strongly to the opening measures, taking apart and clarifying the extremely compact relationships in those measures.

I will not burden the reader by pursuing this verbal review to the very end of the sketch. Suffice it to say that the concepts introduced thus far should prove adequate to the task of understanding the sketch and, therefore, to interpreting the music in its terms.

TOWARD A REEVALUATION OF THE COMPOSER

The technical discussion just concluded strongly suggests, as a point of departure for remarks of a more critical nature, a question regarding the peculiar history of the music's reception. It reveals a composer extremely forward-looking in many respects; so much so, in fact, that one is bidden to ask whether the negative reaction to Bruckner by many musicians involved in the modernist movement in the first sixty years of the century represented an unconscious suppression of their origins. One has only to think of his pioneering simulations of space and distance, of his disjunctive approach to continuity, of his neomodalism and general broadening of the harmonic language of tonality, of his imaginative use of octatonic patterns,[18] and of his experiments in tonal bivalence at pitch-class intervals 1 and 5, which lead directly to the languages of atonal Schoenberg[19] and neoclassical Stravinsky.[20] It is hard to think of any other composer who, notwithstanding an obsessive reliance on a limited class of musical textures, invented so much that proved to be of value to succeeding generations, whether they acknowledge the debt or not.

Undoubtedly it is Bruckner's massive inflation of sonata structures that irked the modernists of the years after World War I, concerned as they were with economy of statement and instrumental resource—that and the political considerations that might have some relevance to the evaluation of Wagner or Strauss but are so irrelevant to the personality or the music of Bruckner as to be not worth the least comment. The view persists, however, although it is less widely held than before, that Bruckner was an awkward, unfinished composer who relied on pretentious length and bombast to mask a paucity of ideas and a lack of feeling for structure.[21]

It is often claimed that particular materials imply a rate of unfolding, and thus a time scale, that is appropriate to them; in other words, length is, or ought to be, a function of thematic material. Indeed, we have all reacted to works as being "too long." A theoretical basis for such claims and intuitions is not easy to formulate, however, but it is important to attempt to do so, in the case of Bruckner, because the property of length has functioned as the main barrier to comprehension of his music and as a principal target of facile criticism.

Most tonal music, ranging from early classicism to the music of

Strauss, is based on a middleground progression of harmonies that moves at a highly differentiated rate. In other words, the middleground is composed of very long and very short chords, as well as chords of medium length. Moreover, structural importance is not correlated with length in this music, at least in any consistent way; shorter chords are often more important structurally than longer ones. Typically, of course, the chords of the middleground—*Stufen,* or scale steps—are not presented as such but are diminuted, generating a surface chord pattern. Since the longer scale steps are normally more intensively diminuted than the shorter ones (i.e., broken into more surface chords), the harmonic rhythm at the surface tends to smooth out the bumpy ride characteristic of the middleground itself.

Conventional tonal music can afford to base itself on middlegrounds in which the lengths of chords are markedly different—for example, a chord occupying fifteen measures followed by one occupying only one measure—because the structure is simple and unambiguous enough to remain clear even when its rhythmic presentation, alternately static and lurching forward, puts durational emphasis at odds with the tonal hierarchy. Virtually any set of durations can be assigned to a tonal middleground without the latter losing a good part of its comprehensibility, even if its artistic merit may suffer in the process.

In Bruckner's case, however, the tonal language is so full of dualistic complexity that to assign to a Brucknerian middleground something like the rhythms of a piece by Mendelssohn would result in disaster. Bruckner showed wisdom and insight in choosing to work with middlegrounds that move very much within a restricted range of durations, even moving for rather long stretches of time mostly in uniform durations. It also made sense for him to keep to a middleground durational range of two to sixteen beats per scale step, thus stretching the classical norm of between one-half and four beats. The result is a rhythmic character that allows an ingenious web of novel tonal relations to be displayed in all of its multivalent complexity without collapsing into incoherence. Those who criticize Bruckner for the plodding quality of his music are probably thinking, whether they know it or not, of the harmonic rhythm of his middlegrounds, without realizing that the somewhat rigid character of these is a sine qua non of intelligibility for this music. This is not to say that, even on its own terms, Bruckner's music is flawless; there are passages in his work that suffer from an inadequate working-out of the larger plan and that substitute empty activity for significant detail, producing an effect of bombast.[22] An example of this in the last movement of the Eighth Symphony is the long dominant preparation leading to the closing horn and flute dialogue of the third theme (the music between N and O). Since such passages are few enough in number, however, and point to nothing basically faulty in the composer's conception, the sympathetic listener may overlook them and imagine that Bruckner would eventually have found better solutions.[23]

Much criticism of Bruckner represents a basic nonacceptance of his resistance to enclosure within the great Viennese symphonic tradition. Although his debt to it is clearly enormous, it should be equally clear that the music diverges radically from this tradition with respect to the perspective it takes on fundamental issues of hierarchy and linearity, and thereby with respect to basic formal problems and solutions. As I indicated previously, Bruckner's approach has its precedents, but on a smaller scale, one confined to the development sections of classical first movements. It is especially in the developments of some of Beethoven's symphonies, notably the Fourth, Sixth, Seventh, and Ninth, that Bruckner finds his source. Whatever one thinks of this approach, it is unfair to criticize a fifteen- or twenty-minute movement constructed along the lines of a massive development section because it lacks the properties of a complete first movement in the classical tradition.

Ultimately, one's critical stance with respect to an artist reflects an underlying sympathy with or antipathy to the spiritual project embodied in the artist's work. Much highly developed tonal music at the end of the nineteenth century may be understood in relation to a project basic to all the arts of romanticism, as well as to much of its philosophy, that of symbolically countering alienation, of making whole again the multiply fractured existence of persons in an increasingly urbanized, industrialized, and bureaucratized society. Music's unique success in this project, by virtue of which it had worked its way into the very center of European intellectual life by the 1890s, resulted from the development of means whereby intellectual and sonic order—and, therefore, symbolic resolution—could be imposed on extremely divergent, even conflicting materials and principles of construction. The symphonies of Mahler represent an obvious extreme in this development, but those of Bruckner, in a more restrained way, address related issues of binding together the incompatible, overcoming the contradictory, and bending centrifugally dissipating elements back toward a center imposed by the force of a compositional design.

The political cataclysms of the early twentieth century, however, rapidly dissolved the faith required to sustain romanticism's project and ushered in a formalist era of parallel projects, all emphasizing the allegedly nonreferential nature of music and thus its susceptibility to

radical redefinition; all reveling in extreme experiment while, paradoxically, finding their roots in the same classical past; and all disdaining as
impure, artificial, and even vulgar any imposition of unity on the totality
of musical experience and withdrawing instead to a world of hermetic
styles, reflective of the larger human context only in their being closed
to one another.

Even if the modernist adventure is today behind us, it is clear that
it has left us with a legacy of "musics" as opposed to "music" and that
any return to the universalizing aims of a century ago, when the Eighth
Symphony was premiered in Vienna, would seem absurdly pretentious.
Nevertheless, we are much more open than was the musical world of
twenty-five, fifty, or seventy-five years ago to appreciating the potential
of music to overflow its systematic boundaries by referring not only to
other works of its kind but also to other kinds of music and to other
dimensions of human experience. This creates a cultural climate much
more hospitable to rhetorically rich and at times extravagant expression
—to what used to be regarded as bombastic excess—a climate in which
it is possible to imagine a warm, even fervent reception for Bruckner's
Eighth Symphony as it begins its second hundred years of life.

NOTES

1. The ascription "tonally deviating" is used as in Harald Krebs, "The Background
Level in Some Tonally Deviating Works of Franz Schubert," *In Theory Only* 8, no. 8
(Dec. 1985): 5–18.

2. See, for example, Leo Treitler, "History, Criticism, and Beethoven's Ninth Symphony," *19th-Century Music* 3, no. 2 (Mar. 1980): 193–210. (Reprinted in Leo Treitler,
Music and the Historical Imagination, 19–45 [Cambridge: Harvard University Press,
1989].)

3. While roughly synonymous with *deviating,* it is obvious that *directional* privileges
the terminal tonality whereas *deviating* seems to imply an emphasis on the original
one. Presumably, context would determine which term, if either, would be more appropriate. I have taken "directional tonality" from William Kinderman, "Directional
Tonality in Chopin," in *Chopin Studies,* ed. Jim Samson, 59–75 (Cambridge: Cambridge University Press, 1988).

4. For a detailed study of this shift, see Leonard Meyer, *Style and Music: Theory,
History, and Ideology* (Philadelphia: University of Pennsylvania Press, 1989), 208–17
and 272–336.

5. John Vincent, *The Diatonic Modes in Modern Music* (Berkeley: University of California Press, 1951). Although still useful as an anthology, particularly of French and
Russian examples, this study is theoretically outdated. It contains only two Bruckner
quotations, neither of which is from a symphony, and makes the unjustifiable statement (p. 246) that "Bruckner is hardly important from a modal standpoint."

6. Deborah Stein, "The Expansion of the Subdominant in the Late Nineteenth
Century," *Journal of Music Theory* 27, no. 2 (fall 1983): 153–80.

7. A particular harmony may of course participate in the expression of more than one tonic, but only by operating at different levels of structure simultaneously.

8. The description given here is meant to suggest a musical surface that is more radical and refractory than those dealt with by Bailey, Kinderman, and others as instances of a double-tonic phenomenon. (See, for example, Robert Bailey's treatment of the Prelude to *Tristan* in "The Genesis of *Tristan and Isolde* and a Study of Wagner's Sketches and Drafts for the First Act" [Ph.D. diss., Princeton University, 1969].) A principal source is Arnold Schoenberg, *Theory of Harmony,* trans. Roy Carter (Berkeley: University of California Press, 1978), which alludes repeatedly to something approaching a true bitonality; see, for example, pp. 128 and 384. Of course, Schoenberg's own tonal music is rich in such relations, examples of which are described in Christopher Lewis, "Mirrors and Metaphors: Reflections on Schoenberg and Nineteenth-Century Tonality," *19th-Century Music* 11, no. 1 (summer 1987): 26–42.

9. Ernst Kurth, *Bruckner,* 2 vols. (Berlin: Max Hesses Verlag, 1925; reprinted Hildesheim: Georg Olms, 1971), 2:1081–84.

10. The rhythmic parallel is noted in Erwin Doernberg, *The Life and Symphonies of Anton Bruckner* (London: Barrie and Rockliff, 1960), 194. On deeper grounds, the harmonic structure of the opening may be viewed as a daring recomposition of Beethoven's opening substituting rising for falling fifths.

11. Doernberg, *The Life and Symphonies,* 94; Robert Simpson, *The Essence of Bruckner: An Essay towards the Understanding of His Music* (London: Victor Gollancz, 1967), 159–78; and Paul Dawson-Bowling, "Thematic and Tonal Unity in Bruckner's Eighth Symphony," *Music Review* 30 (1969): 225–36. The last of these sources makes the conflict of B♭ and C the central tonal issue of the symphony as a whole. Although not without foundation, this viewpoint does not render the opening any less mysterious.

12. Kurth, *Bruckner,* 1:346–55.

13. Robert Haas, *Anton Bruckner,* unnumbered volume in the series Die grossen Meister der Musik (The great masters of music), ed. Ernst Bücken (Potsdam: Akademische Verlagsgesellschaft Athenaion, 1934), 146.

14. There is a striking parallel here to the development section, which ends with an extended tertian sonority on the V of B♭ (mm. 217–24) leading via a threefold sequence to the V of C (m. 249). Regarding this sequence, see also note 17.

15. Especially interesting, if one recalls the tonal outcome of *Tristan und Isolde,* is the penetrating assertion of B tonality in mm. 9–16. If this is viewed as arising from a lower-level elaboration of the V of C, it participates in, and sharpens the latter's prolongational conflict with, the V of B♭ (or IV of C).

16. See the persuasive treatment of this issue in Christopher Lewis's chapter in this volume.

17. The magnificent threefold sequence of this augmented motive in mm. 225–49, with its extraordinary harmonization, is obviously a tribute to Wagner in the form of a rewriting of the opening measures of the *Tristan* Prelude, one that even preserves the intervals of transposition in the latter's sequence pattern (m3, M3).

18. The Eighth Symphony is replete with octatonic patterns, usually associated with the chaining of keys by minor thirds; see, for example, the striking sequence of descending minor sevenths in the upper winds at mm. 103–8. Interestingly, if the last note in this voice in m. 102 (a C♯) and the first in m. 109 (a C♭) are considered along with the six whole notes of the sequence proper, a complete octatonic scale is seen to unfold in these instruments.

19. Regarding tonal bivalence at pitch-class interval 1 in Schoenberg, see my "Epiphanic Tonality: An Approach to Perceptual and Aesthetic Issues in Schoenberg's Music after 1908," a paper read at the conference "Arnold Schoenberg: The Critical Years," University of Victoria, February 1991.

20. Cf. William Benjamin, "Tonality without Fifths: Remarks on the First Movement of Stravinsky's Concerto for Piano and Wind Instruments," *In Theory Only* 2, nos. 11–12 (Feb.–Mar. 1977): 53–70, and 3, no. 2 (May 1977): 9–31.

21. Typical of views widely held in the first half of this century are those expressed in Paul Henry Lang, *Music in Western Civilization* (New York: Norton, 1941), 918–20.

22. Even so ardent a Bruckner admirer as Wilhelm Furtwängler was aware of flaws in the construction of the symphonies. In an address on the composer written in 1939, he says, "Nicht das Fehlen von Mängeln, die Fehlerlosigkeit macht die Bedeutung einer Kunstwerkes aus—das glauben nur geborene Kritikernaturen und Philister—, sondern die Kraft und Größe der Aussage [Not the lack of weaknesses, not the flawlessness represents the significance of an artwork—only born critics and philistines believe that—but the power and greatness of the statement]." See Furtwängler, *Ton und Wort: Aufsätze und Vorträge 1918 bis 1954* (Wiesbaden: F.A. Brockhaus, 1954), 110.

23. In fact, in the 1887 version of the symphony, the dominant preparation of E♭ is extended by a motivic passage of twenty measures, occurring between O and P. In the final (1890) version this passage is dropped, and a neutral four-measure buffer is substituted for it. Compare Anton Bruckner, *Sämtliche Werke* 8 and 8.1 (the 1890 and 1887 versions, respectively), ed. Leopold Nowak (Vienna: Musikwissenschaftlicher Verlag der Internationalen Bruckner-Gesellschaft, 1955 and 1972). The longer passage is preserved in the critical edition prepared by Robert Haas in the 1930s, one that still has partisans among musicians and critics and can therefore still be heard.

Selected Bibliography

Abbate, Carolyn. "Elektra's Voice: Music and Language in Strauss's Opera." In *Richard Strauss, 'Elektra'*, ed. Derrick Puffett, 107–27. Cambridge: Cambridge University Press, 1989.

———. "*Tristan* in the Composition of *Pelléas*." *19th-Century Music* 5, no. 2 (fall 1981): 117–41.

———. *Unsung Voices: Opera and Musical Narrative in the Nineteenth Century.* Princeton: Princeton University Press, 1991.

Abraham, Gerald. *Chopin's Musical Style*. London: Oxford University Press, 1939.

Adler, Guido. "Gustav Mahler." In *Gustav Mahler and Guido Adler: Records of a Friendship,* ed. Edward R. Reilly, 15–73. Cambridge: Cambridge University Press, 1982.

Agawu, V. Kofi. "Extended Tonality in Mahler and Strauss." In *Richard Strauss: New Perspectives on the Composer and his Work,* ed. Bryan Gilliam, 55–76. Durham: Duke University Press, 1992.

———. "Mahler's Tonal Strategies: A Study of the Song Cycles." *Journal of Musicological Research* 6, no. 1 (1986): 1–47.

———. "Theory and Practice in the Analysis of the Nineteenth-Century *Lied*." *Music Analysis* 11, no. 1 (March 1992): 3–36.

———. "Tonal Strategy in the First Movement of Mahler's Tenth Symphony." *19th-Century Music* 9, no. 3 (spring 1986): 222–33.

Antokoletz, Elliott. "Verdi's Dramatic Use of Harmony and Tonality in *Macbeth*." *In Theory Only* 4, no. 6 (November–December 1978): 17–28.

Atlas, Allan W. "Crossed Stars and Crossed Tonal Areas in Puccini's *Madama Butterfly*." *19th-Century Music* 14, no. 2 (fall 1990): 186–96.

Bailey, Robert. "An Analytical Study of the Sketches and Drafts." In *Wagner: Prelude and Transfiguration from "Tristan and Isolde,"* ed. Robert Bailey, 113–46. New York: Norton, 1985.

———. "Form and Musical Language in Brahms's Fourth Symphony." Paper read at the International Brahms Congress, Washington DC, April 1980.

———. *The Genesis of 'Tristan und Isolde' and a Study of Wagner's Sketches and Drafts for the First Act.* (Ph.D. diss., Princeton University, 1969.) 70–8346. Ann Arbor: UMI.

———. "*Das Lied von der Erde:* Tonal Language and Formal Design." Paper read at the Forty-fourth Annual Meeting of the American Musicological Society, Minneapolis, 21 October 1978.

———. "Musical Language and Structure in the Third Symphony." In *Brahms Studies: Analytical and Historical Perspectives: Papers Delivered at the International Brahms Conference, Washington* DC, *5–8 May 1983,* ed. George S. Bozarth, 405–21. Oxford: Clarendon, 1990.

———. "The Structure of the *Ring* and Its Evolution." *19th-Century Music* 1, no.1 (July 1977): 48–61.

Ballan, Harry R. *Schoenberg's Expansion of Tonality, 1899–1908.* (Ph.D. diss., Yale University, 1986.) DA8627258. Ann Arbor: UMI.

Bass, Richard. "Prokofiev's Technique of Chromatic Displacement." *Music Analysis* 7, no.2 (July 1988): 197–214.

Bekker, Paul. *Richard Wagner: His Life in His Work.* Trans. Mildred M. Bozman. London: Dent, 1931.

———. "Zum Gedächtnis Karl Friedrich Weitzmanns" (In memory of K. F. Weitzmann). *Allgemeine Musik-Zeitung* 35, nos.32–33 (7–14 August 1908): 577–78.

Benary, Peter. "Zu Anton Bruckners Personalstil" (On Bruckner's style). *Musiktheorie* 8, no.2 (1993): 119–30.

Benjamin, William E. "Epiphanic Tonality: An Approach to Perceptual and Aesthetic Issues in Schoenberg's Music after 1908." Paper read at the conference Arnold Schoenberg: The Critical Years. University of Victoria, February 1991.

———. "Interlocking Diatonic Collections as a Source of Chromaticism in Late Nineteenth-Century Music." *In Theory Only* 1, nos.11–12 (February–March 1976): 31–51.

———. "Pitch-class Counterpoint in Tonal Music." In *Music Theory: Special Topics,* ed. Richmond Browne, 1–32. New York: Academic, 1981.

———. "Tonality without Fifths: Remarks on the First Movement of Stravinsky's Concerto for Piano and Wind Instruments." *In Theory Only* 2, nos.11–12 (February–March 1977): 53–70, and 3, no.2 (May 1977): 9–31.

Bergquist, Peter. "The First Movement of Mahler's Tenth Symphony: An Analysis and an Examination of the Sketches." *Music Forum* 5 (1980): 335–94.

Bieri, Georg. "Hugo Wolfs Lieder nach verschiedenen Dichtern" (Wolf's lieder based on various poets). *Schweizerische Musikzeitung* 75, no.11 (1 June 1935): 401–7.

Bloom, Peter A. *François-Joseph Fétis and the "Revue Musicale" (1827–1835).* (Ph.D. diss., University of Pennsylvania, 1972.) 72–25,546. Ann Arbor: UMI.

Booth, Paul J. "Hindemith's Analytical Method and an Alternative: Two Views of His *Concerto for Orchestra.*" *Soundings* 7 (June 1978): 117–36.

Boretz, Benjamin. "Meta-Variations: Studies in the Foundations of Musical Thought (I)." *Perspectives of New Music* 8, no. 1 (fall–winter 1969): 1–74.

Bourniquel, Camille. *Chopin.* Trans. Sinclair Road. New York: Grove, 1960.

Brinkmann, Reinhold. *Musik-Konzepte 70: Johannes Brahms, die Zweite Symphonie: Späte Idylle* (Brahms, the Second Symphony). Ed. Heinz-Karl Metzger and Rainer Riehn. Munich: edition text + kritik, 1990. Trans. by Peter Palmer as *Late Idyll: The Second Symphony of Johannes Brahms.* Cambridge: Harvard University Press, 1995.

Brown, Matthew. "The Diatonic and the Chromatic in Schenker's Theory of Harmonic Relations." *Journal of Music Theory* 30, no. 1 (spring 1986): 1–34.

Bruns, Steven M. *Mahler's Motivically Expanded Tonality: An Analytical Study of the Adagio of the "Tenth Symphony."* (Ph.D. diss., University of Wisconsin–Madison, 1989.) DA8917090. Ann Arbor: UMI.

Budde, Elmar. *Anton Weberns Lieder Op. 3. Untersuchungen zur frühen Atonalität bei Webern* (Webern's Songs Op. 3. A study of Webern's early atonality). Wiesbaden: Franz Steiner Verlag, 1971.

Burkhart, Charles. "Departures from the Norm in Two Songs from Schumann's *Liederkreis.*" In *Schenker Studies,* ed. Hedi Siegel, 146–64. Cambridge: Cambridge University Press, 1990.

Burstein, L. Poundie. "The Non-Tonic Opening in Classical and Romantic Music." Ph.D. diss., City University of New York, 1988. DA8915577.

Busoni, Ferruccio B. *The Essence of Music and Other Papers.* Trans. Rosamond Ley. New York: Dover, 1965.

———. *Sketch of a New Esthetic of Music.* Trans. T. Baker. New York: Schirmer, 1911; rpt., New York: Dover, 1962.

Carew, Derek. "An Examination of the Composer/Performer Relationship in the Piano Style of J. N. Hummel." Ph.D. diss., University of Leicester, 1981.

Carpenter, Tethys. "The Musical Language of 'Elektra.'" In *Richard Strauss, 'Elektra,'* ed. Derrick Puffett, 74–106. Cambridge: Cambridge University Press, 1989.

Cheong, Wai-Ling. "Structural Coherence and the Two-Key Scheme: A Study of Selected Cases from the Nineteenth Century." Master's thesis, Cambridge University, 1988.

Chominski, Józef. *Sonaty Chopina* (Chopin's sonatas). Krakow: Polskie wyd-wo muzyczne, 1960.

Cinnamon, Howard. "Chromaticism and Tonal Coherence in Liszt's Sonetto 104 del Petrarca." *In Theory Only* 7, no. 3 (August 1983): 3–19.

———. *Third-relations as Structural Elements in Book II of Liszt's "Années de Pelerinage" and Three Later Works.* (Ph.D. diss., University of Michigan, 1984.) DA8502781. Ann Arbor: UMI.

———. "Tonic Arpeggiation and Successive Equal Third Relations as Elements of Tonal Evolution in the Music of Franz Liszt." *Music Theory Spectrum* 8 (1986): 1–24.

Clarke, Frederick R. "Schubert's Use of Tonality: Some Unique Features." CAUSM/ACEUM (Canadian Association of University Schools of Music/Association Canadienne des Écoles Universitaires de Musique) 1, no. 2 (fall 1971): 25–38.

Cone, Edward T. "On the Road to *Otello:* Tonality and Structure in *Simon Boccanegra.*" *Studi verdiani* 1 (1982): 72–98.

———. "Schubert's Promissory Note: An Essay in Musical Hermeneutics." *19th-Century Music* 5, no. 3 (spring 1982): 233–41.

———. "Three Ways of Reading a Detective Story—or a Brahms Intermezzo." *Georgia Review* 31, no. 3 (fall 1977): 554–74. Rpt. in *Music: A View from Delft. Selected Essays,* ed. Robert P. Morgan, 77–93. Chicago and London: University of Chicago Press, 1989.

Crotty, John. "Symbolist Influences in Debussy's *Prelude to the Afternoon of a Faun.*" *In Theory Only* 6, no. 2 (Feb. 1982): 17–30.

Cuyler, Louise E. "Progressive Concepts of Pitch Relationships as Observed in the Symphonies of Brahms." In *Essays on Music for Charles Warren Fox,* ed. Jerald C. Graue, 164–80. Rochester: Eastman School of Music Press, 1979.

Czerny, Carl. *A Systematic Introduction to Improvisation on the Pianoforte.* Trans. and ed. Alice L. Mitchell. New York: Longman, 1983.

Dahlhaus, Carl, and John Deathridge. *The New Grove Wagner.* London: Macmillan, 1984.

Danuser, Hermann. "Musical Manifestations of the End in Wagner and in Post-Wagnerian *Weltanschauungsmusik.*" *19th-Century Music* 18, no. 1 (summer 1994): 64–82.

Darcy, Warren. *Wagner's 'Das Rheingold.'* Oxford: Clarendon, 1993.

Daverio, John. Review of George S. Bozarth, ed., *Brahms Studies: Analytical and Historical Perspectives. 19th-Century Music* 15, no. 3 (spring 1992): 246–54.

Dawson-Bowling, Paul. "Thematic and Tonal Unity in Bruckner's Eighth Symphony." *Music Review* 30 (1969): 225–36.

Decsey, Ernst. *Hugo Wolf.* 3 vols. Leipzig and Berlin: Schuster and Loeffler, 1903–4.

Denny, Thomas. "Directional Tonality in Schubert's Lieder." In *Franz Schubert —Der Fortschrittliche? Analysen-Perspectiven-Fakten* (Schubert—the progressive?), ed. Erich W. Partsch, 37–53. Veröffentlichungen des Internationalen Franz-Schubert-Instituts 4. Tutzing: Hans Schneider, 1989.

Deutsch, Diana. "Two Issues Concerning Tonal Hierarchies: Comment on Castellano, Bharucha, and Krumhansl." *Journal of Experimental Psychology: General* 113, no. 3 (1984): 413–16.

Deutsch, Otto E. "Ein unbekanntes Goethe-Lied von Schubert" (An unknown Goethe song by Schubert). *Schweizerische Musikzeitung* 92, no. 11 (1 Nov. 1952): 446–48.

Doernberg, Erwin. *The Life and Symphonies of Anton Bruckner.* London: Barrie and Rockliff, 1960.

Drabkin, William. "Characters, Key Relations and Tonal Structure in *Il trovatore*." *Music Analysis* 1, no. 2 (July 1982): 143–53.

Draeseke, Felix. *Schriften 1855–1861*. Ed. Martella Gutiérrez-Denhoff and Helmut Loos. Bad Honnef: Gudrun Schröder Verlag, 1987.

Eigeldinger, Jean-Jacques. *Chopin: Pianist and Teacher as Seen by His Pupils*. Trans. Naomi Shohet with Krysia Osostowicz and Roy Howat. Ed. Roy Howat. Cambridge: Cambridge University Press, 1986.

Floros, Constantin. "Die Faust-Symphonie von Franz Liszt: Eine semantische Analyse." In *Musik-Konzepte 12: Franz Liszt,* ed. Heinz-Karl Metzger and Rainer Riehn, 42–87. Munich: edition text + kritik, 1980.

———. *Die Symphonien*. Vol. 3 of *Gustav Mahler*. 3 vols. Wiesbaden: Breitkopf und Härtel, 1985.

Forte, Allen. "Liszt's Experimental Idiom and Music of the Early Twentieth Century." *19th-Century Music* 10, no. 3 (spring 1987): 209–28. Reprinted as "Liszt's Experimental Idiom and Twentieth-Century Music," in *Music at the Turn of the Century,* ed. Joseph Kerman, 93–112. California Studies in 19th Century Music, vol. 6. Berkeley: University of California Press, 1990.

Frisch, Walter. *The Early Works of Arnold Schoenberg, 1893–1908* Berkeley: University of California Press, 1993.

Furtwängler, Wilhelm. *Ton und Wort: Aufsätze und Vorträge 1918 bis 1954* (Tone and word: essays and lectures). Wiesbaden: F. A. Brockhaus, 1954.

Gal, Hans. *Johannes Brahms: His Work and Personality*. Trans. Joseph Stein. New York: Knopf, 1963.

George, Graham. *Tonality and Musical Structure*. London: Faber & Faber, 1970.

Gerlach, Reinhard. *Musik und Jugendstil der Wiener Schule 1900–1908* (Music and "Jugendstil" of the Vienna School 1900–1908). Laaber: Laaber Verlag, 1985.

———. "Mystik und Klangmagie in Anton von Weberns hybrider Tonalität" (Mysticism and magical sound in Webern's hybrid tonality). *Archiv für Musikwissenschaft* 33, no. 1 (1976): 1–27.

———. "Die Orchesterkomposition als musikalisches Drama. Die Teil-Tonalitäten der 'Gestalten' und der bitonale Kontrapunkt in *Ein Heldenleben* von Richard Strauss" (Orchestral composition as music drama. The partial tonics of the "characters" and bitonal counterpoint in *Ein Heldenleben*). *Musiktheorie* 6, no. 1 (1991): 55–78.

Gerstenberg, Walter. "Der Rahmen der Tonalität im Liede Schuberts." (The frame of tonality in the Schubert song). In *Musicae Scientiae Collectanae, Festschrift Karl Gustav Fellerer, zum 70. Geburtstag,* ed. Heinrich Hüschen, 147–55. Cologne: Arno-Volk-Verlag, 1973.

Gilliam, Bryan, ed. *Richard Strauss and His World*. Princeton: Princeton University Press, 1992.

———. *Richard Strauss's "Elektra."* Oxford: Clarendon, 1991.

Glauert, Amanda. "The Double Perspective in Beethoven's Opus 131." *19th-Century Music* 4, no. 2 (fall 1980): 113–20.

———. "Hugo Wolf: Poet or Musician?" Paper presented at the Conference of Nineteenth-Century Music, University of Birmingham, July 1986.

Göllerich, August. *Franz Liszt.* Leipzig: Reclam, 1908.

Gut, Serge. *Franz Liszt: Les Éléments du langage musical.* Paris: Klincksieck, 1975.

Haar, James. "Pace non trovo: A Study in Literary and Musical Parody." *Musica Disciplina* 20 (1966), 95–149.

Haas, Robert. *Anton Bruckner.* Unnumbered volume in the series *Die grossen Meister der Musik,* ed. Ernst Bücken. Potsdam: Akademische Verlagsgesellschaft Athenaion, 1934.

Hasty, Christopher. "Segmentation and Process in Post-Tonal Music." *Music Theory Spectrum* 3 (1981): 54–73.

———. "On the Problem of Succession and Continuity in Twentieth-Century Music." *Music Theory Spectrum* 8 (1986): 58–74.

Hefling, Stephen E. "Miners Digging from Opposite Sides? Mahler, Strauss, and the Problem of Program Music." In *Richard Strauss: New Perspectives on the Composer and His Work,* ed. Bryan Gilliam, 41–54. Durham: Duke University Press, 1992.

Hepokoski, James. "Structure and Program in *Macbeth:* A Proposed Hearing of Strauss's First Symphonic Poem." In *Richard Strauss and His World,* ed. Bryan Gilliam, 67–89. Princeton: Princeton University Press, 1992.

Hiatt, James S. *Form and Tonal Organization in the Late Instrumental Works of Carl Nielsen.* (Ph.D. diss., Indiana University, 1986.) DA8627992. Ann Arbor: UMI.

Howell, Tim. Review of Deborah J. Stein, *Hugo Wolf's "Lieder" and Extensions of Tonality. Music Analysis* 7, no.1 (Mar. 1988): 93–99.

Hoyt, Reed J. "Chopin's Prelude in A Minor Revisited: The Issue of Tonality." *In Theory Only* 8, no.6 (Apr. 1985): 7–16.

Jackson, Timothy L. "Schubert's Revisions of *Der Jüngling und der Tod,* D 545a-b, and *Meeresstille,* D 216a-b." *Musical Quarterly* 75, no.3 (fall 1991): 336–61.

Johnson, Steven P. *Thematic and Tonal Processes in Mahler's "Third Symphony"* (Ph.D. diss., University of California, Los Angeles, 1989.) DA9005187. Ann Arbor: UMI.

Jones, William Isaac. *A Study of Tonality in the Symphonies of Carl Nielsen.* (Ph.D. diss., Florida State University, Tallahassee, 1973.) DA73-25118. Ann Arbor: UMI.

Jordan, Roland, and Emma Kafalenos. "The Double Trajectory: Ambiguity in Brahms and Henry James." *19th-Century Music* 13, no.2 (fall 1989): 129–44.

Kallberg, Jeffrey. "Chopin's Last Style." *Journal of the American Musicological Society.* 38, no.2 (summer 1985): 264–315.

Kaplan, Richard A. "The Interaction of Diatonic Collections in the Adagio of Mahler's Tenth Symphony." *In Theory Only* 6, no.1 (Nov. 1981): 29–39.

———. "Interpreting Surface Harmonic Connections in the Adagio of Mahler's Tenth Symphony." *In Theory Only* 4, no.2 (May–June 1978): 32–44.

———. "The Musical Language of *Elektra:* A Study in Chromatic Harmony." Ph.D. diss., University of Michigan, Ann Arbor, 1985. DA8512443.

Kerman, Joseph. *Opera as Drama*. New York: Knopf, 1956; rpt. Westport, CN: Greenwood, 1981.

———. "Viewpoint." *19th-Century Music* 2, no. 2 (Nov. 1978): 186–91.

Kinderman, William. "Directional Tonality in Chopin." In *Chopin Studies,* ed. Jim Samson, 59–75. Cambridge: Cambridge University Press, 1988.

———. "Draesekes Klaviersonate op. 6." In *Zum Schaffen von Felix Draeseke: Instrumentalwerke und geistliche Musik. Tagungen 1990 in Coburg und 1991 in Dresden* (The works of Felix Draeseke: instrumental and sacred music. Conferences in Coburg, 1990, and Dresden, 1991), ed. Helmut Loos, 3–17. Veröffentlichungen der Internationalen Draeseke-Gesellschaft, vol. 5. Bonn: Gudrun Schröder Verlag, 1994. A version of this essay in English appears in the booklet accompanying the recording of the Draeseke Sonata by Claudius Tanski (Altarus AIR-CD-9030 1992).

———. "Dramatic Recapitulation in Wagner's *Götterdämmerung.*" *19th-Century Music* 4, no. 2 (fall 1980): 101–12.

———. "Die Entstehung der *Parsifal*-Musik" (The genesis of the music to *Parsifal*). *Archiv für Musikwissenschaft* 52, no. 1 (1995): 66–97; and 52, no. 2 (1995): 145–65.

———. "Das 'Geheimnis der Form' in Wagners *Tristan und Isolde*" (The "secret" of form in Wagner's *Tristan and Isolde*). *Archiv für Musikwissenschaft* 40, no. 3 (1983): 174–88.

———. "Hans Sachs's 'Cobbler's Song,' *Tristan,* and the 'Bitter Cry of the Resigned Man.'" *Journal of Musicological Research* 13, nos. 3–4 (1993): 161–84.

———. "Wagner's *Parsifal:* Musical Form and the Drama of Redemption." *The Journal of Musicology* 4, no. 4 (fall 1985–86): 431–46; corrigenda in *Journal of Musicology* 5, no. 2 (spring 1987): 315–16.

———. "Zwischen Schumann und Hugo Wolf: *Das verlassene Mägdlein von Felix Draeseke*" (Between Schumann and Hugo Wolf: *The Forsaken Maiden* by Felix Draeseke). In *Draeseke und Liszt. Draesekes Liedschaffen. Tagungen 1987 und 1988 in Coburg* (Draeseke and Liszt. Draeseke's songs. Conferences in Coburg, 1987 and 1988), ed. Helga Lühning and Helmut Loos, 205–17. Bad Honnef: Gudrun Schröder Verlag, 1988 [Veröffentlichungen der Internationalen Draeseke-Gesellschaft, vol. 2].

Kissler, John M. "The *Four Last Songs* by Richard Strauss: A Formal and Tonal Perspective." *Music Review* 50 (1989): 231–39.

Knapp, Raymond. "The Tonal Structure of *Tristan und Isolde:* A Sketch." *Music Review* 45 (1984): 11–25.

Korsyn, Kevin E. *Integration in Works of Beethoven's Final Period.* (Ph.D. diss., Yale University, 1983.) DA8411528. Ann Arbor: UMI.

———. "J. W. N. Sullivan and the *Heiliger Dankgesang:* Questions of Meaning in Late Beethoven." In *Beethoven Forum 2,* ed. Christopher Reynolds, 133–74. Lincoln: University of Nebraska Press, 1993.

———. "Towards a New Poetics of Musical Influence." *Music Analysis* 10, nos. 1–2 (Mar.–July 1991): 3–72.

Kramer, Jonathan. *The Time of Music: New Meanings, New Temporalities, New Listening Strategies.* New York: Schirmer, 1988.

Kramer, Lawrence. "Decadence and Desire: The *Wilhelm Meister* Songs of Wolf and Schubert." *19th-Century Music* 10, no. 3 (spring 1987): 229–42.

———. "The Mirror of Tonality: Transitional Features of Nineteenth-Century Harmony." *19th-Century Music* 4, no. 3 (spring 1981): 191–208.

———. "Musical Narratology: A Theoretical Outline." *Indiana Theory Review* 12 (spring and fall 1991): 141–62.

———. *Music as Cultural Practice, 1800–1900.* California Studies in 19th-Century Music, 8. Berkeley: University of California Press, 1990.

———. "The Schubert Lied: Romantic Form and Romantic Consciousness." In *Schubert: Critical and Analytical Studies,* ed. Walter Frisch, 200–236. Lincoln: University of Nebraska Press, 1986.

———. "The Shape of Post-Classical Music." *Critical Inquiry* 6 (1979): 144–52.

Kraus, Joseph C. "Tonal Plan and Narrative Plot in Tchaikovsky's Symphony No. 5 in E Minor." *Music Theory Spectrum* 13, no. 1 (spring 1991): 21–47.

Krebs, Harald. "Alternatives to Monotonality in Early Nineteenth-Century Music." *Journal of Music Theory* 25, no. 1 (spring 1981): 1–16.

———. "The Background Level in Some Tonally Deviating Works of Franz Schubert." *In Theory Only* 8, no. 8 (Dec. 1985): 5–18.

———. "Techniques of Unification in Tonally Deviating Works." *Canadian University Music Review* 10, no. 1 (1990): 55–70.

———. *Third Relation and Dominant in Late Eighteenth- and Early Nineteenth-Century Music.* (Ph.D. diss., Yale University, 1980.) 8025208. Ann Arbor: UMI.

———. "Tonal and Formal Dualism in Chopin's Scherzo, Op. 31." *Music Theory Spectrum* 13, no. 1 (spring 1991): 48–60.

———. "Tonal Structure in Nielsen's Symphonies." In *A Carl Nielsen Companion,* ed. Mina Miller, 208–49. London: Faber and Faber, 1994.

———. "Tonart und Text in Schuberts Liedern mit abweichenden Schlüssen" (Tonality and text in Schuberts directionally tonal songs). *Archiv für Musikwissenschaft* 47, no. 4 (1990): 264–71.

Krebs, Wolfgang. "Terzenfolgen und Doppelterzklänge in den "Gezeichneten" von Franz Schreker—Versuch einer energetisch—psychoanalytischen Betrachtungsweise" (Third progressions and double-third triads in *The Branded Ones*—attempt at an energetic-psychoanalytic interpretation). *Die Musikforschung* 47, no. 4 (October–December 1994): 365–83.

Krumhansl, Carol L., and Mark A. Schmuckler "The *Petrouchka* Chord: A Perceptual Investigation." *Music Perception* 4, no. 2 (winter 1986): 153–84.

Kurth, Ernst. *Bruckner.* 2 vols. Berlin: Max Hesses Verlag, 1925; rpt. Hildesheim: Georg Olms, 1971.

———. *Romantische Harmonik und ihre Krise in Wagners "Tristan"* (Romantic harmony and its crisis in Wagner's *Tristan*). 2d ed. Berlin: Max Hesses Verlag, 1923; facsimile, Hildesheim: Georg Olms Verlag, 1968.

La Motte, Diether de. *Harmonielehre* (Harmony). 2d ed. Kassel: Bärenreiter Verlag, 1978.

LaRue, Jan. "Bifocal Tonality: An Explanation for Ambiguous Baroque Cadences." In *Essays on Music in Honor of Archibald Thompson Davison*, 173–84. Cambridge: Department of Music, Harvard University, 1957.

Lau, Robert Clark. *Initial versus Ultimate Tonality in Instrumental Music of the Classic and Romantic Periods.* (Ph.D. diss., Catholic University of America, 1979.) DA7918576. Ann Arbor: UMI.

Lawton, David. "On the 'Bacio' Theme in *Otello*." *19th-Century Music* 1, no. 3 (Mar. 1978): 211–20.

Lemoine, Bernard C. "Tonal Organization in Selected Late Piano Works of Franz Liszt." In *Liszt-Studien 2: Referate des 2. Liszt-Symposions,* ed. Serge Gut, 123–31. Munich: Emil Katzbichler, 1981.

Lerdahl, Fred. "Tonal Pitch Space." *Music Perception* 5, no. 3 (spring 1988): 315–49.

Levarie, Siegmund. "Key Relations in Verdi's *Un ballo in maschera*." *19th-Century Music* 2, no. 2 (Nov. 1978): 143–47.

Lewin, David. "Amfortas's Prayer to Titurel and the Role of D in *Parsifal:* The Tonal Spaces of the Drama and the Enharmonic Cb/B." *19th-Century Music* 7, no. 3 (April 1984): 336–49.

———. "Music Theory, Phenomenology, and Modes of Perception." *Music Perception* 3, no. 4 (summer 1986): 327–92.

Lewis, Christopher O. "Mirrors and Metaphors: Reflections on Schoenberg and Nineteenth-Century Tonality." *19th-Century Music* 11, no. 1 (summer 1987): 26–42. Rpt. as "Mirrors and Metaphors: On Schoenberg and Nineteenth-Century Tonality," in *Music at the Turn of the Century,* ed. Joseph Kerman, 15–31. California Studies in 19th-Century Music, 6. Berkeley: University of California Press, 1990.

———. *Tonal Coherence in Mahler's Ninth Symphony.* Studies in Musicology, no. 79. Ann Arbor: UMI Research Press, 1984.

Longyear, Rey M. "Unusual Tonal Procedures in Schumann's Sonata-type Cycles." *In Theory Only* 3, no. 12 (March 1978): 22–30.

Longyear, Rey M., and Kate Covington. "Liszt, Mahler and a Remote Tonal Relationship in Sonata Form." In *Virtuosität und Avantgarde: Untersuchungen zum Klavierwerk Franz Liszts* (Virtuosity and avantagarde: studies of Franz Liszt's piano music), ed. Zsolt Gardonyi and Siegfried Mauser, 32–59. Mainz: Schott, 1988.

Lorenz, Alfred. *Das Geheimnis der Form bei Richard Wagner.* 4 vols. Berlin: Max Hesses Verlag, 1924–33; rpt. Tutzing: Hans Schneider, 1966.

McClary, Susan. *Feminine Endings: Music, Gender, and Sexuality.* Minneapolis: University of Minnesota Press, 1991.

McCreless, Patrick. "Motive and Magic: A Referential Dyad in *Parsifal*." *Music Analysis* 9, no. 3 (October 1990): 227–65.

———. "Schenker and the Norns." In *Analyzing Opera: Verdi and Wagner,* ed. Carolyn Abbate and Roger Parker, 276–97. California Studies in 19th-Century Music, 6. Berkeley: University of California Press, 1989.

———. "Syntagmatics and Paradigmatics: Some Implications for the Analysis of Chromaticism in Tonal Music." *Music Theory Spectrum* 13, no. 2 (fall 1991): 147–78.

———. *Wagner's "Siegfried": Its Drama, History and Music.* Studies in Musicology, no. 59. Ann Arbor: UMI, 1982.

McNamee, Ann K. "Bitonality, Mode, and Interval in the Music of Karol Szymanowski." *Journal of Music Theory* 29, no. 1 (spring 1985): 61–84.

Martin, Henry. "A Structural Model for Schoenberg's 'Der verlorene Haufen,' op. 12, no. 2." *In Theory Only* 3, no. 3 (June 1977): 4–22.

Meyer, Leonard B. *Style and Music: Theory, History, and Ideology.* Philadelphia: University of Pennsylvania Press, 1989.

Mitchell, William J. "The Tristan Prelude: Techniques and Structure." *Music Forum* 1 (1967): 162–203.

Morgan, Robert. "Dissonant Prolongations: Theoretical and Compositional Precedents." *Journal of Music Theory* 20, no. 1 (spring 1976): 49–91.

Murphy, Edward. "Tonal Organization in Five Strauss Tone Poems." *Music Review* 44 (1983): 223–33.

———. "Tonality and Form in *Salome*." *Music Review* 50 (1989): 215–30.

Nagler, Norbert. "Die verspätete Zukunftsmusik" (Belated music of the future). In *Musik-Konzepte 12: Franz Liszt*, ed. Heinz-Karl Metzger and Rainer Riehn, 4–41. Munich: edition text + kritik, 1980.

Nelson, John C. "Progressive Tonality in the Finale of the Piano Quintet, Op. 44 of Robert Schumann." *Indiana Theory Review* 13 (1992): 41–52.

Newcomb, Anthony. "The Birth of Music out of the Spirit of Drama." *19th-Century Music* 5, no. 1 (summer 1981): 38–66.

Newlin, Dika. *Bruckner, Mahler, Schoenberg.* New York: King's Crown, 1947.

Niemöller, Karl. "Zur nicht-tonalen Thema-Struktur von Liszts Faust-Symphonie" (On the nontonal thematic structure of Liszt's "Faust" Symphony). *Die Musikforschung* 22 (1969): 69–72.

Norton, Richard. *Tonality in Western Culture: A Critical and Historical Perspective* (University Park: Pennsylvania State University Press, 1984).

Nowik, Wojciech. "Proces twórczy Fryderyka Chopina w swietle jego autografów muzycznych" (The creative process of Frederic Chopin in light of his musical manuscripts). Ph.D. diss., University of Warsaw, 1978.

Nüll, Edwin von der. *Moderne Harmonik* (Modern harmony). Leipzig: Fr. Kistner and C. F. W. Siegel, 1932.

Osthoff, Wolfgang. "Pfitzner und der 'Historische Materialstand'" (Pfitzner and the "historical situation"). In *Symposium Hans Pfitzner Berlin 1981*, ed. Wolfgang Osthoff, 115–46. Tutzing: Hans Schneider, 1984.

Parkany, Stephen. "Kurth's *Bruckner* and the Adagio of the Seventh Symphony." *19th-Century Music* 11, no. 3 (spring 1988): 262–81.

Parker, Roger, and Allan W. Atlas. "A Key for *Chi?* Tonal Areas in Puccini." *19th-Century Music* 15, no. 3 (spring 1992): 229–34.

Phillips, Edward R. "Smoke, Mirrors and Prisms: Tonal Contradiction in Fauré." *Music Analysis* 12, no. 1 (Mar. 1993): 3–24.

Phipps, Graham H. "The Logic of Tonality in Strauss's *Don Quixote:* A Schoenbergian Evaluation." *19th-Century Music* 9, no. 3 (spring 1986): 189–205.

Pohl, Richard. "Liszts Faust-Symphonie (1862)." In *Franz Liszt: Studien und Erinnerungen* (Liszt: studies and recollections), vol. 2 of *Gesammelte Schriften über Musik und Musiker* (Collected works about music and musicians), 247–320. Leipzig: Bernhard Schlicke (1883), 247–320.

Poniatowska, Irena. "Improwizacja fortepianowa w okresie romantyzmu" (Piano improvisation in the romantic period). *Szkice o kulturze muzycznej XIXw* (Profiles of musical culture of the 19th century). Warsaw: Institut Sztuki (1980), 4:7–26.

Poos, Heinrich. "Zur Tristanharmonik" (On the harmony of *Tristan*). In *Festschrift Ernst Pepping,* ed. Heinrich Poos, 269–97. Berlin: Verlag Merseburger, 1971.

Proctor, Gregory M. "Technical Bases of Nineteenth-Century Chromatic Tonality: A Study in Chromaticism." Ph.D diss., Princeton University, 1978. 7807490.

Ratner, Leonard G. *Classic Music: Expression, Form and Style.* New York: Schirmer, 1980.

Rink, John S. "Chopin's Ballades and the Dialectic: Analysis in Historical Perspective." *Music Analysis* 13, no. 1 (March 1994): 99–115. A French translation of an earlier version of this article appeared in *Analyse musicale* 27 (1992); a Polish translation appeared in *Rocznik Chopinowski* 21 (1994).

———. "The Evolution of Chopin's 'Structural Style' and Its Relation to Improvisation." Ph.D. diss., Cambridge University, 1989.

Ritterman, Janet. "Piano Music and the Public Concert." In *The Cambridge Companion to Chopin,* ed. Jim Samson, 11–31. Cambridge: Cambridge University Press, 1992.

Ritzel, Fred. "Materialdenken bei Liszt: Eine Untersuchung des 'Zwölftonthemas' der Faust-Symphonie" (Constructive principles in Liszt: an investigation of the "twelve-tone theme" of the "Faust" Symphony). *Die Musikforschung* 20 (1967): 289–94.

Rogers, Michael R. "Chopin, Prelude in A Minor, Op. 28, No. 2." *19th-Century Music* 4, no. 3 (spring 1981): 244–50.

Rosen, Charles. *The Classical Style: Haydn, Mozart, Beethoven.* New York: Viking, 1971.

Saint-Saëns, Camille. "A Chopin M. S.: The F Major Ballade in the Making." In *Outspoken Essays on Music,* trans. Fred Rothwell, 97–105. London: Kegan Paul, Trench, Trubner, 1922.

Sams, Eric. *The Songs of Hugo Wolf.* London: Methuen, 1961; rpt. London: Faber, 1992.

Samson, Jim. "Chopin and Genre." *Music Analysis* 8, no.3 (October 1989): 213–31.

———. "The Composition-Draft of the Polonaise-Fantasy: The Issue of Tonality." In *Chopin Studies,* 41–58. Cambridge: Cambridge University Press, 1988.

———. *Music in Transition: A Study of Tonal Expansion and Atonality, 1900–1920.* London: Dent, 1977.

———. *The Music of Chopin.* London: Routledge & Kegan Paul, 1985.

Schachter, Carl. "Analysis by Key: Another Look at Modulation." *Music Analysis* 6, no.3 (October 1987): 289–318.

———. "Chopin's Fantasy, op.49: The Two-Key Scheme." In *Chopin Studies,* ed. Jim Samson, 221–53. Cambridge: Cambridge University Press, 1988.

Schenker, Heinrich. *Counterpoint.* Trans. John Rothgeb and Jürgen Thym. 2 vols. New York: Schirmer, 1987.

———. *Free Composition.* Trans. and ed. Ernst Oster. 2 vols. New York and London: Longman, 1979.

———. *Harmony.* Trans. Elisabeth Mann Borgese, ed. and annotated Oswald Jonas. Cambridge: MIT Press, 1973.

Schoenberg, Arnold. *Structural Functions of Harmony.* Ed. and revised Leonard Stein. New York: Norton, 1969.

———. *Theory of Harmony.* Trans. Roy E. Carter. Berkeley: University of California Press, 1978.

Searle, Humphrey. "Liszt." *The New Grove Early Romantic Masters I,* ed. Stanley Sadie, rev. Sharon Winklhofer, 237–378. London: Macmillan, 1985.

Simpson, Robert. *Carl Nielsen, Symphonist.* 2d ed. London: Kahn and Averill, 1979.

———. *The Essence of Bruckner: An Essay towards the Understanding of His Music.* London: Victor Gollancz, 1967.

Sine, Nadine. *The Evolution of Symphonic Worlds: Tonality in the Symphonies of Gustav Mahler, with Emphasis on the First, Third and Fifth.* (Ph.D. diss., New York University, 1983.) DA84-05807. Ann Arbor: UMI.

Sisman, Elaine. "Brahms's Slow Movements: Reinventing the 'Closed' Forms." In *Brahms Studies: Analytical and Historical Perspectives,* ed. George Bozarth, 79–103. Oxford: Clarendon, 1990.

Skoumal, Zdenek. "Liszt's Androgynous Harmony." *Music Analysis* 13, no.1 (March 1994): 51–72.

Smith, Charles J. "The Functional Extravagance of Chromatic Chords." *Music Theory Spectrum* 8 (1986): 94–139.

Sobaskie, James W. *A Theory of Associative Harmony for Tonal Music.* (Ph.D. diss., University of Wisconsin–Madison, 1985.) DA8601123. Ann Arbor: UMI.

———. "Associative Harmony: The Reciprocity of Ideas in Musical Space." *In Theory Only* 10, nos.1–2 (Aug. 1987): 31–64.

Stein, Deborah J. "The Expansion of the Subdominant in the Late Nineteenth Century." *Journal of Music Theory* 27, no.2 (fall 1983): 153–80.

————. *Hugo Wolf's "Lieder" and Extensions of Tonality.* Studies in Musicology, no. 72. Ann Arbor: UMI, 1985.

Stein, Jack M. "Poem and Music in Hugo Wolf's Mörike Songs." *Musical Quarterly* 53, no. 1 (January 1967): 22–38.

Straus, Joseph. "The 'Anxiety of Influence' in Early 20th-Century Music." Paper read to the Society of Music Theory, Austin, October 1989.

————. *Remaking the Past: Musical Modernism and the Influence of the Tonal Tradition.* Cambridge: Harvard University Press, 1990.

————. "Stravinsky's Tonal Axis." *Journal of Music Theory* 26, no. 2 (fall 1982): 261–90.

Subotnik, Rose. "Tonality, Autonomy, and Competence in Postclassical Music." In Subotnik, *Developing Variations: Style and Ideology in Western Music,* 195–205 (Minneapolis: University of Minnesota Press, 1991). This essay first appeared in *Critical Inquiry* 6 (1979).

Swift, Richard. "1-XII-99: Tonal Relations in Schönberg's *Verklärte Nacht.*" *19th-Century Music* 1, no. 1 (July 1977): 3–14. Rpt. in *Music at the Turn of the Century,* ed. Joseph Kerman, 3–14. California Studies in 19th-Century Music, 6. Berkeley: University of California Press, 1990.

Szabolcsi, Bence. *The Twilight of Ferenc Liszt.* Trans. András Deák. Budapest: Akadémiai Kiadó, 1959.

Taruskin, Richard. "Chernomor to Kashchei: Harmonic Sorcery; or, Stravinsky's 'Angle.'" *Journal of the American Musicological Society* 38, no. 1 (spring 1985): 72–142.

Tausche, Anton. *Hugo Wolfs Mörikelieder in Dichtung, Musik und Vortrag* (Wolf's "Mörike songs" in poetry, music, and performance). Vienna: Amandus-Edition, 1947.

Tischler, Hans. "Key Symbolism versus 'Progressive Tonality.'" *Musicology* 2, no. 4 (July 1949): 383–88.

————. "Mahler's Impact on the Crisis of Tonality." *Music Review* 12 (1951): 113–21.

Todd, R. Larry. "Liszt, Fantasy and Fugue for Organ on 'Ad nos, ad salutarem undam.'" *19th-Century Music* 4, no. 3 (spring 1981): 250–61.

————. "Strauss before Liszt and Wagner: Some Observations." In *Richard Strauss: New Perspectives on the Composer and His Work,* ed. Bryan Gilliam, 3–40. Durham: Duke University Press, 1992.

————. "The 'Unwelcome Guest' Regaled: Franz Liszt and the Augmented Triad." *19th-Century Music* 12, no. 2 (fall 1988): 93–115.

Torkewitz, Dieter. "Die Erstfassung der *Harmonies poétiques et réligieuses* von Liszt" (The first version of Liszt's *Harmonies poétiques*). In *Liszt-Studien 2: Referate des 2. Liszt-Symposions,* ed. Serge Gut, 220–36. Munich: Emil Katzbichler, 1981.

————. *Harmonisches Denken im Frühwerk Franz Liszts* (Harmonic principles in Liszt's early works). Ed. Heinrich Eggebrecht. Freiburger Schriften zur Musikwissenschaft, vol. 10. Munich: Emil Katzbichler, 1978.

Tovey, Sir Donald F. *The Main Stream of Music and Other Essays.* New York: Oxford University Press, 1949.

Treitler, Leo. "History, Criticism, and Beethoven's Ninth Symphony." *19th-Century Music* 3, no. 2 (Mar. 1980): 193–210. Rpt. in Treitler, *Music and the Historical Imagination,* 19–45. Cambridge: Harvard University Press, 1989.

Truscott, Harold. "Some Aspects of Mahler's Tonality." *Monthly Musical Record* 87/984 (November–December 1957): 203–8.

Vincent, John. *The Diatonic Modes in Modern Music.* Berkeley: University of California Press, 1951.

Walker, Frank. *Hugo Wolf: A Biography.* Rev. ed. London: Dent, 1968.

Weitzmann, Karl Friedrich. *Geschichte des Septimen-Akkordes* (History of the seventh chord). Berlin: J. Guttentag, 1854.

———. *Der übermässige Dreiklang* (The augmented triad). Berlin: J. Guttentag, 1853.

———. *Der verminderte Septimen-Akkord* (The diminished-seventh chord). Berlin: Herman Peters, 1854.

Werba, Erik. "Hugo Wolfs Liedschaffen aus der Sicht von Heute" (A modern view of Hugo Wolf's songs). *Österreichische Musikzeitschrift* 33, no. 2 (February 1978): 57–64.

Whittall, Arnold. "Dramatic Structure and Tonal Organisation." In *Richard Strauss, 'Elektra,'* ed. Derrick Puffett, 55–73. Cambridge: Cambridge University Press, 1989.

Williamson, John. "Mahler, Hermeneutics and Analysis." *Music Analysis* 10, no. 3 (October 1991): 357–73.

———. *The Music of Hans Pfitzner.* Oxford: Clarendon, 1992.

Contributors

William E. Benjamin, professor of music at the University of British Columbia in Vancouver, has recently completed papers on musical cognition and music in cognitive evolution and continues his work on the atonal music of Schoenberg. He has also published recently on sociocultural aspects of contemporary concert music.

William Kinderman is professor of music at the University of Victoria and taught during 1993–94 at the Hochschule der Künste, Berlin. His most recent work includes the comprehensive monograph *Beethoven* and a CD of Beethoven's Diabelli Variations (Hyperion CDA66763).

Kevin Korsyn is associate professor of music at the University of Michigan. He received the Young Scholar Award from the Society for Music Theory for his article "Schenker and Kantian Epistomology" in *Theoria* 3 (1988) and has recently published articles in *Music Analysis* and *Beethoven Forum.*

Harald Krebs, an associate professor at the University of Victoria, has written widely on harmonic, rhythmic, and metrical aspects of nineteenth-century music, as well as on Schoenberg and Nielsen. His recent research centers on metrical "dissonance" in the music of Schumann.

Christopher Lewis was professor of music at the University of Alberta until his unexpected death in 1992. His most important writings include "Mirrors and Metaphors: On Schoenberg and Nineteenth-Century Tonality," in *Music at the Turn of the Century: A 19th-Century Music Reader,* ed. Joseph Kerman, and *Tonal Coherence in Mahler's Ninth Symphony.*

Patrick McCreless is associate professor of Music Theory at the University of Texas at Austin. His work focuses on the tonal language of nineteenth-century music, literary and narrative models for musical analysis, and the operas of Wagner; his publications in the last category include *Wagner's 'Siegfried': Its Drama, History and Music.*

Jim Samson is professor of music at the University of Bristol. His most recent books include *The Music of Szymanowski,* and *The Music of Chopin;* he is the editor of *Chopin Studies* (1988), *Man and Music Volume 7: The Late-Romantic Era,* and *The Cambridge Companion to Chopin.*

R. Larry Todd, professor of music at Duke University, has written extensively about Mendelssohn, Liszt, Webern, and Obrecht. He is the general editor of the series Studies in Musical Genres and Repertories (Schirmer-Macmillan) and the editor of *Mendelssohn and His World,* a collection of essays published by Princeton University Press.

John Williamson is senior lecturer at the University of Liverpool. He is the author of studies of Liszt, Mahler, Richard Strauss, and other composers of the late-nineteenth and early-twentieth centuries and has recently published a comprehensive volume entitled *The Music of Hans Pfitzner,* as well as *Strauss: "Also Sprach Zarathustra."*

Index of Names and Works